PYTHON

PRACTICE MAKES A MASTER

{ 'BEGINNER', 'INTERMEDIATE', 'ADVANCED' }

CUANTUM

MACHINE LEARNING, NATURAL LANGUAGE GENERATION, AND MUCH MORE

120 'REAL WORLD' EXERCISES
WITH MORE THAN 220 CONCEPTS EXPLAINED

First edition: March 2023
Published by Cuantum Technologies LLC.
Dallas, TX.
ISBN 979-8-89496-837-7

"Learning to write programs stretches your mind, and helps you think better, creates a way of thinking about things that I think is helpful in all domains."- Bill Gates

YOUR JOURNEY STARTS HERE…

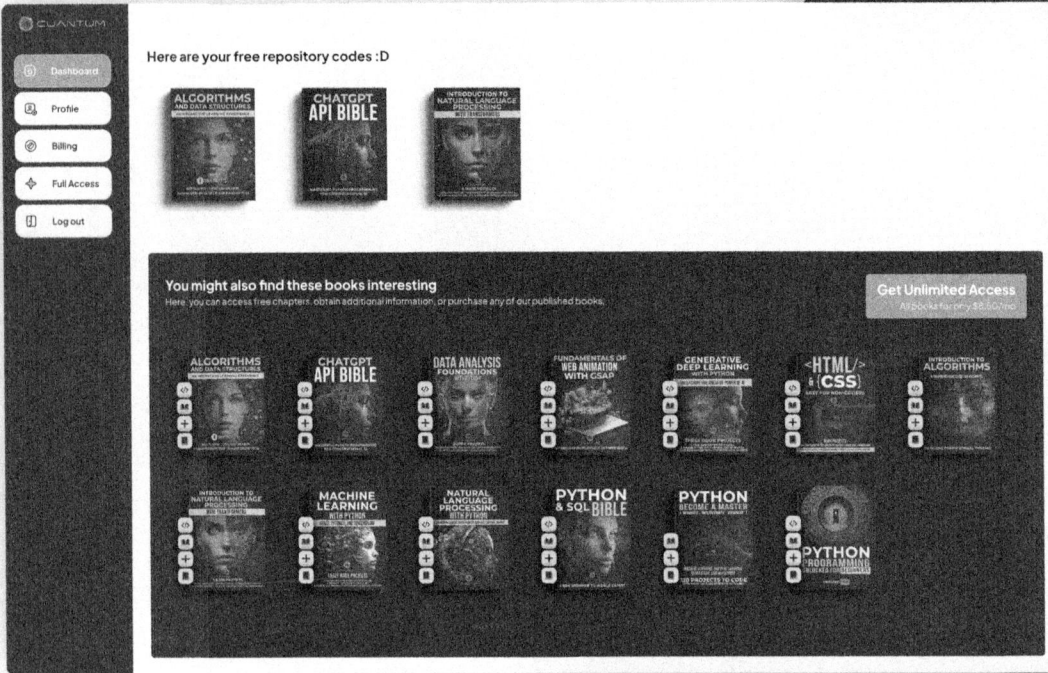

Get access to all the benefits of being one of our valuable readers through our new **eLearning Platform**:

1. Free code repository of this book

2. Access to a **free example chapter** of any of our books.

3. Access to the **free repository code** of any of our books.

4. Premium customer support by writing to **books@cuantum.tech**

And much more…

HERE IS YOUR
FREE ACCESS

www.cuantum.tech/books/python-become-a-master/code/

TABLE OF CONTENTS

BEGINNER LEVEL 21

Pg   **CONCEPTS**
23   Beginner Level Concepts

Pg   **EXERCISES**
43   Exercise 1: Calculate the Area of a Circle
43   Exercise 2: Word Frequency Counter
44   Exercise 3: Simple Temperature Converter
44   Exercise 4: Odd or Even Number Checker
45   Exercise 5: Simple File Operations
46   Exercise 6: List of Multiples
46   Exercise 7: Palindrome Checker
47   Exercise 8: Simple Interest Calculator
47   Exercise 9: Fibonacci Sequence Generator
48   Exercise 10: Leap Year Checker
48   Exercise 11: Prime Number Checker
49   Exercise 12: Count Vowels in a String
50   Exercise 13: Calculate the Factorial of a Number
50   Exercise 14: Sum of Digits in a Number
51   Exercise 15: Caesar Cipher Encoder
52   Exercise 16: Reverse a String
52   Exercise 17: Count Occurrences of a Character
52   Exercise 18: Print the ASCII Value of a Character
53   Exercise 19: Simple Calculator
54   Exercise 20: Longest Word in a Sentence
55   Exercise 21: Calculate the Average of Numbers in a List
55   Exercise 22: Common Elements in Two Lists
56   Exercise 23: Find the Smallest and Largest Numbers in a List
56   Exercise 24: Remove Duplicates from a List
57   Exercise 25: Sorting a List in Ascending and Descending Order
57   Exercise 26: Square and Cube of Numbers in a List
58   Exercise 27: Count the Number of Words in a Sentence
58   Exercise 28: Swapping Two Variables
59   Exercise 29: Distance Between Two Points
59   Exercise 30: Convert Temperature from Celsius to Fahrenheit and Vice Versa

INTERMEDIATE LEVEL **61**

Pg   **CONCEPTS**
63   Intermediate Level Concepts

Pg   **EXERCISES**
121   Exercise 1: Web Scraping
121   Exercise 2: File I/O
122   Exercise 3: Data Analysis
122   Exercise 4: Command-Line Interface
123   Exercise 5: API Integration
124   Exercise 6: Regular Expressions
124   Exercise 7: Object-Oriented Programming
125   Exercise 8: Concurrency
126   Exercise 9: Testing
126   Exercise 10: Data Visualization
127   Exercise 11: Database Operations
128   Exercise 12: Networking
129   Exercise 13: Data Science
129   Exercise 14: Web Development
130   Exercise 15: Asynchronous Programming
131   Exercise 16: Image Processing
132   Exercise 17: Email Sending
132   Exercise 18: Web API Integration
133   Exercise 19: Data Encryption
134   Exercise 20: GUI Programming
135   Exercise 21: File I/O
135   Exercise 22: Logging
136   Exercise 23: Web Scraping
136   Exercise 24: Concurrency with asyncio
137   Exercise 25: Data Analysis with Pandas
138   Exercise 26: Regular Expressions
138   Exercise 27: Database ORM
139   Exercise 28: Web Scraping with Selenium
140   Exercise 29: Natural Language Processing
141   Exercise 30: Machine Learning

INTERMEDIATE LEVEL   **61**

Pg	**EXERCISES**
142	Exercise 31: Image Recognition with Deep Learning
143	Exercise 32: Web APIs with Flask
144	Exercise 33: GUI Programming with PyQt
145	Exercise 34: Web Scraping with Beautiful Soup and Requests
145	Exercise 35: Data Visualization with Matplotlib
146	Exercise 36: Data Analysis with NumPy
146	Exercise 37: Object-Oriented Programming
148	Exercise 38: Regular Expressions
148	Exercise 39: File I/O
149	Exercise 40: Data Manipulation with Pandas

ADVANCED LEVEL **151**

Pg **CONCEPTS**
153 Advanced Level Concepts

Pg **EXERCISES**
269 Exercise 1: File Parsing
269 Exercise 2: Data Analysis
270 Exercise 3: Web Scraping
271 Exercise 4: Multithreading
271 Exercise 5: Machine Learning
272 Exercise 6: Natural Language Processing
273 Exercise 7: Web Development
274 Exercise 8: Data Visualization
275 Exercise 9: Machine Learning
276 Exercise 10: Data Analysis
278 Exercise 11: Computer Vision
279 Exercise 12: Natural Language Processing
280 Exercise 13: Web Scraping
281 Exercise 14: Big Data Processing
282 Exercise 15: DevOps
283 Exercise 16: Reinforcement Learning
284 Exercise 17: Time Series Analysis
286 Exercise 18: Computer Networking
287 Exercise 19: Data Analysis and Visualization
288 Exercise 20: Machine Learning
289 Exercise 21: Natural Language Processing
291 Exercise 22: Web Scraping
292 Exercise 23: Database Interaction
293 Exercise 24: Parallel Processing
294 Exercise 25: Image Processing
295 Exercise 26: Machine Learning
297 Exercise 27: Web Development
298 Exercise 28: Data Streaming
299 Exercise 29: Natural Language Processing
300 Exercise 30: Distributed Systems

ADVANCED LEVEL 151

Pg   **EXERCISES**

301   Exercise 31: Data Visualization

302   Exercise 32: Data Engineering

303   Exercise 33: Natural Language Generation

304   Exercise 34: Machine Learning

305   Exercise 35: Computer Vision

307   Exercise 36: Network Programming

308   Exercise 37: Cloud Computing

309   Exercise 38: Natural Language Processing

310   Exercise 39: Deep Learning

311   Exercise 40: Data Analysis

312   Exercise 41: Data Science

313   Exercise 42: Machine Learning

314   Exercise 43: Web Scraping

315   Exercise 44: Database Programming

316   Exercise 45: Cloud Computing

317   Exercise 46: Natural Language Processing

318   Exercise 47: Big Data

319   Exercise 48: Cybersecurity

320   Exercise 49: Machine Learning

321   Exercise 50: Computer Vision

CLAIM YOUR
FREE MONTH

As part of our reward program for our readers, we want to give you a **full free month** of...

www.cuantum.ai

THE PROCESS IS SIMPLE

1 Go to Amazon and leave us your amazing book review

2 Send us your name and date of review to books@cuantum.tech

3 Join **cuantum.ai** and we will activate the Creator Plan for you, free of charge.

What is CuantumAI?

All-in-one AI powered content generator and money factory

A complete Eco-system

AI Powerded Chatbot Mentors - Templates - Documents - Images - Audio/Text Transcriptions - And more...

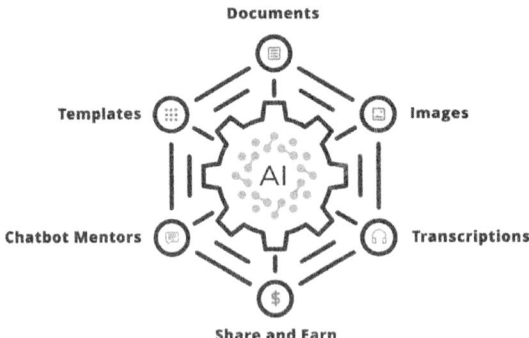

Get all your AI needs in one place to boost productivity, advance your career, or start an AI-powered business.

Do the research - Write the content - Generate the Image - Publish - Earn Money

CLAIM IT TODAY! LIMITED AVAILABILITY

WHO WE ARE

Welcome to this book created by Cuantum Technologies. We are a team of passionate developers who are committed to creating software that delivers creative experiences and solves real-world problems. Our focus is on building high-quality web applications that provide a seamless user experience and meet the needs of our clients.

At our company, we believe that programming is not just about writing code. It's about solving problems and creating solutions that make a difference in people's lives. We are constantly exploring new technologies and techniques to stay at the forefront of the industry, and we are excited to share our knowledge and experience with you through this book.

Our approach to software development is centered around collaboration and creativity. We work closely with our clients to understand their needs and create solutions that are tailored to their specific requirements. We believe that software should be intuitive, easy to use, and visually appealing, and we strive to create applications that meet these criteria.

In this book, we aim to provide you with a practical and hands-on approach to practice Python programming. Whether you are a beginner with no programming

OUR PHILOSOPHY

At the heart of Cuantum, we believe that the best way to create software is through collaboration and creativity. We value the input of our clients, and we work closely with them to create solutions that meet their needs. We also believe that software should be intuitive, easy to use, and visually appealing, and we strive to create applications that meet these criteria.

We also believe that programming is a skill that can be learned and developed over time. We encourage our developers to explore new technologies and techniques, and we provide them with the tools and resources they need to stay at the forefront of the industry. We also believe that programming should be fun and rewarding, and we strive to create a work environment that fosters creativity and innovation.

OUR EXPERTISE

At our software company, we specialize in building web applications that deliver creative experiences and solve real-world problems. Our developers have expertise in a wide range of programming languages and frameworks, including Python, Django, React, Three.js, and Vue.js, among others. We are constantly exploring new technologies and techniques to stay at the forefront of the industry, and we pride ourselves on our ability to create solutions that meet our clients' needs.

We also have extensive experience in data analysis and visualization, machine learning, and artificial intelligence. We believe that these technologies have the potential to transform the way we live and work, and we are excited to be at the forefront of this revolution.

In conclusion, our company is focused on creating software web for creative experiences and solving real-world problems. We believe in collaboration and creativity, and we strive to create solutions that are intuitive, easy to use, and visually appealing. We are passionate about programming, and we are excited to share our knowledge and experience with you through this book. Whether you are a beginner or an experienced programmer, we hope that you find this book to be a valuable resource in your journey to become a proficient Python programmer.

INTRODUCTION

Welcome to the world of Python programming! Python is an extremely popular, versatile, and easy-to-learn programming language. It is used for a wide range of applications, including web development, data science, machine learning, and artificial intelligence, among others. Python's popularity stems from its simple syntax, vast libraries and frameworks, and its ability to handle complex tasks with ease.

"Python, Practice Makes a Master" is a resource designed to help Python enthusiasts of all levels. Whether you are a novice with no programming experience, an intermediate programmer looking to enhance your skills, or an advanced programmer seeking to challenge yourself with complex exercises, this book has something to offer you.

The exercises in this book are practical and relevant, designed to help you master the essential concepts of Python programming while also giving you the opportunity to apply those concepts to real-world problems. The exercises are divided into three sections, each covering a different level of difficulty.

The beginner exercises are designed for those who have little to no programming experience. This section covers the basic building blocks of Python programming, such as variables, data types, loops, conditional statements, functions, and file handling. The exercises are designed to be simple and easy to understand, allowing you to build a solid foundation in Python programming.

The intermediate exercises are designed for those who have some programming experience and are familiar with the basic concepts of Python programming. This section covers more advanced topics such as object-oriented programming, regular expressions, web scraping, data analysis, and data visualization. The exercises in this section are more challenging than those in the beginner section, but they are still designed to be accessible and practical.

The advanced exercises are designed for experienced programmers who are looking to challenge themselves and expand their skills. This section covers advanced topics such as concurrency, network programming, machine learning, and natural language processing.

The exercises in this section are challenging and require a deep understanding of Python programming concepts.

In "**Python, Practice Makes a Master,**" we aim to provide practical exercises for those studying Python, as well as for intermediate or advanced level programmers with a thirst for more knowledge or who want to challenge themselves with complex problems to solve. Whether you are seeking to practice and learn Python programming, improve your Python skills, or use the exercises as a reference, we hope you find this book to be a valuable resource in your journey to become a proficient Python programmer.

This book is designed to help you become a proficient Python programmer, no matter your current skill level. Whether you are a beginner with no programming experience, an intermediate programmer looking to improve your skills, or an advanced programmer seeking to challenge yourself with complex exercises, this book has something for you.

The exercises in this book are practical and relevant, designed to help you master the essential concepts of Python programming while also giving you the opportunity to apply those concepts to real-world problems. The exercises are divided into three sections, with each section covering a different level of difficulty.

SECTION 1: BEGINNER EXERCISES

The beginner exercises are designed for those who have little to no programming experience. This section covers the basic building blocks of Python programming, such as variables, data types, loops, conditional statements, functions, and file handling. The exercises are designed to be simple and easy to understand, allowing you to build a solid foundation in Python programming.

SECTION 2: INTERMEDIATE EXERCISES

The intermediate exercises are designed for those who have some programming experience and are familiar with the basic concepts of Python programming. This section covers more advanced topics such as object-oriented programming, regular expressions, web scraping, data analysis, and data visualization. The exercises in this section are more challenging than those in the beginner section, but they are still designed to be accessible and practical.

SECTION 3: ADVANCED EXERCISES

The advanced exercises are designed for experienced programmers who are looking to challenge themselves and expand their skills. This section covers advanced topics such as concurrency, network programming, machine learning, and natural language processing.

The exercises in this section are challenging and require a deep understanding of Python programming concepts.

HOW TO USE THIS BOOK

This book is designed to be a practical resource for Python programmers and students of all levels. You can use this book in a number of ways:

1. **Practice and learn Python Programming**: If you are new to programming, start with the beginner exercises and work your way up to the advanced exercises. Each exercise is designed to be self-contained, so you can work through the exercises at your own pace.

2. **Improve Your Python Skills**: If you are an intermediate programmer, you can use this book to improve your Python skills. Work through the exercises in the intermediate and advanced sections to challenge yourself and expand your knowledge.

3. **Use as a Reference**: Even if you are an experienced Python programmer, you may find the exercises in this book to be useful as a reference. The exercises cover a wide range of topics, and you can use them as a starting point for your own projects.

WHAT IS THIS BOOK NOT ABOUT?

One of the biggest challenges that people face when learning a new programming language is figuring out how to put what they've learned into practice. While it's important to study and understand the core concepts and syntax of a language, it's equally important to practice using that knowledge in real-world scenarios.

This is where this book comes in. The exercises in this book are designed to help you practice your Python programming skills in a practical way. Rather than simply presenting you with abstract concepts and syntax rules, the exercises in this book challenge you to apply what you've learned to real-world problems.

It's important to note that this book is not designed to be a comprehensive guide to Python programming. While it covers a wide range of topics, it's not meant to be a substitute for more in-depth study and research. Instead, the exercises in this book are meant to complement your learning by providing you with practical, hands-on experience with the language. The exercises in this book are also not meant to be completed in a specific order or as a linear progression. While we've divided the exercises into beginner, intermediate, and advanced sections, you're free to pick and choose which exercises you want to work on based on your own needs and interests.

By practicing your Python programming skills through the exercises in this book, you'll gain a deeper understanding of the language and its capabilities. You'll also develop problem-solving skills that will be invaluable as you continue to work on more complex projects.

It's important to note that practicing programming skills requires patience and persistence. You may not get the correct answer on the first try, and that's okay. The exercises in this book are designed to challenge you, and it's through struggling with difficult problems that you'll truly learn and grow as a programmer.

In summary, this book is not a traditional study guide for Python programming. Instead, it's a collection of practical exercises designed to help you practice and develop your programming skills. By working through these exercises, you'll gain real-world experience with Python and develop the problem-solving skills that are essential for success in programming.

THE BOTTOM LINE IS...

Python is an exceptionally versatile programming language and can be used to create a wide range of applications. Whether you are a beginner, intermediate, or advanced programmer, this book is designed to help you master Python programming. It is a comprehensive guide, covering not only the basics but also more advanced topics, such as object-oriented programming and database management.

In addition to providing thorough explanations of Python programming concepts, this book also includes practical exercises that are designed to help you put your knowledge into practice. These exercises are relevant to real-world problems, so you can be sure that you are learning skills that will be useful to you in your career as a Python programmer.

We hope that you find this book to be a valuable resource in your journey to becoming a proficient Python programmer. With its clear and concise explanations, comprehensive coverage of both basic and advanced topics, and practical exercises that allow you to apply what you've learned, we believe that this book will be an indispensable tool for anyone looking to improve their Python programming skills.

LET'S START

BEGINNER LEVEL
CHAPTER 1

BEGINNER LEVEL CONCEPTS

Here you can see the **20 concepts** that you will learn/practice during the next **30 beginner level exercises**. These exercises will guide you through each concept, providing detailed explanations and examples so that you can gain a solid understanding of each one. By the end of the 30 exercises, you will have not only learned 20 new concepts, but you will also have developed the skills to apply them in real-world situations. This will give you a strong foundation on which to build as you continue to advance your knowledge and abilities in this field.

Concepts List:

1. Basic arithmetic 25
2. Conditional statements 25
3. Dictionaries 26
4. Exception handling 26
5. File I/O 27
6. Functions 28
7. Input/output 28
8. Lists 29
9. Loops 30
10. Match module 30
11. min() and max() functions 31
12. Modular arithmetic 33
13. ord() function 33
14. Sets 34
15. Slicing 35
16. String manipulation 36
17. Strings 36
18. Tuples 37
19. User input 38
20. Variables 39

1. Basic Arithmetic:

Basic arithmetic in Python involves performing mathematical operations like addition, subtraction, multiplication, and division. These operations can be performed using the appropriate mathematical symbols (+ for addition, - for subtraction, * for multiplication, / for division).

For example, if you want to add two numbers (let's say 5 and 3), you can write:

```
5 + 3
```

This will give you the result of 8. Similarly, if you want to subtract two numbers (let's say 7 and 4), you can write:

```
7 - 4
```

This will give you the result of 3.

2. Conditional Statements:

Conditional statements allow your code to make decisions based on certain conditions. In Python, you can use `if` statements to check a condition and execute a block of code if the condition is true, and optionally execute a different block of code if the condition is false.

For example, you can use an `if` statement to check if a number is positive or negative:

```
num = -5
if num > 0:
    print("The number is positive")
else:
    print("The number is negative")
```

This will print "The number is negative", since `-5` is less than zero.

You can also use `elif` statements to check multiple conditions:

```
num = 0
if num > 0:
    print("The number is positive")
elif num < 0:
    print("The number is negative")
else:
    print("The number is zero")
```

This will print "The number is zero", since `0` is neither positive nor negative.

3. Dictionaries:

Dictionaries are collections of key-value pairs that allow you to store and retrieve data based on keys rather than indices. You can create a dictionary by enclosing a comma-separated list of key-value pairs in curly braces ({...}).

For example, you can create a dictionary that maps English words to their Spanish translations like this:

```
translations = {"hello": "hola", "goodbye": "adios", "thank you": "gracias"}
```

You can then retrieve a value from the dictionary by using its corresponding key, like this:

```
print(translations["hello"])
```

This will print the value "hola", which is the Spanish translation of "hello".

4. Exception Handling:

Exception handling allows your Python code to gracefully handle errors and unexpected situations that may arise during execution. You can use `try` and `except` blocks to catch and handle exceptions that may occur during your code's execution.

For example, you can catch a `ValueError` exception that may be raised if you try to convert a non-numeric string to a number:

```
string = "hello"
try:
    num = int(string)
except ValueError:
    print("The string is not a number.")
```

This will attempt to convert the string `"hello"` to an integer using the `int()` function. If a `ValueError` is raised, the code inside the `except` block will execute, printing the message "The string is not a number."

Exception handling is useful for ensuring that your code can handle unexpected situations and continue to run smoothly even if errors occur.

5. File I/O:

File I/O, or input/output, allows your Python code to read and write data to files on your computer's file system. You can use the built-in functions `open()` and `close()` to open and close files, and `read()`, `readline()`, and `write()` to read and write data to and from files.

For example, you can read data from a text file like this:

```
file = open("example.txt", "r")
  content = file.read()
file.close()
print(content)
```

This will open the file `"example.txt"` in read mode (`"r"`), read the contents of the file into the `content` variable, and then close the file. Finally, it will print the contents of the file to the console.

You can also write data to a text file like this:

```
file = open("example.txt", "w")
  file.write("Hello, world!")
file.close()
```

This will open the file `"example.txt"` in write mode (`"w"`), write the string `"Hello, world!"` to the file, and then close the file.

6. Functions:

Functions are blocks of code that perform a specific task and can be called from other parts of your code. Functions can be defined using the `def` keyword, followed by the function name and any arguments it takes in parentheses. The code block for the function is indented below the `def` statement.

For example, you can define a function called `square` that takes in a number and returns its square like this:

```python
def square(num):
    return num * num
```

You can then call this function from other parts of your code, passing in a number as an argument:

```python
result = square(5)
print(result)  # prints 25
```

This will call the `square` function with the argument `5` and store the result in the variable `result`.

7. Input/Output:

Input and output (or I/O) refers to how a program interacts with the user. In Python, you can use the `input()` function to get input from the user, and the `print()` function to display output to the user.

For example, if you want to ask the user to enter their name, you can write:

```python
name = input("Please enter your name: ")
```

This will prompt the user to enter their name, and store their input in the variable `name`. You can then use the `print()` function to display a message to the user, like:

```
print("Hello, " + name + "!")
```

This will display a message that says "Hello, " followed by the user's name.

8. Lists:

Lists are one of the most common and useful data structures in Python. A list is an ordered collection of items, which can be of any data type, including numbers, strings, and even other lists. You can create a list by enclosing a comma-separated sequence of items in square brackets `[...]`.

For example, you can create a list called `numbers` that contains a sequence of integers like this:

```
numbers = [1, 2, 3, 4, 5]
```

You can then access individual elements of the list using their index (starting from 0), like this:

```
print(numbers[0])  # prints 1
print(numbers[2])  # prints 3
```

You can also modify elements of the list by assigning a new value to their index, like this:

```
numbers[1] = 10
print(numbers)  # prints [1, 10, 3, 4, 5]
```

Lists are versatile and useful data structures that can be used in a wide variety of programming applications.

9. Loops:

Loops allow you to execute a block of code repeatedly, either a fixed number of times or until a certain condition is met. There are two main types of loops in Python: `for` loops and `while` loops.

For example, you can use a `for` loop to iterate over a sequence of values, such as a list or a string:

```python
fruits = ["apple", "banana", "cherry"]
for fruit in fruits:
    print(fruit)
```

This will print each element of the `fruits` list on a separate line.

You can also use a `while` loop to repeatedly execute a block of code until a certain condition is met:

```python
count = 0
while count < 5:
    print(count)
    count += 1
```

This will print the numbers 0 to 4 on separate lines.

10. Math module

The math module in Python is a built-in module that provides a variety of mathematical functions and constants. You can use the functions and constants in the math module to perform advanced mathematical calculations in your Python code.

To use the math module in your code, you first need to import it using the `import` statement. For example:

```python
import math
```

This will import the math module, allowing you to use its functions and constants in your code.

Some of the most commonly used functions in the math module include:

- `math.sqrt(x)` : returns the square root of x
- `math.sin(x)` : returns the sine of x (in radians)
- `math.cos(x)` : returns the cosine of x (in radians)
- `math.tan(x)` : returns the tangent of x (in radians)
- `math.log(x)` : returns the natural logarithm of x
- `math.exp(x)` : returns the exponential of x
- `math.pow(x, y)` : returns x raised to the power of y
- `math.degrees(x)` : converts x from radians to degrees
- `math.radians(x)` : converts x from degrees to radians

In addition to these functions, the math module also provides several constants, such as `math.pi` (which represents the value of pi) and `math.e` (which represents the value of the mathematical constant e).

Here's an example of using the math module to calculate the sine and cosine of an angle in radians:

```python
import math

angle = math.pi / 4  # calculate the angle in radians
sin_value = math.sin(angle)  # calculate the sine of the angle
cos_value = math.cos(angle)  # calculate the cosine of the angle

print(sin_value)  # prints 0.7071067811865475
print(cos_value)  # prints 0.7071067811865476
```

This will calculate the sine and cosine of an angle of 45 degrees (converted to radians), using the `math.sin()` and `math.cos()` functions from the math module.

The math module is a powerful tool for performing advanced mathematical calculations in Python, and it is commonly used in scientific computing, data analysis, and other fields.

11. min() and max() functions

The `min()` and `max()` functions in Python are built-in functions that allow you to find the minimum and maximum values in a sequence of numbers. You can use these functions to quickly and easily find the smallest and largest values in a list, tuple, set, or other iterable data type.

The `min()` function takes one or more arguments, which can be numbers or iterable data types, and returns the smallest value. For example:

```
numbers = [1, 2, 3, 4, 5]
smallest = min(numbers)
print(smallest)  # prints 1
```

This will find the smallest value in the list `numbers` , which is `1` .

The `max()` function works similarly, but it returns the largest value instead. For example:

```
numbers = [1, 2, 3, 4, 5]
  largest = max(numbers)
print(largest)  # prints 5
```

This will find the largest value in the list `numbers` , which is `5` .

You can also use the `min()` and `max()` functions with strings, since strings are iterable data types. When used with strings, `min()` and `max()` return the character with the smallest and largest Unicode code point, respectively. For example:

```
string = "hello"
smallest_char = min(string)
largest_char = max(string)
print(smallest_char)  # prints 'e'
print(largest_char)  # prints 'o'
```

This will find the smallest and largest characters in the string `"hello"` , which are `'e'` and `'o'` , respectively.

The `min()` and `max()` functions are useful for finding the smallest and largest values in a sequence of numbers or other iterable data types, and they are commonly used in many different programming applications.

12. Modular Arithmetic:

Modular arithmetic is a system of arithmetic for integers, where numbers "wrap around" after reaching a certain value called the modulus. In Python, you can perform modular arithmetic using the modulo operator `%`.

For example, if you want to calculate the remainder when `10` is divided by `3`, you can write:

```
remainder = 10 % 3
print(remainder)  # prints 1
```

This will calculate the remainder of `10` divided by `3`, which is `1`.

Modular arithmetic is useful in many applications, such as cryptography, computer graphics, and game development.

13. ord() function

The `ord()` function in Python is a built-in function that returns the Unicode code point of a single character. Unicode is a standard that assigns a unique code point to every character in every language, and the `ord()` function allows you to access these code points in your Python code.

The `ord()` function takes a single argument, which is a string containing a single character. For example:

```
print(ord('A'))  # prints 65
```

This will print the Unicode code point for the capital letter "A", which is `65`.

You can also use the `chr()` function to convert a Unicode code point back into its corresponding character. For example:

```
print(chr(65))  # prints 'A'
```

This will print the character corresponding to the Unicode code point `65`, which is the capital letter "A".

The `ord()` function is useful for working with Unicode text data in Python, and it is commonly used in applications such as natural language processing and web development.

14. Sets

In Python, a set is an unordered collection of unique elements. Sets are similar to lists and tuples, but they differ in two key ways: sets are unordered, and they cannot contain duplicate elements.

You can create a set in Python using curly braces `{...}` or the `set()` function. For example:

```
set1 = {1, 2, 3, 4, 5}
set2 = set([3, 4, 5, 6, 7])
```

These two examples both create sets containing the integers 1 through 5, but they use different syntax to do so.

You can perform various operations on sets in Python, such as adding elements, removing elements, and performing set operations like union, intersection, and difference. Here are some examples:

```
set1.add(6)  # adds the element 6 to the set
set2.remove(7)  # removes the element 7 from the set
union_set = set1.union(set2)  # creates a new set containing all elements from set1 and se
t2
intersection_set = set1.intersection(set2)  # creates a new set containing only elements t
hat are in both set1 and set2
difference_set = set1.difference(set2)  # creates a new set containing only elements that
 are in set1 but not in set2
```

Sets are useful for various applications in Python, such as removing duplicates from a list, performing set operations, and finding unique elements in a dataset.

15. Slicing:

Slicing is a way to extract a portion of a sequence (such as a string or a list) in Python. You can use slicing notation, which uses square brackets and colons to specify the start and end indices of the slice.

The general syntax for slicing is:

```
sequence[start:end:step]
```

where `start` is the index of the first element to include in the slice, `end` is the index of the first element to exclude from the slice, and `step` is the stride or increment for the slice.

For example, if you have a list of numbers:

```
numbers = [1, 2, 3, 4, 5]
```

You can slice the list to extract a portion of it:

```
slice = numbers[1:4]
print(slice)  # prints [2, 3, 4]
```

This will create a new list called `slice` that contains the elements at indices 1, 2, and 3 of the original `numbers` list.

You can also use negative indices to slice from the end of the sequence, like this:

```
slice = numbers[-3:-1]
print(slice)  # prints [3, 4]
```

This will create a new list called `slice` that contains the elements at indices -3 and -2 of the original `numbers` list.

Slicing is a powerful and versatile tool for working with sequences in Python, and it is commonly used in a wide variety of programming applications.

16. String Manipulation:

String manipulation involves modifying and transforming strings in various ways. In Python, you can use various built-in string methods to manipulate strings, such as `split()`, `join()`, `replace()`, and `strip()`.

For example, you can split a string into a list of substrings based on a delimiter like this:

```python
string = "apple,banana,cherry"
fruits = string.split(",")
print(fruits)  # prints ["apple", "banana", "cherry"]
```

This will split the string `"apple,banana,cherry"` into a list of substrings based on the `,` delimiter.

You can also replace a substring with another substring like this:

```python
string = "Hello, world!"
new_string = string.replace("world", "John")
print(new_string)  # prints "Hello, John!"
```

This will replace the substring `"world"` with `"John"` in the string `"Hello, world!"`, resulting in the new string `"Hello, John!"`.

String manipulation is useful for processing and transforming text data in your Python code.

17. Strings:

Strings are sequences of characters that are used to represent text in Python. You can create a string by enclosing a sequence of characters in either single quotes ('...') or double quotes ("...").

For example, you can create a string called `message` that contains the text "Hello, world!" like this:

```
message = "Hello, world!"
```

You can then use various methods to manipulate and work with strings, such as concatenation (combining two strings with the `+` operator), slicing (extracting a portion of a string using the `[]` operator), and formatting (replacing parts of a string with variables using the `format()` method).

For example, you can concatenate two strings like this:

```
greeting = "Hello"
name = "John"
message = greeting + ", " + name + "!"
```

This will create a string called `message` that contains the text "Hello, John!".

18. Tuples

In Python, a tuple is a collection of ordered, immutable elements. Tuples are similar to lists, but they differ in two key ways: tuples are immutable (which means you cannot change their contents once they are created), and they are typically used to group together related pieces of data.

You can create a tuple in Python using parentheses `(...)` or the `tuple()` function. For example:

```
tuple1 = (1, 2, 3)
tuple2 = tuple(['a', 'b', 'c'])
```

These two examples both create tuples containing three elements, but they use different syntax to do so.

You can access individual elements of a tuple using their index (starting from 0), just like you can with a list. For example:

```
print(tuple1[0])  # prints 1
```

You can also use slicing notation to extract a portion of a tuple, just like you can with a list. For example:

```
tuple3 = tuple1[1:]
print(tuple3)  # prints (2, 3)
```

This will create a new tuple called `tuple3` that contains the elements at indices 1 and 2 of the original `tuple1` tuple.

Because tuples are immutable, you cannot modify their contents once they are created. However, you can create a new tuple by concatenating existing tuples together, like this:

```
tuple4 = tuple1 + tuple2
print(tuple4)  # prints (1, 2, 3, 'a', 'b', 'c')
```

This will create a new tuple called `tuple4` that contains all the elements of `tuple1` followed by all the elements of `tuple2`.

Tuples are useful for various applications in Python, such as storing related pieces of data together, passing multiple values as a single argument to a function, and returning multiple values from a function.

19. User Input:

User input allows your code to get input from the user at runtime. In Python, you can use the `input()` function to prompt the user for input and store their response in a variable.

For example, you can ask the user for their name and store it in a variable like this:

```
name = input("What is your name? ")
print("Hello, " + name + "!")
```

This will prompt the user for their name and store their response in the `name` variable, which is then used to print a personalized greeting.

20. Variables:

Variables are used to store data in Python. You can think of a variable as a container that holds a value. In Python, you can create a variable by giving it a name and assigning a value to it using the `=` symbol.

For example, if you want to store the value 10 in a variable called x, you can write:

```
x = 10
```

You can then use the variable x in your code to refer to the value 10. For example, you can add 5 to x by writing:

```
x = x + 5
```

This will update the value of x to be 15. You can then use x in your code to refer to the updated value of 15.

30 BEGINNER LEVEL EXERCISES

The exercises in this book, and this section, are not arranged in any particular order according to the difficulty level. This may seem unorganized, but in fact, it grants readers the flexibility to skip ahead and find the information that they need at that particular moment. Furthermore, this is especially beneficial for students or readers who are more advanced in their studies as they may not need to cover the basics.

In this way, you can focus on the more challenging areas of the subject matter and progress at your own pace, which can be very rewarding. Ultimately, the lack of a prescribed order can be an advantage rather than a disadvantage, offering you the ability to customize your learning experience and make the most of your time and effort.

You can follow the order if you want, but you can also go directly to the exercise that you need to focus on.

The best way to learn is to enjoy yourself, so have fun coding your future.

LET'S START.

Beginner Level Exercises

Exercise 1: Calculate the Area of a Circle

Concepts:

- Basic arithmetic

- Input/output

- Variables

Description: Write a Python program that takes the radius of a circle as input from the user and calculates its area.

Solution:

```python
import math

radius = float(input("Enter the radius of the circle: "))
area = math.pi * (radius ** 2)

print(f"The area of the circle with radius {radius} is {area:.2f}")
```

Exercise 2: Word Frequency Counter

Concepts:

- Strings

- Dictionaries

- Loops

Description: Write a Python program that takes a string as input and counts the frequency of each word in the string.

Solution:

```
input_string = input("Enter a sentence: ")
words = input_string.lower().split()
word_count = {}

for word in words:
    if word in word_count:
        word_count[word] += 1
    else:
        word_count[word] = 1

print("Word frequencies:", word_count)
```

Exercise 3: Simple Temperature Converter

Concepts:

- Functions

- Conditional statements

- User input

Description: Write a Python program that converts temperatures between Celsius and Fahrenheit. The program should ask the user for the temperature unit and the value to be converted.

Solution:

```
def celsius_to_fahrenheit(celsius):
    return (celsius * 9/5) + 32

def fahrenheit_to_celsius(fahrenheit):
    return (fahrenheit - 32) * 5/9

unit = input("Enter the temperature unit (C for Celsius, F for Fahrenheit): ")
value = float(input("Enter the temperature value to be converted: "))

if unit.upper() == "C":
    print(f"{value} Celsius is {celsius_to_fahrenheit(value):.2f} Fahrenheit.")
elif unit.upper() == "F":
    print(f"{value} Fahrenheit is {fahrenheit_to_celsius(value):.2f} Celsius.")
else:
    print("Invalid temperature unit.")
```

Exercise 4: Odd or Even Number Checker

Concepts:

- Modular arithmetic

- Conditional statements

Description: Write a Python program that checks whether a given number is odd or even.

Solution:

```python
number = int(input("Enter an integer: "))

if number % 2 == 0:
    print(f"{number} is even.")
else:
    print(f"{number} is odd.")
```

Exercise 5: Simple File Operations

Concepts:

- File I/O

- Exception handling

- String manipulation

Description: Write a Python program that reads a text file, converts its content to uppercase, and writes the result to a new file. If the input file does not exist, display an error message.

Solution:

```python
input_file = input("Enter the name of the input file: ")
output_file = input("Enter the name of the output file: ")

try:
    with open(input_file, "r") as infile:
        content = infile.read()
    uppercase_content = content.upper()

    with open(output_file, "w") as outfile:
        outfile.write(uppercase_content)

    print("The content has been converted to uppercase and saved in the output file.")
```

```
except FileNotFoundError:
    print(f"The file '{input_file}' does not exist.")
```

Exercise 6: List of Multiples

Concepts:

- Loops

- Lists

- Arithmetic

Description: Write a Python program that takes a number as input and returns a list of its first 10 multiples.

Solution:

```
number = int(input("Enter a number: "))
multiples = [number * i for i in range(1, 11)]

print(f"The first 10 multiples of {number} are: {multiples}")
```

Exercise 7: Palindrome Checker

Concepts:

- Strings

- Conditional statements

- String manipulation

Description: Write a Python program that checks whether a given word or phrase is a palindrome. Ignore spaces, punctuation, and capitalization.

Solution:

```
import re

input_string = input("Enter a word or phrase: ")
processed_string = re.sub(r'\W+', '', input_string.lower())
reversed_string = processed_string[::-1]
```

```
if processed_string == reversed_string:
    print(f"'{input_string}' is a palindrome.")
else:
    print(f"'{input_string}' is not a palindrome.")
```

Exercise 8: Simple Interest Calculator

Concepts:

- Arithmetic

- Input/output

- Variables

Description: Write a Python program that calculates the simple interest for a given principal amount, rate of interest, and number of years.

Solution:

```
principal = float(input("Enter the principal amount: "))
rate = float(input("Enter the rate of interest (percentage): "))
years = int(input("Enter the number of years: "))

interest = principal * rate * years / 100
total_amount = principal + interest

print(f"The simple interest is: {interest:.2f}")
print(f"The total amount after {years} years is: {total_amount:.2f}")
```

Exercise 9: Fibonacci Sequence Generator

Concepts:

- Loops

- Lists

- Functions

Description: Write a Python program that generates the first n numbers of the Fibonacci sequence, where n is provided by the user.

Solution:

```python
def generate_fibonacci(n):
    sequence = [0, 1]

    for i in range(2, n):
        sequence.append(sequence[-1] + sequence[-2])

    return sequence[:n]

n = int(input("Enter the number of Fibonacci numbers to generate: "))
fibonacci_sequence = generate_fibonacci(n)

print(f"The first {n} Fibonacci numbers are: {fibonacci_sequence}")
```

Exercise 10: Leap Year Checker

Concepts:

- Conditional statements

- Modular arithmetic

Description: Write a Python program that checks whether a given year is a leap year.

Solution:

```python
year = int(input("Enter a year: "))

if (year % 4 == 0 and year % 100 != 0) or (year % 400 == 0):
    print(f"{year} is a leap year.")
else:
    print(f"{year} is not a leap year.")
```

Exercise 11: Prime Number Checker

Concepts:

- Loops

- Conditional statements

- Functions

Description: Write a Python program that checks whether a given number is a prime number.

Solution:

```python
def is_prime(number):
    if number <= 1:
        return False

    for i in range(2, number):
        if number % i == 0:
            return False
    return True

number = int(input("Enter a number: "))

if is_prime(number):
    print(f"{number} is a prime number.")
else:
    print(f"{number} is not a prime number.")
```

Exercise 12: Count Vowels in a String

Concepts:

- Strings

- Loops

- Dictionaries

Description: Write a Python program that counts the number of vowels in a given string.

Solution:

```python
input_string = input("Enter a string: ").lower()
vowels = "aeiou"
vowel_count = {}

for char in input_string:
    if char in vowels:
        if char in vowel_count:
            vowel_count[char] += 1
        else:
            vowel_count[char] = 1

print("Vowel count:", vowel_count)
```

Exercise 13: Calculate the Factorial of a Number

Concepts:

- Loops

- Conditional statements

- Functions

Description: Write a Python program that calculates the factorial of a given number using loops.

Solution:

```python
def factorial(number):
    if number == 0 or number == 1:
        return 1

    result = 1
    for i in range(2, number + 1):
        result *= i

    return result

number = int(input("Enter a number: "))
print(f"The factorial of {number} is {factorial(number)}")
```

Exercise 14: Sum of Digits in a Number

Concepts:

- Loops

- Arithmetic

- Strings

Description: Write a Python program that calculates the sum of the digits of a given integer.

Solution:

```python
number = int(input("Enter an integer: "))
```

```
sum_of_digits = sum(int(digit) for digit in str(number))

print(f"The sum of the digits of {number} is {sum_of_digits}")
```

Exercise 15: Caesar Cipher Encoder

Concepts:

- Strings

- Loops

- Modular arithmetic

Description: Write a Python program that implements a simple Caesar cipher. The program should take a string and an integer shift value as input, and return the encoded string.

Solution:

```
def caesar_cipher(text, shift):
    encrypted = []

    for char in text:
        if char.isalpha():
            shift_amount = shift % 26
            new_ord = ord(char) + shift_amount

            if char.islower():
                if new_ord > ord("z"):
                    new_ord -= 26
            else:
                if new_ord > ord("Z"):
                    new_ord -= 26

            encrypted.append(chr(new_ord))
        else:
            encrypted.append(char)

    return "".join(encrypted)

text = input("Enter a string: ")
shift = int(input("Enter the shift value: "))

encoded_text = caesar_cipher(text, shift)
print(f"The encoded text is: {encoded_text}")
```

Exercise 16: Reverse a String

Concepts:

- Strings

- Loops

- Slicing

Description: Write a Python program that reverses a given string.

Solution:

```python
input_string = input("Enter a string: ")
reversed_string = input_string[::-1]

print(f"The reversed string is: {reversed_string}")
```

Exercise 17: Count Occurrences of a Character

Concepts:

- Strings

- Loops

- Dictionaries

Description: Write a Python program that counts the occurrences of a specific character in a given string.

Solution:

```python
input_string = input("Enter a string: ")
target_char = input("Enter a character to count: ")

count = input_string.lower().count(target_char.lower())
print(f"The character '{target_char}' occurs {count} times in the string.")
```

Exercise 18: Print the ASCII Value of a Character

Concepts:

- Input/output

- ord() function

Description: Write a Python program that takes a single character as input and prints its ASCII value.

Solution:

```python
char = input("Enter a single character: ")

if len(char) == 1:
    print(f"The ASCII value of '{char}' is {ord(char)}")
else:
    print("Invalid input. Please enter a single character.")
```

Exercise 19: Simple Calculator

Concepts:

- Functions

- Input/output

- Conditional statements

Description: Write a Python program that creates a simple calculator that can perform addition, subtraction, multiplication, and division. The program should ask the user for the operation, the two numbers, and then display the result.

Solution:

```python
def add(x, y):
    return x + y

def subtract(x, y):
    return x - y

def multiply(x, y):
    return x * y

def divide(x, y):
```

```
        return x / y

operation = input("Enter the operation (add, subtract, multiply, divide): ")
num1 = float(input("Enter the first number: "))
num2 = float(input("Enter the second number: "))

if operation.lower() == "add":
    print(f"The result is: {add(num1, num2)}")
elif operation.lower() == "subtract":
    print(f"The result is: {subtract(num1, num2)}")
elif operation.lower() == "multiply":
    print(f"The result is: {multiply(num1, num2)}")
elif operation.lower() == "divide":
    if num2 == 0:
        print("Error: Division by zero is not allowed.")
    else:
        print(f"The result is: {divide(num1, num2)}")
else:
    print("Invalid operation.")
```

Exercise 20: Longest Word in a Sentence

Concepts:

- Strings

- Loops

- String manipulation

Description: Write a Python program that takes a sentence as input and returns the longest word in the sentence.

Solution:

```
input_sentence = input("Enter a sentence: ")
words = input_sentence.split()

longest_word = ""
max_length = 0

for word in words:
    if len(word) > max_length:
        max_length = len(word)
        longest_word = word

print(f"The longest word in the sentence is: {longest_word}")
```

Exercise 21: Calculate the Average of Numbers in a List

Concepts:

- Lists

- Loops

- Arithmetic

Description: Write a Python program that calculates the average of a list of numbers.

Solution:

```python
numbers = [float(x) for x in input("Enter a list of numbers separated by spaces: ").split
()]
average = sum(numbers) / len(numbers)

print(f"The average of the numbers is: {average:.2f}")
```

Exercise 22: Common Elements in Two Lists

Concepts:

- Lists

- Loops

- Sets

Description: Write a Python program that takes two lists and returns a list of common elements.

Solution:

```python
list1 = input("Enter the first list of numbers separated by spaces: ").split()
list2 = input("Enter the second list of numbers separated by spaces: ").split()

common_elements = list(set(list1) & set(list2))
print(f"The common elements in the two lists are: {common_elements}")
```

Exercise 23: Find the Smallest and Largest Numbers in a List

Concepts:

- Lists

- Loops

- min() and max() functions

Description: Write a Python program that takes a list of numbers as input and returns the smallest and largest numbers in the list.

Solution:

```python
numbers = [float(x) for x in input("Enter a list of numbers separated by spaces: ").split
()]

smallest_number = min(numbers)
largest_number = max(numbers)

print(f"The smallest number is: {smallest_number}")
print(f"The largest number is: {largest_number}")
```

Exercise 24: Remove Duplicates from a List

Concepts:

- Lists

- Sets

- List comprehensions

Description: Write a Python program that takes a list and returns a new list without duplicates.

Solution:

```python
input_list = input("Enter a list of elements separated by spaces: ").split()
unique_list = list(dict.fromkeys(input_list))
```

```
print(f"The list without duplicates is: {unique_list}")
```

Exercise 25: Sorting a List in Ascending and Descending Order

Concepts:

- Lists

- Sorting

Description: Write a Python program that takes a list of numbers as input and returns the same list sorted in ascending and descending order.

Solution:

```
numbers = [float(x) for x in input("Enter a list of numbers separated by spaces: ").split
()]

ascending_sorted_list = sorted(numbers)
descending_sorted_list = sorted(numbers, reverse=True)

print(f"The list sorted in ascending order is: {ascending_sorted_list}")
print(f"The list sorted in descending order is: {descending_sorted_list}")
```

Exercise 26: Square and Cube of Numbers in a List

Concepts:

- Lists

- Loops

- List comprehensions

Description: Write a Python program that takes a list of numbers and returns a new list containing the square and cube of each number.

Solution:

```
numbers = [int(x) for x in input("Enter a list of numbers separated by spaces: ").split()]
```

```
squares_and_cubes = [(x**2, x**3) for x in numbers]

print(f"The squares and cubes of the numbers are: {squares_and_cubes}")
```

Exercise 27: Count the Number of Words in a Sentence

Concepts:

- Strings

- String manipulation

Description: Write a Python program that takes a sentence as input and counts the number of words in the sentence.

Solution:

```
input_sentence = input("Enter a sentence: ")
words = input_sentence.split()
word_count = len(words)

print(f"The number of words in the sentence is: {word_count}")
```

Exercise 28: Swapping Two Variables

Concepts:

- Variables

- Tuples

Description: Write a Python program that takes two variables as input and swaps their values.

Solution:

```
x = input("Enter the value of x: ")
y = input("Enter the value of y: ")

print(f"Before swapping: x = {x}, y = {y}")

x, y = y, x
```

```
print(f"After swapping: x = {x}, y = {y}")
```

Exercise 29: Distance Between Two Points

Concepts:

- Functions

- Input/output

- Math module

Description: Write a Python program that calculates the distance between two points in a 2D space. The coordinates of the points should be provided by the user.

Solution:

```
import math

def distance(x1, y1, x2, y2):
    return math.sqrt((x2 - x1)**2 + (y2 - y1)**2)

x1, y1 = map(float, input("Enter the coordinates of the first point (x1, y1): ").split())
x2, y2 = map(float, input("Enter the coordinates of the second point (x2, y2): ").split())

result = distance(x1, y1, x2, y2)
print(f"The distance between the two points is: {result:.2f}")
```

Exercise 30: Convert Temperature from Celsius to Fahrenheit and Vice Versa

Concepts:

- Functions

- Input/output

- Conditional statements

Description: Write a Python program that converts temperatures between Celsius and Fahrenheit. The user should provide the temperature value and the unit.

Solution:

```python
def celsius_to_fahrenheit(celsius):
    return (celsius * 9/5) + 32

def fahrenheit_to_celsius(fahrenheit):
    return (fahrenheit - 32) * 5/9

temperature = float(input("Enter the temperature value: "))
unit = input("Enter the unit (C for Celsius, F for Fahrenheit): ")

if unit.upper() == "C":
    result = celsius_to_fahrenheit(temperature)
    print(f"{temperature} Celsius is equal to {result:.2f} Fahrenheit")
elif unit.upper() == "F":
    result = fahrenheit_to_celsius(temperature)
    print(f"{temperature} Fahrenheit is equal to {result:.2f} Celsius")
else:
    print("Invalid unit. Please enter 'C' for Celsius or 'F' for Fahrenheit.")
```

INTERMEDIATE LEVEL
CHAPTER 2

INTERMEDIATE LEVEL CONCEPTS

In this chapter you will practice **63 intermediate level python concepts** during the next **40 intermediate level exercises**. These exercises will guide you through each concept, providing detailed explanations and examples so that you can gain a solid understanding of each one. By the end of the 40 exercises, you will have not only practice 63 (maybe new) concepts, but you will also have developed the skills to apply them in real-world situations. This will give you a strong foundation on which to build as you continue to advance your knowledge and abilities in this field.

The concepts are organized alphabetically.

Concepts List:

1. Asynchronous programming using asyncio 66
2. Basic data analysis using Pandas 66
3. Browser automation and DOM manipulation 67
4. Classes, objects, and inheritance 68
5. Command-line arguments using the argparse module 69
6. Connecting to a database using the SQLite3 module 70
7. Convolutional neural networks and image recognition 70
8. Coroutines 72
9. Creating and manipulating arrays 72
10. Creating tables and inserting data 73
11. Creating tables and querying data 74
12. Data analysis using Pandas 75
13. Data analysis with NumPy 75
14. Data encryption using the cryptography library 76
15. Data manipulation using NumPy and Pandas 77

16. Data manipulation using Pandas 78
17. Data preparation, model training, and prediction 79
18. Data visualization with Matplotlib 80
19. Deep learning with Keras 81
20. Email sending using the smtplib library 82
21. Event loops 83
22. File I/O in Python 83
23. GUI programming using the Tkinter library 84
24. GUI programming with PyQt 85
25. HTML parsing and navigation 86
26. HTML parsing using BeautifulSoup 87
27. HTTP methods and routing 88
28. HTTP requests using the requests module 88
29. Image manipulation and conversion 89
30. Image processing using the Pillow library 90
31. JSON parsing 91
32. Line plots and labels 91
33. Loading and manipulating data with DataFrames 92
34. Log levels and handlers 93
35. Logging in Python 94
36. Machine learning using scikit-learn 95
37. Natural language processing using the NLTK library 96
38. Object-oriented programming in Python 97
39. Object-relational mapping using SQLAlchemy 97
40. Pattern matching and substitution 98
41. Querying data using SQL 99
42. Reading and filtering data 100
43. Reading and writing files 100
44. Reading and writing files using Python's built-in open() function 102
45. Reading and writing text files 102
46. Reading data from a CSV file using Pandas 103
47. Regular expressions in Python 104
48. RESTful APIs and HTTP requests 105
49. RESTful architecture and HTTP methods 105
50. Searching for patterns in text 107
51. Server-client architecture 108
52. SMTP servers and email authentication 109

53. Socket programming using the socket module 110
54. String manipulation 111
55. Symmetric and asymmetric encryption 111
56. Tokenization, stemming, and POS tagging 112
57. Web API integration using the requests library 113
58. Web APIs with Flask 113
59. Web development using the Flask framework 114
60. Web scraping using BeautifulSoup 115
61. Web scraping with Beautiful Soup and Requests 116
62. Web scraping with Selenium 117
63. Widgets and event handling 118

Intermediate Level - Concepts

1. Asynchronous programming using asyncio

Asynchronous programming is a programming paradigm that allows you to write programs that can execute multiple tasks concurrently, without blocking the main thread of execution. Python provides a built-in module called `asyncio` that allows you to write asynchronous programs using coroutines and event loops. Here's an example:

```python
import asyncio

async def say_hello():
    print('Hello')
    await asyncio.sleep(1)
    print('World')

async def main():
    await asyncio.gather(say_hello(), say_hello())

asyncio.run(main())
```

In this example, we define two coroutines (`say_hello()` and `main()`) that use the `async` keyword to indicate that they can be executed asynchronously. Inside the `say_hello()` coroutine, we print 'Hello', wait for 1 second using the `asyncio.sleep()` function, and then print 'World'.

In the `main()` coroutine, we use the `asyncio.gather()` function to execute the `say_hello()` coroutine twice concurrently. Finally, we use the `asyncio.run()` function to execute the `main()` coroutine in an event loop.

2. Basic data analysis using Pandas

Pandas also provides tools for basic data analysis, such as calculating summary statistics and creating plots. Here are some examples:

- Summary statistics: You can calculate summary statistics for a DataFrame or a specific column using methods like `describe()`, `mean()`, `median()`, `std()`, and `var()`.

For example, to calculate the mean and standard deviation of a column, you can use the following code:

```python
mean = df['column_name'].mean()
 std = df['column_name'].std()
```

- Plotting: You can create various types of plots using the `plot()` method of a DataFrame or a specific column. Pandas uses Matplotlib to create the plots. For example, to create a line plot of a column, you can use the following code:

```python
df['column_name'].plot(kind='line')
```

You can also customize the plot by passing additional parameters to the `plot()` method.

3. Browser automation and DOM manipulation

Browser automation and DOM manipulation are techniques for interacting with web pages using automated scripts or tools. Python's `selenium` library provides a powerful and flexible framework for automating web browsers and performing web scraping tasks.

Here's an example of using `selenium` to automate a web browser and manipulate the DOM:

```python
from selenium import webdriver

# Create a webdriver instance and load a website
driver = webdriver.Chrome()
driver.get('https://www.example.com')

# Find an element on the page using a CSS selector and set its value
element = driver.find_element_by_css_selector('#search')
element.send_keys('python')

# Submit a form on the page
form = driver.find_element_by_css_selector('#search-form')
form.submit()
```

```
# Wait for some time to let the search results load
driver.implicitly_wait(10)

# Find a list of links on the search results page and click the first one
links = driver.find_elements_by_css_selector('.result a')
links[0].click()

# Wait for some time to let the new page load
driver.implicitly_wait(10)

# Print the title of the new page
print(driver.title)

# Close the browser window
driver.quit()
```

In this example, we create a `webdriver` instance using the Chrome browser driver, and load a website named `https://www.example.com` . We use various methods provided by `Selenium` to interact with elements on the page, such as finding an element by its CSS selector, setting its value, submitting a form, and clicking a link. We then wait for some time to let the search results and the new page load, and print the title of the new page using the `title` attribute of the `webdriver` instance. Finally, we close the browser window using the `quit()` method.

4. Classes, objects, and inheritance

Classes, objects, and inheritance are fundamental concepts in object-oriented programming (OOP). A class is a blueprint for creating objects, which are instances of the class. A class defines the attributes (data) and methods (functions) of an object. Inheritance is a mechanism in OOP that allows one class to inherit the attributes and methods of another class.

Here's an example of using Python to define classes, objects, and inheritance:

```
class Animal:     def __init__(self, name):
        self.name = name

    def speak(self):
        print(f"{self.name} makes a sound.")

class Dog(Animal):
    def __init__(self, name):
```

```
        super().__init__(name)

    def speak(self):
        print(f"{self.name} barks.")

# Create objects and call their methods
a = Animal("Generic animal")
a.speak()
d = Dog("Rover")
d.speak()
```

In this example, we define two classes: `Animal` and `Dog`. The `Animal` class has an `__init__()` method that initializes the `name` attribute, and a `speak()` method that prints a generic message. The `Dog` class inherits from the `Animal` class and overrides the `speak()` method with a specific message. We create objects of both classes and call their `speak()` methods. This example demonstrates the basic principles of classes, objects, and inheritance in Python.

5. Command-line arguments using the argparse module

The `argparse` module provides a way to parse command-line arguments in a Python script. It allows you to define the arguments that your script expects and their types, and it generates help messages and error messages for the user. Here's an example:

```
import argparse

parser = argparse.ArgumentParser(description='Description of your script')
parser.add_argument('-f', '--file', type=str, required=True, help='Path to the input fil
e')
parser.add_argument('-n', '--number', type=int, default=10, help='Number of items to proce
ss')
args = parser.parse_args()

print(args.file)
print(args.number)
```

In this example, the script expects two arguments: `-f/--file`, which is a required argument of type string, and `-n/--number`, which is an optional argument of type integer with a default value of 10. When the script is run with the `-h` or `--help` option, argparse generates a help message based on the arguments that you defined.

6. Connecting to a database using the SQLite3 module

The `sqlite3` module in Python provides a simple way to work with SQLite databases. SQLite is a lightweight, serverless database engine that stores data in a single file on disk. The `sqlite3` module allows you to create and manipulate databases, and execute SQL commands against them.

Here's an example of using Python to connect to an SQLite database:

```python
pythonCopy code
import sqlite3

# Connect to a database (or create it if it doesn't exist)
conn = sqlite3.connect('example.db')

# Create a table and insert some data
c = conn.cursor()
c.execute('''CREATE TABLE users (id INTEGER PRIMARY KEY, name TEXT, email TEXT)''')
c.execute('''INSERT INTO users (name, email) VALUES (?, ?)''', ('John', 'john@example.com'))
c.execute('''INSERT INTO users (name, email) VALUES (?, ?)''', ('Jane', 'jane@example.com'))

# Commit the changes and close the connection
conn.commit()
conn.close()
```

In this example, we use the `connect()` method from the `sqlite3` module to connect to an SQLite database `example.db`. If the database does not exist, it will be created. We then create a table `users` with three columns: `id`, `name`, and `email`. We insert two rows of data into the table using the `execute()` method and placeholders for the values. Finally, we commit the changes and close the connection. This example demonstrates the basic principles of connecting to a database using the `sqlite3` module in Python.

7. Convolutional neural networks and image recognition

Convolutional neural networks (CNNs) are a type of neural network that are particularly suited for image recognition and classification tasks. CNNs consist of convolutional layers that apply filters to input images, pooling layers that downsample the outputs of the convolutional layers, and fully connected layers that perform the final classification. Python's `Keras` library provides a high-level API for building and training CNNs, with support for a wide range of network architectures, layers, activations, optimizers, loss functions, and metrics.

Here's an example of using `Keras` to build and train a CNN for image recognition:

```python
pythonCopy code
from keras.models import Sequential
from keras.layers import Conv2D, MaxPooling2D, Flatten, Dense
from keras.optimizers import SGD
from keras.datasets import mnist
from keras.utils import to_categorical

# Load the MNIST dataset
(X_train, y_train), (X_test, y_test) = mnist.load_data()

# Preprocess the images and labels
X_train = X_train.reshape((X_train.shape[0], 28, 28, 1))
X_test = X_test.reshape((X_test.shape[0], 28, 28, 1))
X_train = X_train.astype('float32') / 255
X_test = X_test.astype('float32') / 255
y_train = to_categorical(y_train)
y_test = to_categorical(y_test)

# Define a CNN model
model = Sequential()
model.add(Conv2D(32, (3, 3), activation='relu', input_shape=(28, 28, 1)))
model.add(MaxPooling2D((2, 2)))
model.add(Conv2D(64, (3, 3), activation='relu'))
model.add(MaxPooling2D((2, 2)))
model.add(Conv2D(64, (3, 3), activation='relu'))
model.add(Flatten())
model.add(Dense(64, activation='relu'))
model.add(Dense(10, activation='softmax'))

# Compile the model with an optimizer, loss function, and metric
model.compile(optimizer=SGD(lr=0.01), loss='categorical_crossentropy', metrics=['accurac
y'])

# Train the model on the training set
model.fit(X_train, y_train, epochs=5, batch_size=64)

# Evaluate the model on the testing set
loss, accuracy = model.evaluate(X_test, y_test)

# Print the results
print('Loss:', loss)
print('Accuracy:', accuracy)
```

In this example, we load the MNIST dataset using the `mnist.load_data()` function, preprocess the images and labels, and define a CNN model using the `Sequential()` class and the appropriate `Conv2D()`, `MaxPooling2D()`, `Flatten()`, and `Dense()` layers. We then compile the model with an optimizer, loss function, and metric using the `compile()` method, and train the model on the training set using the `fit()` method. Finally, we evaluate the model on the testing set using the `evaluate()` method, and print the loss and accuracy of the model to the console.

This example demonstrates the basic steps involved in building and training a CNN using `Keras`, as well as the importance of data preprocessing and model evaluation in the machine learning workflow.

8. Coroutines

A coroutine is a special type of function that can be paused and resumed while it's running. Coroutines are used extensively in asynchronous programming to allow multiple tasks to execute concurrently without blocking the main thread of execution. Here's an example of a coroutine:

```
scssCopy code
import asyncio

async def say_hello():
    print('Hello')
    await asyncio.sleep(1)
    print('World')

asyncio.run(say_hello())
```

In this example, we define a coroutine called `say_hello()` using the `async` keyword. Inside the coroutine, we print 'Hello', wait for 1 second using the `asyncio.sleep()` function, and then print 'World'. We then execute the coroutine using the `asyncio.run()` function.

Coroutines are similar to regular functions, but they use the `await` keyword to indicate that they are waiting for a result or a task to complete. Coroutines can be executed concurrently using an event loop.

9. Creating and manipulating arrays

Arrays are a fundamental data structure in computer programming, and are widely used for a range of data analysis tasks. Python provides a comprehensive set of tools for creating and manipulating arrays, including the `list` and `array` classes, as well as specialized libraries like NumPy and Pandas.

Here's an example of using Python to create and manipulate arrays:

```php
phpCopy code
import array

# Create a Python array
a = array.array('i', [1, 2, 3, 4, 5])

# Print the array and its properties
print(a)
print(a.typecode)
print(len(a))

# Manipulate the array
a[2] = 6
b = a[1:4]
c = array.array('i', [6, 7, 8])
d = a + c

# Print the results
print(a)
print(b)
print(d)
```

In this example, we use the `array` class from the Python standard library to create a Python array `a`, and print its type code and length. We then manipulate the array by changing one of its elements, creating a slice of the array, and adding another array to it. Finally, we print the results of these operations. This example demonstrates the basic principles of creating and manipulating arrays in Python.

10. Creating tables and inserting data

When working with relational databases, you typically create tables to store your data. You can create tables and insert data using SQL statements. Here's an example:

```python
pythonCopy code
import sqlite3

# Connect to the database
```

```python
conn = sqlite3.connect('example.db')

# Create a cursor object to execute SQL queries
c = conn.cursor()

# Create a table
c.execute('''CREATE TABLE users
             (id INTEGER PRIMARY KEY, name TEXT, age INTEGER)''')

# Insert data into the table
c.execute("INSERT INTO users VALUES (1, 'John', 30)")
c.execute("INSERT INTO users VALUES (2, 'Jane', 25)")

# Commit the changes
conn.commit()

# Close the connection
conn.close()
```

In this example, we first connect to a database named `example.db`. We then create a table named `users` with three columns (`id`, `name`, and `age`) and insert two rows of data into it. We commit the changes to the database and then close the connection to the database.

11. Creating tables and querying data

Creating tables and querying data are fundamental operations in relational databases. Python's `sqlite3` library provides a lightweight and easy-to-use interface for working with SQLite databases, which are a popular choice for small to medium-sized projects.

Here's an example of creating a database table and querying data using `sqlite3`:

```python
import sqlite3

# Connect to a database
conn = sqlite3.connect('example.db')

# Create a database table
conn.execute('CREATE TABLE users (id INTEGER PRIMARY KEY, name TEXT, email TEXT)')

# Insert some data into the table
conn.execute('INSERT INTO users (name, email) VALUES (?, ?)', ('John Doe', 'john@example.com'))
conn.execute('INSERT INTO users (name, email) VALUES (?, ?)', ('Jane Smith', 'jane@example.com'))
conn.commit()
```

```
# Query the data from the table
cursor = conn.execute('SELECT name, email FROM users')
rows = cursor.fetchall()
for row in rows:
    print(row[0], row[1])
```

In this example, we connect to a SQLite database named `'example.db'` using the `sqlite3.connect()` function. We create a database table named `'users'` using the `execute()` method of the connection object, and insert some data into the table using the `execute()` method and SQL queries. Finally, we query the data from the table using the `execute()` method and a SELECT statement, and print the results using a for loop.

Note that the `execute()` method returns a cursor object, which we can use to fetch the results of a query. The `fetchall()` method of the cursor object returns a list of tuples, where each tuple contains the values of a row in the result set.

12. Data analysis using Pandas

Pandas is a powerful data analysis library for Python. Here are some examples of what you can do with Pandas:

- Data cleaning: You can use Pandas to clean and preprocess your data. This includes handling missing values, transforming data types, and dealing with outliers and errors.

- Data exploration: Pandas provides tools for exploring and visualizing your data. This includes calculating summary statistics, creating histograms and scatter plots, and grouping and aggregating data.

- Data modeling: You can use Pandas to build and evaluate predictive models. This includes feature engineering, model selection, and hyperparameter tuning.

Overall, Pandas provides a comprehensive set of tools for working with data in Python.

13. Data analysis with NumPy

NumPy is a popular numerical computing library for Python, which provides a high-performance array object and a comprehensive set of tools for working with arrays. NumPy arrays are used for a wide range of data analysis tasks, including statistical analysis, data processing, and scientific computing.

Here's an example of using NumPy to create and manipulate arrays:

```python
import numpy as np

# Create a NumPy array
a = np.array([1, 2, 3, 4, 5])

# Print the array and its properties
print(a)
print(a.shape)
print(a.dtype)

# Perform array operations
b = a + 1
c = a * 2
d = np.sqrt(a)
e = np.sum(a)

# Print the results
print(b)
print(c)
print(d)
print(e)
```

In this example, we use the `numpy` library to create a NumPy array `a`, and print its shape and data type. We then perform a range of operations on the array, including addition, multiplication, square root, and sum. Finally, we print the results of these operations. This example demonstrates the basic principles of using NumPy for data analysis.

14. Data encryption using the cryptography library

Data encryption is the process of converting plain text into a secret code to protect it from unauthorized access. Python's `cryptography` library provides a wide range of cryptographic primitives, such as ciphers, hashes, and message authentication codes, to help you implement encryption and decryption algorithms in your Python programs.

Here's an example of encrypting and decrypting data using the `cryptography` library:

```python
from cryptography.fernet import Fernet

# Generate a secret key
```

```
key = Fernet.generate_key()

# Create a Fernet cipher object
cipher = Fernet(key)

# Encrypt the data
data = b'some plain text data'
encrypted_data = cipher.encrypt(data)

# Decrypt the data
decrypted_data = cipher.decrypt(encrypted_data)
```

In this example, we generate a secret key using the `Fernet.generate_key()` function and create a Fernet cipher object using the key. We use the `encrypt()` method to encrypt some plain text data and store the encrypted data in the `encrypted_data` variable. We then use the `decrypt()` method to decrypt the encrypted data and store the decrypted data in the `decrypted_data` variable.

The `cryptography` library provides many other functions and algorithms for data encryption and decryption, including symmetric and asymmetric encryption.

15. Data manipulation using NumPy and Pandas

NumPy and Pandas are popular libraries in Python for data manipulation and analysis. NumPy provides support for multidimensional arrays and mathematical operations on arrays, while Pandas provides support for data frames and data manipulation operations on data frames.

Here's an example of using NumPy and Pandas to manipulate data:

```
import numpy as np
import pandas as pd

# Create a NumPy array
arr = np.array([[1, 2], [3, 4], [5, 6]])

# Print the array
print(arr)

# Compute the mean and standard deviation of the array
print(np.mean(arr))
print(np.std(arr))

# Create a Pandas data frame
df = pd.DataFrame({'name': ['Alice', 'Bob', 'Charlie'], 'age': [25, 30, 35], 'gender':
```

```
 ['F', 'M', 'M']})

# Print the data frame
print(df)

# Filter the data frame to include only rows with age greater than 30
df_filtered = df[df['age'] > 30]

# Print the filtered data frame
print(df_filtered)
```

In this example, we use NumPy to create a two-dimensional array `arr` and compute its mean and standard deviation. We then use Pandas to create a data frame `df` with three columns: `name`, `age`, and `gender`. We filter the data frame to include only rows with age greater than 30, and store the filtered data frame in a new variable `df_filtered`. Finally, we print the array and the data frames. This example demonstrates the basic principles of data manipulation using NumPy and Pandas.

16. Data manipulation using Pandas

Pandas provides many powerful tools for manipulating data in a DataFrame. Here are some examples:

- Filtering: You can filter rows in a DataFrame based on certain criteria using boolean indexing. For example, to filter a DataFrame to only include rows where a certain column has a value greater than a certain number, you can use the following code:

```
filtered_df = df[df['column_name'] > 10]
```

- Grouping: You can group rows in a DataFrame based on the values in one or more columns, and then apply aggregation functions to the groups. For example, to group a DataFrame by the values in a column and calculate the mean of another column for each group, you can use the following code:

```
grouped_df = df.groupby('column_name')['other_column'].mean()
```

- Merging: You can combine two or more DataFrames based on a common column or index. For example, to merge two DataFrames on a common column, you can use the following code:

```
merged_df = pd.merge(df1, df2, on='column_name')
```

- Reshaping: You can reshape a DataFrame using methods like `pivot()`, `melt()`, and `stack()`. These methods allow you to transform a DataFrame from a wide format to a long format or vice versa. For example, to pivot a DataFrame from long to wide format, you can use the following code:

```
pivoted_df = df.pivot(index='index_column', columns='column_name', values='value_colu
mn')
```

17. Data preparation, model training, and prediction

Data preparation, model training, and prediction are common steps in machine learning workflows. Python's `scikit-learn` library provides a powerful and easy-to-use framework for implementing machine learning algorithms and models, as well as functions and classes for data preprocessing, feature selection, model selection, and model evaluation.

Here's an example of using `scikit-learn` to prepare data, train a model, and make predictions on new data:

```
from sklearn.datasets import load_iris
from sklearn.model_selection import train_test_split
from sklearn.tree import DecisionTreeClassifier from sklearn.metrics import accuracy_score

# Load the Iris dataset
iris = load_iris()

# Split the dataset into training and testing sets
X_train, X_test, y_train, y_test = train_test_split(iris.data, iris.target, test_size=0.3,
random_state=42)
```

```
# Train a decision tree classifier on the training set
clf = DecisionTreeClassifier()
clf.fit(X_train, y_train)

# Make predictions on new data
new_data = [[5.1, 3.5, 1.4, 0.2], [6.2, 2.9, 4.3, 1.3], [7.7, 3.8, 6.7, 2.2]]
new_predictions = clf.predict(new_data)

# Print the results
print('New data:', new_data)
print('New predictions:', new_predictions)
```

In this example, we load the Iris dataset using the `load_iris()` function, split the dataset into training and testing sets using the `train_test_split()` function, and train a decision tree classifier on the training set using the `DecisionTreeClassifier()` class. We then use the trained model to make predictions on new data using the `predict()` method of the classifier object. Finally, we print the new data and the corresponding predictions to the console. This example demonstrates the basic workflow of data preparation, model training, and prediction in machine learning.

18. Data visualization with Matplotlib

Matplotlib is a popular data visualization library for Python, which provides a comprehensive set of tools for creating a wide range of charts, graphs, and plots. Matplotlib is designed to be easy to use and highly customizable, and supports a wide range of data formats and output formats.

Here's an example of using Matplotlib to create a simple line plot:

```
import matplotlib.pyplot as plt

# Define the data to be plotted
x = [1, 2, 3, 4, 5]
y = [10, 8, 6, 4, 2]

# Create a Matplotlib figure and axis
fig, ax = plt.subplots()

# Plot the data as a line
ax.plot(x, y)

# Set the axis labels and title
ax.set_xlabel('X axis')
ax.set_ylabel('Y axis')
```

```
ax.set_title('My plot')

# Show the plot
plt.show()
```

In this example, we define the data to be plotted as two lists (`x` and `y`), and create a Matplotlib figure and axis using the `subplots()` method. We plot the data as a line using the `plot()` method, and set the axis labels and title using the `set_xlabel()` , `set_ylabel()` , and `set_title()` methods. Finally, we show the plot using the `show()` method. This example demonstrates the basic principles of data visualization using Matplotlib.

19. Deep learning with Keras

Deep learning is a subfield of machine learning that involves the use of artificial neural networks to model and solve complex problems. Python's `Keras` library provides a high-level API for building and training deep neural networks, with support for a wide range of network architectures, layers, activations, optimizers, loss functions, and metrics.

Here's an example of using `Keras` to build and train a simple neural network:

```
from keras.models import Sequential
from keras.layers import Dense
from keras.optimizers import SGD
from sklearn.datasets import load_iris
from sklearn.model_selection import train_test_split

# Load the Iris dataset
iris = load_iris()

# Split the dataset into training and testing sets
X_train, X_test, y_train, y_test = train_test_split(iris.data, iris.target, test_size=0.3,
random_state=42)

# Define a neural network model
model = Sequential()
model.add(Dense(units=10, activation='relu', input_dim=4))
model.add(Dense(units=3, activation='softmax'))

# Compile the model with an optimizer, loss function, and metric
sgd = SGD(lr=0.01)
model.compile(optimizer=sgd, loss='categorical_crossentropy', metrics=['accuracy'])

# Train the model on the training set
model.fit(X_train, y_train, epochs=100, batch_size=32)
```

```
# Evaluate the model on the testing set
loss, accuracy = model.evaluate(X_test, y_test)

# Print the results
print('Loss:', loss)
print('Accuracy:', accuracy)
```

In this example, we load the Iris dataset using the `load_iris()` function, split the dataset into training and testing sets using the `train_test_split()` function, and define a neural network model using the `Sequential()` class and the `Dense()` class for the layers. We then compile the model with an optimizer, loss function, and metric using the `compile()` method, and train the model on the training set using the `fit()` method. Finally, we evaluate the model on the testing set using the `evaluate()` method, and print the loss and accuracy of the model to the console.

20. Email sending using the smtplib library

Python's `smtplib` library allows you to send emails using the Simple Mail Transfer Protocol (SMTP). Here's an example:

```
import smtplib

# Define the email message
subject = 'Test email'
body = 'This is a test email'
sender_email = 'your_email@example.com'
receiver_email = 'recipient@example.com'
message = f'Subject: {subject}\n\n{body}'

# Create a SMTP server object
smtp_server = smtplib.SMTP('smtp.gmail.com', 587)

# Start the TLS encryption
smtp_server.starttls()

# Log in to the SMTP server
smtp_server.login(sender_email, 'your_password')

# Send the email
smtp_server.sendmail(sender_email, receiver_email, message)

# Quit the SMTP server
smtp_server.quit()
```

In this example, we define the email message including the subject, body, sender email, and recipient email. We then create an SMTP server object using the `smtplib.SMTP()` function and specify the SMTP server and port number to use. We start the TLS encryption using the `starttls()` method and log in to the SMTP server using the `login()` method.

We then use the `sendmail()` method to send the email and specify the sender email, recipient email, and message. Finally, we quit the SMTP server using the `quit()` method.

21. Event loops

An event loop is a programming construct that allows you to execute multiple tasks concurrently in a single thread of execution. In Python's asyncio module, an event loop is an object that manages the execution of coroutines and other asynchronous tasks.

Here's an example of using an event loop to execute a coroutine:

```python
import asyncio

async def say_hello():
    print('Hello')
    await asyncio.sleep(1)
    print('World')

loop = asyncio.get_event_loop()
loop.run_until_complete(say_hello())
loop.close()
```

In this example, we define a coroutine called `say_hello()`. We then create an event loop using the `asyncio.get_event_loop()` function and use the `run_until_complete()` method to execute the `say_hello()` coroutine. Finally, we close the event loop using the `close()` method.

Event loops allow you to execute multiple coroutines and other asynchronous tasks concurrently, without blocking the main thread of execution. You can also use event loops to handle I/O operations, network connections, and other types of asynchronous tasks.

22. File I/O in Python

File I/O (Input/Output) refers to the process of reading from and writing to files on disk or other storage devices. Python's built-in `open()` function allows you to open files in different modes, such as read-only, write-only, or append mode.

Here's an example of opening a file for reading and reading its contents:

```python
# Open a file for reading
with open('file.txt', 'r') as file:
    # Read the entire contents of the file
    contents = file.read()
    # Print the contents of the file
    print(contents)
```

In this example, we use the `open()` function to open a file named `file.txt` in read-only mode using the `'r'` mode specifier. We use a `with` statement to ensure that the file is closed automatically when the block is exited. We read the entire contents of the file using the `read()` method and store them in the `contents` variable. We then print the contents of the file.

23. GUI programming using the Tkinter library

GUI (Graphical User Interface) programming allows you to create interactive and user-friendly applications with buttons, menus, text boxes, and other visual elements. Python's `Tkinter` library provides a simple and easy-to-use interface for creating GUI applications in Python.

Here's an example of creating a simple GUI application using `Tkinter`:

```python
import tkinter as tk

# Create a new window
window = tk.Tk()

# Create a label
label = tk.Label(window, text='Hello, Tkinter!')

# Add the label to the window
label.pack()

# Start the main event loop
window.mainloop()
```

In this example, we create a new window using the `tk.Tk()` function and create a label using the `tk.Label()` function. We add the label to the window using the `pack()` method and start the main event loop using the `mainloop()` method.

`Tkinter` provides many other widgets and options for creating GUI applications, such as buttons, menus, text boxes, and images. You can also use `Tkinter` to bind events and callbacks to user actions, such as button clicks or menu selections.

24. GUI programming with PyQt

PyQt is a set of Python bindings for the Qt application framework, which is widely used for building graphical user interfaces (GUIs) in a variety of programming languages. PyQt provides a high-level API for building GUI applications using a combination of Qt widgets and Python code, with support for a wide range of widgets, layouts, signals, slots, and event handling.

Here's an example of using PyQt to create a simple GUI application:

```
from PyQt5.QtWidgets import QApplication, QWidget, QLabel, QVBoxLayout

# Define the PyQt application
app = QApplication([])

# Define a PyQt widget with a layout and a label
widget = QWidget()
layout = QVBoxLayout()
label = QLabel('Hello, world!')
layout.addWidget(label)
widget.setLayout(layout)
widget.show()

# Run the PyQt application
app.exec_()
```

In this example, we create a simple PyQt application using the `QApplication()` class, and define a `QWidget()` widget with a `QVBoxLayout()` layout and a `QLabel()` label. We add the label to the layout using the `addWidget()` method, and set the layout of the widget using the `setLayout()` method. Finally, we show the widget using the `show()` method, and run the PyQt application using the `exec_()` method. This example demonstrates the basic structure of a PyQt application, and how to create and display widgets using layouts and event handling.

25. HTML parsing and navigation

HTML parsing and navigation is the process of extracting specific data from HTML documents by identifying and manipulating their structural elements, such as tags, attributes, and content. Python's `BeautifulSoup` library provides a flexible and powerful interface for parsing and navigating HTML documents.

Here's an example of using `BeautifulSoup` to parse and navigate an HTML document:

```python
from bs4 import BeautifulSoup

# Load an HTML document
html = """
<html>
  <head>
    <title>My Page</title>
  </head>
  <body>
    <h1>Welcome to my page!</h1>
    <p>This is some text.</p>
    <ul>
      <li>Item 1</li>
      <li>Item 2</li>
      <li>Item 3</li>
    </ul>
  </body>
</html>
"""

# Parse the HTML document using BeautifulSoup
soup = BeautifulSoup(html, 'html.parser')

# Find the title tag
title = soup.title

# Find the h1 tag
h1 = soup.h1

# Find the first li tag
li = soup.li

# Find all the li tags
lis = soup.find_all('li')

# Print the results
```

```
print(title.text)
print(h1.text)
print(li.text)
for li in lis:
    print(li.text)
```

In this example, we load an HTML document as a string and parse it using the
`BeautifulSoup` library. We use various methods and functions provided by `BeautifulSoup`
to extract specific elements from the HTML document, such as the title, h1, and li tags.
We then print the text content of these elements.

26. HTML parsing using BeautifulSoup

BeautifulSoup is a Python library that allows you to parse HTML and XML documents. It
makes it easy to extract data from HTML documents by providing a simple way to
navigate and search the document's structure. To use BeautifulSoup, you first need to
install it:

```
pip install beautifulsoup4
```

Then, you can create a BeautifulSoup object from an HTML string or file:

```
from bs4 import BeautifulSoup

# Parse an HTML string
html = '<html><body><h1>Hello, world!</h1></body></html>'
soup = BeautifulSoup(html, 'html.parser')

# Parse an HTML file
with open('example.html') as f:
    soup = BeautifulSoup(f, 'html.parser')
```

Once you have a BeautifulSoup object, you can use its methods and properties to
navigate the document's structure and extract data. For example, to get the text of an
element with a specific tag name, you can use the `find()` method:

```
h1_element = soup.find('h1')
```

```
text = h1_element.text
```

27. HTTP methods and routing

HTTP (Hypertext Transfer Protocol) is the protocol used for transferring data over the web. HTTP requests can use different methods, such as GET, POST, PUT, and DELETE, to perform different actions on a resource. Here's an example of routing HTTP requests using the Flask framework:

```
from flask import Flask, request

app = Flask(__name__)

@app.route('/', methods=['GET', 'POST'])
def index():
    if request.method == 'GET':
        return 'This is a GET request'
    elif request.method == 'POST':
        return 'This is a POST request'
if __name__ == '__main__':       app.run()
```

In this example, we define a route for the root URL (/) and specify that it can handle both GET and POST requests using the `methods` parameter. Inside the route function, we use the `request.method` attribute to determine the type of request and return a different response depending on the method.

You can use routing to handle different types of requests and perform different actions based on the requested URL and data.

28. HTTP requests using the requests module

When you want to access data from a website, you can send an HTTP request to the website's server. The requests module in Python allows you to do this. To make a request using requests, you first need to import the module:

```
import requests
```

Then, you can use the `requests.get()` method to send a GET request to a URL and retrieve the response:

```python
response = requests.get('https://www.example.com')
```

You can then access the response's content, status code, headers, and other information using the properties of the `response` object. For example, to get the HTML content of the response, you can use the `text` property:

```python
html_content = response.text
```

29. Image manipulation and conversion

Pillow provides many functions for manipulating and converting images. Here are some examples:

- Cropping: You can crop an image using the `crop()` method. For example:

```python
from PIL import Image

# Open an image file
image = Image.open('image.jpg')

# Crop the image
image = image.crop((100, 100, 300, 300))

# Save the image to a file
image.save('image_cropped.jpg')
```

- Rotating: You can rotate an image using the `rotate()` method. For example:

```python
from PIL import Image

# Open an image file
image = Image.open('image.jpg')

# Rotate the image
```

```
image = image.rotate(45)

# Save the image to a file
image.save('image_rotated.jpg')
```

- Converting formats: You can convert an image to a different format using the `save()` method and specifying the format in the file name. For example:

```
from PIL import Image

# Open an image file
image = Image.open('image.jpg')
# Convert the image to PNG format
image.save('image.png')
```

Pillow provides many other functions for working with images, including resizing, filtering, and enhancing.

30. Image processing using the Pillow library

Pillow is a popular Python library for working with images. It provides a wide range of functions for opening, manipulating, and saving image files in various formats. Here's an example:

```
from PIL import Image

# Open an image file
image = Image.open('image.jpg')
# Resize the image
image = image.resize((500, 500))

# Convert the image to grayscale
image = image.convert('L')

# Save the image to a file
image.save('image_processed.jpg')
```

In this example, we open an image file using the `Image.open()` function and resize it using the `resize()` method. We then convert the image to grayscale using the `convert()`

method and save it to a file using the `save()` method. Pillow provides many other functions for working with images, including cropping, rotating, and filtering.

31. JSON parsing

JSON (JavaScript Object Notation) is a lightweight data interchange format that is widely used in web applications. Python provides a built-in module called `json` that allows you to parse and generate JSON data. Here are some examples:

- Parsing: You can parse a JSON string into a Python object using the `json.loads()` function. For example:

```python
import json

json_string = '{"name": "John", "age": 30, "city": "New York"}'
data = json.loads(json_string)

print(data['name'])
print(data['age'])
print(data['city'])
```

- Generating: You can generate a JSON string from a Python object using the `json.dumps()` function. For example:

```python
import json

data = {
    'name': 'John',
    'age': 30,
    'city': 'New York'
}

json_string = json.dumps(data)
print(json_string)
```

The `json` module also provides various other functions for encoding and decoding JSON data with more advanced features.

32. Line plots and labels

Line plots are a common type of chart used for visualizing data over time, and are widely used in scientific, financial, and engineering applications. Line plots typically show the relationship between two variables (x and y), with one variable plotted along the horizontal axis and the other variable plotted along the vertical axis. Line plots can be customized with a wide range of labels and annotations, including axis labels, titles, legends, and annotations.

Here's an example of using Matplotlib to create a line plot with labels:

```python
import matplotlib.pyplot as plt

# Define the data to be plotted
x = [1, 2, 3, 4, 5]  y = [10, 8, 6, 4, 2]

# Create a Matplotlib figure and axis
fig, ax = plt.subplots()

# Plot the data as a line with labels
ax.plot(x, y, label='My line plot')

# Set the axis labels, title, and legend
ax.set_xlabel('X axis')
ax.set_ylabel('Y axis')
ax.set_title('My plot')
ax.legend()

# Show the plot
plt.show()
```

In this example, we define the data to be plotted as two lists (x and y), and create a Matplotlib figure and axis using the subplots() method. We plot the data as a line with a label using the plot() method and the label parameter. We set the axis labels, title, and legend using the set_xlabel() , set_ylabel() , set_title() , and legend() methods. Finally, we show the plot using the show() method. This example demonstrates the basic principles of creating a line plot with labels using Matplotlib.

33. Loading and manipulating data with DataFrames

DataFrames are a data structure provided by the pandas library that allows you to store and manipulate tabular data, similar to a spreadsheet or database table. DataFrames provide many built-in functions and methods for data manipulation, such as filtering, sorting, grouping, and aggregation.

Here's an example of loading data from a CSV file into a DataFrame and manipulating the data:

```python
import pandas as pd

# Load data from a CSV file into a DataFrame
df = pd.read_csv('data.csv')

# Print the first five rows of the DataFrame
print(df.head())

# Filter the data to only show rows where the value in column A is greater than 10
filtered = df[df['A'] > 10]

# Group the data by the values in column B and calculate the mean of column C for each group
grouped = df.groupby('B')['C'].mean()

# Sort the data by the values in column A in descending order
sorted = df.sort_values('A', ascending=False)

# Save the filtered, grouped, and sorted data to new CSV files
filtered.to_csv('filtered.csv', index=False)
grouped.to_csv('grouped.csv')
sorted.to_csv('sorted.csv', index=False)
```

In this example, we use the `pandas` library to load data from a CSV file named `data.csv` into a DataFrame. We then manipulate the data in various ways, such as filtering, grouping, and sorting the data. We save the manipulated data to new CSV files named `filtered.csv`, `grouped.csv`, and `sorted.csv`.

34. Log levels and handlers

The `logging` module supports different levels of logging, which can be used to control the verbosity and severity of log messages. Here are the standard logging levels supported by the `logging` module, in increasing order of severity:

- `DEBUG`

- `INFO`

- WARNING

- ERROR

- CRITICAL

You can configure the logging level for your program using the `basicConfig()` function or by creating a custom `Logger` object.

The `logging` module also supports different handlers, which can be used to specify where log messages should be sent, such as a file, console, or network socket. Some of the built-in handlers supported by the `logging` module include:

- `StreamHandler` : Sends log messages to the console.

- `FileHandler` : Sends log messages to a file.

- `SMTPHandler` : Sends log messages to an email address.

- `SysLogHandler` : Sends log messages to the system log.

You can configure the logging handlers for your program using the `basicConfig()` function or by creating a custom `Logger` object.

35. Logging in Python

Logging is the process of recording messages or events from a program to a file or console for later analysis and debugging. Python's built-in `logging` module provides a powerful and flexible logging framework that you can use to log messages at different levels of severity, such as debug, info, warning, error, and critical.

Here's an example of using the `logging` module to log messages to a file and console:

```python
import logging

# Configure the logging system
logging.basicConfig(filename='example.log', level=logging.DEBUG)

# Log some messages
logging.debug('This is a debug message')
logging.info('This is an info message')
logging.warning('This is a warning message')
logging.error('This is an error message')
logging.critical('This is a critical message')
```

In this example, we use the `basicConfig()` function to configure the logging system to write messages to a file named `example.log` and set the logging level to `DEBUG`. We then use the logging functions `debug()`, `info()`, `warning()`, `error()`, and `critical()` to log messages at different levels of severity.

36. Machine learning using scikit-learn

Machine learning is a subfield of artificial intelligence that involves the development of algorithms and models that can learn from data and make predictions or decisions based on that data. Python's `scikit-learn` library provides a powerful and easy-to-use framework for implementing machine learning algorithms and models.

Here's an example of using `scikit-learn` to perform supervised learning on a dataset:

```
from sklearn.datasets import load_iris
from sklearn.model_selection import train_test_split
from sklearn.tree import DecisionTreeClassifier from sklearn.metrics import accuracy_score

# Load the Iris dataset
iris = load_iris()

# Split the dataset into training and testing sets
X_train, X_test, y_train, y_test = train_test_split(iris.data, iris.target, test_size=0.3,
random_state=42)

# Train a decision tree classifier on the training set
clf = DecisionTreeClassifier()
clf.fit(X_train, y_train)

# Make predictions on the testing set and calculate the accuracy
y_pred = clf.predict(X_test)
accuracy = accuracy_score(y_test, y_pred)

# Print the results
print('Accuracy:', accuracy)
```

In this example, we load the Iris dataset using the `load_iris()` function, split the dataset into training and testing sets using the `train_test_split()` function, and train a decision tree classifier on the training set using the `DecisionTreeClassifier()` class. We then make predictions on the testing set using the `predict()` method of the classifier object, and calculate the accuracy of the predictions using the `accuracy_score()` function. Finally, we print the accuracy of the model to the console.

37. Natural language processing using the NLTK library

Natural language processing (NLP) is the study of computational methods for understanding and generating human language. Python's NLTK (Natural Language Toolkit) library provides a comprehensive set of tools and resources for NLP, such as text preprocessing, part-of-speech tagging, named entity recognition, sentiment analysis, and machine learning algorithms.

Here's an example of using NLTK to perform text preprocessing and analysis on a piece of text:

```python
import nltk
from nltk.tokenize import word_tokenize
from nltk.corpus import stopwords
from nltk.stem import WordNetLemmatizer
from nltk.sentiment import SentimentIntensityAnalyzer

# Download and install required resources
nltk.download('punkt')
nltk.download('stopwords')
nltk.download('wordnet')
nltk.download('vader_lexicon')

# Define some text to analyze
text = 'This is a sample sentence for NLP analysis.'

# Tokenize the text into words
tokens = word_tokenize(text)

# Remove stop words from the tokens
stop_words = set(stopwords.words('english'))
filtered_tokens = [word for word in tokens if word.lower() not in stop_words]

# Lemmatize the filtered tokens
lemmatizer = WordNetLemmatizer()
lemmatized_tokens = [lemmatizer.lemmatize(word) for word in filtered_tokens]
# Perform sentiment analysis on the text
analyzer = SentimentIntensityAnalyzer()
scores = analyzer.polarity_scores(text)

# Print the results
print('Original text:', text)
print('Tokenized text:', tokens)
print('Filtered text:', filtered_tokens)
print('Lemmatized text:', lemmatized_tokens)
print('Sentiment scores:', scores)
```

In this example, we use various functions and resources provided by NLTK to preprocess and analyze a piece of text. We tokenize the text into words using the word_tokenize() function, remove stop words from the tokens using the stopwords corpus, and lemmatize the filtered tokens using the WordNetLemmatizer class. We then perform sentiment analysis on the text using the SentimentIntensityAnalyzer class, which uses a lexicon-based approach to assign scores to the text based on its positive, negative, and neutral polarity. Finally, we print the results of each step to the console.

38. Object-oriented programming in Python

Object-oriented programming (OOP) is a programming paradigm that is widely used for building complex software systems. OOP involves organizing code into objects, which are instances of classes that encapsulate data and behavior. Python provides full support for OOP, including classes, objects, inheritance, and polymorphism.

Here's an example of using Python to define a simple class:

```python
class Person:
    def __init__(self, name, age):
        self.name = name
        self.age = age

    def say_hello(self):
        print(f"Hello, my name is {self.name} and I am {self.age} years old.")

# Create a Person object and call its methods
p = Person("John", 30)
p.say_hello()
```

In this example, we define a simple Person class that has a name and age attribute, and a say_hello() method that prints a message. We create a Person object p with the name "John" and age 30, and call its say_hello() method. This example demonstrates the basic principles of object-oriented programming in Python. OOP can help to organize code, make it more modular and reusable, and create complex systems that are easier to understand and maintain.

39. Object-relational mapping using SQLAlchemy

Object-relational mapping (ORM) is a programming technique that allows you to map relational database tables to objects in your code, and vice versa. Python's SQLAlchemy library provides a powerful and flexible ORM framework that allows you to interact with databases using Python objects and SQL queries.

Here's an example of using SQLAlchemy to create a database table and query data:

```python
from sqlalchemy import create_engine, Column, Integer, String
  from sqlalchemy.orm import sessionmaker
from sqlalchemy.ext.declarative import declarative_base

# Create a database engine and session
engine = create_engine('sqlite:///example.db')
Session = sessionmaker(bind=engine)
session = Session()

# Define a database table using a declarative base
Base = declarative_base()
class User(Base):
    __tablename__ = 'users'
    id = Column(Integer, primary_key=True)
    name = Column(String)
    email = Column(String)

# Create the database table Base.metadata.create_all(engine)

# Add some data to the table
user1 = User(name='John Doe', email='john@example.com')
user2 = User(name='Jane Smith', email='jane@example.com')
session.add(user1)
session.add(user2)
session.commit()

# Query the data from the table
users = session.query(User).all()
for user in users:
    print(user.name, user.email)
```

In this example, we create a database table named 'users' using a declarative base class. We add some data to the table using a Session object and SQL queries. Finally, we query the data from the table using the query() method of the Session object, and print the results.

40. Pattern matching and substitution

Pattern matching and substitution are techniques for finding and replacing specific patterns in text using regular expressions or other matching algorithms. Python's re module provides a powerful set of functions and methods for pattern matching and substitution.

Here's an example of using pattern matching and substitution in Python:

```python
import re

# Find all email addresses in a string and replace them with 'redacted'
string = 'My email is john@example.com and my friend\'s email is jane@example.com'
redacted = re.sub(r'\b[\w.-]+@[\w.-]+\.[\w.-]+\b', 'redacted', string)
print(redacted)
```

In this example, we use a regular expression to match all email addresses in a string, and replace them with the word `'redacted'`. The regular expression uses a pattern that matches any string that looks like an email address, such as `'john@example.com'` and `'jane@example.com'`.

41. Querying data using SQL

After you've inserted data into a table, you can retrieve it using SQL queries. Here's an example:

```python
import sqlite3

# Connect to the database
conn = sqlite3.connect('example.db')

# Create a cursor object to execute SQL queries
c = conn.cursor()

# Execute a SELECT query
c.execute("SELECT * FROM users")
rows = c.fetchall()
for row in rows:
    print(row)

# Close the connection
conn.close()
```

In this example, we first connect to the `example.db` database and create a cursor object. We then execute a SELECT query to retrieve all rows from the `users` table, fetch the results using the `fetchall()` method, and print them out. Finally, we close the connection to the database.

You can also use SQL to filter, sort, and aggregate data, and to perform more complex operations on your data.

42. Reading and filtering data

Reading and filtering data is a common task in data analysis and processing. Python provides a wide range of tools for reading and filtering data, including the `csv` module, the `pandas` library, and the built-in `filter()` function.

Here's an example of using Python to read and filter data:

```python
import csv

# Read a CSV file and filter its contents
with open('data.csv', 'r') as f:
    reader = csv.DictReader(f)
    data = [row for row in reader if row['score'] > '90']

# Print the filtered data
for row in data:
    print(row['name'], row['score'])
```

In this example, we use the `csv` module to read the contents of a CSV file `data.csv` and store them in a list of dictionaries. We then filter the list to include only rows with a score greater than 90, and print the filtered data. This example demonstrates the basic principles of reading and filtering data in Python.

43. Reading and writing files

In addition to reading and writing files, you can also append to files, create new files, and delete files using Python's `open()` function. Here are some examples:

Appending to a file:

```python
# Open a file for appending
```

```python
with open('file.txt', 'a') as file:
    # Append some text to the file
    file.write('Hello, again!')
```

In this example, we use the `open()` function to open a file named `file.txt` in append mode using the `'a'` mode specifier. We use a `with` statement to ensure that the file is closed automatically when the block is exited. We append some text to the file using the `write()` method.

Creating a new file:

```python
# Open a new file for writing
with open('new_file.txt', 'w') as file:
    # Write some text to the file
    file.write('This is a new file!')
```

In this example, we use the `open()` function to open a new file named `new_file.txt` in write mode using the `'w'` mode specifier. We use a `with` statement to ensure that the file is closed automatically when the block is exited. We write some text to the file using the `write()` method.

Deleting a file:

```python
import os

# Delete a file
os.remove('file.txt')
```

In this example, we use the `os.remove()` function to delete a file named `file.txt` from the file system.

Python's `open()` function also allows you to specify additional parameters such as encoding, buffering, and newline options. It's important to ensure that files are closed properly and that file paths and permissions are handled correctly to avoid errors and security issues.

44. Reading and writing files using Python's built-in open() function

Python's built-in `open()` function allows you to read and write files. To open a file for reading, you can use the following code:

```
with open('file.txt', 'r') as f:
    content = f.read()
```

The first argument to `open()` is the file name, and the second argument is the mode. `'r'` indicates that the file should be opened for reading. You can also open files for writing, appending, or in binary mode by specifying a different mode.

To write to a file, you can use the following code:

```
with open('file.txt', 'w') as f:
    f.write('Hello, world!')
```

This will open the file for writing and write the string `'Hello, world!'` to it.

45. Reading and writing text files

Reading and writing text files is a common task in many applications, including data processing, log analysis, and report generation. Python provides a wide range of tools for reading and writing text files, including the built-in `open()` function and the `csv` module.

Here's an example of using Python to read and write text files:

```
# Read a text file
with open('input.txt', 'r') as f:
    data = f.read()

# Print the data
print(data)

# Write a text file
```

```
with open('output.txt', 'w') as f:
    f.write('Hello, world!')
```

In this example, we use the built-in `open()` function to read the contents of a text file `input.txt`, and store them in a variable `data`. We then print the contents of the file. We also use the `open()` function to create a new text file `output.txt` and write the string "Hello, world!" to it. This example demonstrates the basic principles of reading and writing text files in Python.

46. Reading data from a CSV file using Pandas

Pandas is a Python library that provides data manipulation and analysis tools. It also provides a convenient way to read and write CSV files.

Pandas provides the `read_csv()` function to read data from a CSV file into a Pandas DataFrame. To use it, you first need to import the Pandas library:

```
import pandas as pd
```

Then, you can use the `read_csv()` function to read the CSV file:

```
df = pd.read_csv('data.csv')
```

By default, `read_csv()` assumes that the first row of the CSV file contains column headers. If your CSV file doesn't have column headers, you can use the `header=None` parameter to indicate this:

```
df = pd.read_csv('data.csv', header=None)
```

You can also use other parameters to customize the behavior of `read_csv()`, such as specifying the delimiter, encoding, and data types of the columns.

Once you have a DataFrame, you can use its methods and properties to manipulate and analyze the data. For example, you can get the first few rows of the DataFrame using the `head()` method:

```
makefileCopy code
first_few_rows = df.head()
```

Or you can get the mean of a column using the `mean()` method:

```
mean_of_column = df['column_name'].mean()
```

Overall, Pandas provides a powerful and flexible way to work with tabular data in Python.

47. Regular expressions in Python

Regular expressions are a powerful and flexible tool for matching and manipulating text patterns in Python. Python's built-in `re` module provides a rich set of functions and methods for working with regular expressions.

Here's an example of using regular expressions in Python to match and manipulate text:

```
import re

# Match a string that contains 'cat'
string = 'The cat in the hat'
match = re.search('cat', string)
if match:
    print('Match found:', match.group(0))

# Replace all occurrences of 'cat' with 'dog'
new_string = re.sub('cat', 'dog', string)
print('New string:', new_string)
```

In this example, we use the `re.search()` function to search for the pattern `'cat'` in the string `'The cat in the hat'`. If a match is found, we print the matched substring using the `group()` method. We then use the `re.sub()` function to replace all occurrences of `'cat'` with `'dog'` in the original string, and print the resulting new string.

Regular expressions provide many powerful features for matching and manipulating text patterns, such as character classes, repetition operators, anchors, groups, and backreferences. It's important to use regular expressions carefully and correctly, as they can be complex and difficult to debug.

48. RESTful APIs and HTTP requests

A RESTful API (Representational State Transfer Application Programming Interface) is an architectural style for building web services that allows clients to interact with server resources using HTTP requests. RESTful APIs use HTTP methods (such as GET, POST, PUT, and DELETE) to perform operations on resources (such as retrieving, creating, updating, and deleting data).

HTTP (Hypertext Transfer Protocol) is the protocol used for transferring data over the web. HTTP requests consist of a request method (such as GET, POST, PUT, or DELETE), a URL (Uniform Resource Locator) that identifies the resource to access, and optional request headers and data.

Here's an example of sending an HTTP GET request to a RESTful API:

```
import requests

response = requests.get('https://api.example.com/resource')
data = response.json()
```

In this example, we use the `requests.get()` function to send an HTTP GET request to the `https://api.example.com/resource` URL. We store the response object in the `response` variable and extract the response data in JSON format using the `response.json()` method.

RESTful APIs can be used for a wide range of applications, including web and mobile applications, Internet of Things (IoT) devices, and more.

49. RESTful architecture and HTTP methods

REST (Representational State Transfer) is a popular architectural style for building web services that provide access to data and resources over the internet. RESTful APIs use HTTP methods (GET, POST, PUT, DELETE, etc.) to perform CRUD (Create, Read,

Update, Delete) operations on resources, and typically use JSON or XML as the data format. RESTful APIs are designed to be stateless, scalable, and cacheable, and can be accessed from a wide range of clients and platforms.

Here's an example of a simple RESTful API using the Flask micro-framework:

```python
from flask import Flask, jsonify, request

# Define the Flask app
app = Flask(__name__)

# Define a list of users
users = [
    {'id': 1, 'name': 'John', 'email': 'john@example.com'},
    {'id': 2, 'name': 'Jane', 'email': 'jane@example.com'},
    {'id': 3, 'name': 'Bob', 'email': 'bob@example.com'} ]

# Define a route for getting all users
@app.route('/users', methods=['GET'])
def get_users():
    return jsonify(users)

# Define a route for getting a single user
@app.route('/users/<int:user_id>', methods=['GET'])
def get_user(user_id):
    for user in users:
        if user['id'] == user_id:
            return jsonify(user)
    return jsonify({'error': 'User not found'})

# Define a route for creating a new user
@app.route('/users', methods=['POST'])
def create_user():
    user = request.json
    user['id'] = len(users) + 1
    users.append(user)
    return jsonify(user)

# Define a route for updating an existing user
@app.route('/users/<int:user_id>', methods=['PUT'])
def update_user(user_id):
    user = request.json
    for i, u in enumerate(users):
        if u['id'] == user_id:                users[i] = user
            return jsonify(user)
    return jsonify({'error': 'User not found'})

# Define a route for deleting an existing user
```

```python
@app.route('/users/<int:user_id>', methods=['DELETE'])
def delete_user(user_id):
    for i, user in enumerate(users):
        if user['id'] == user_id:
            del users[i]
            return jsonify({'message': 'User deleted'})
    return jsonify({'error': 'User not found'})

# Run the Flask app
if __name__ == '__main__':
    app.run()
```

In this example, we define a simple RESTful API using the `Flask` micro-framework, with routes for getting all users, getting a single user, creating a new user, updating an existing user, and deleting an existing user. Each route corresponds to an HTTP method (GET, POST, PUT, DELETE), and returns JSON data or an error message depending on the outcome of the operation.

50. Searching for patterns in text

Searching for patterns in text is a common task in many applications, including text processing, data analysis, and natural language processing. Python provides a wide range of tools for searching for patterns in text, including regular expressions, string methods, and third-party libraries like NLTK and SpaCy.

Here's an example of using Python to search for a pattern in text:

```python
import re

# Define a regular expression pattern
pattern = r'\d+'

# Search for the pattern in a string
text = "There are 123 apples and 456 oranges."
matches = re.findall(pattern, text)

# Print the matches
print(matches)
```

In this example, we define a regular expression pattern that matches one or more digits. We search for this pattern in a string using the `findall()` method from the `re` module, which returns a list of all matches. Finally, we print the matches. This example demonstrates the basic principles of searching for patterns in text using regular expressions.

51. Server-client architecture

The server-client architecture is a common design pattern for networked applications. In this architecture, a server program provides services to multiple client programs over a network. The clients send requests to the server, and the server responds with the requested information or service.

The client program can be running on a different computer or device than the server program. The communication between the server and the client is typically done using a communication protocol, such as TCP/IP or HTTP.

Here's an example of a simple server-client architecture:

```python
# Server program
import socket

# Create a socket object
serversocket = socket.socket(socket.AF_INET, socket.SOCK_STREAM)

# Get the local machine name and port number
host = socket.gethostname()
port = 9999

# Bind the socket to a specific address and port
serversocket.bind((host, port))

# Start listening for incoming connections
serversocket.listen(1)

# Wait for a client to connect
clientsocket, address = serversocket.accept()

# Send a message to the client
clientsocket.send('Hello, client!'.encode())

# Close the connection
clientsocket.close()

# Client program
import socket

# Create a socket object
clientsocket = socket.socket(socket.AF_INET, socket.SOCK_STREAM)
```

```
# Get the server hostname and port number
host = socket.gethostname()
port = 9999

# Connect to the server
clientsocket.connect((host, port))

# Receive the server's message
data = clientsocket.recv(1024)

# Print the message
print(data.decode())

# Close the connection
clientsocket.close()
```

In this example, we have a server program and a client program that communicate over a network using sockets. The server program creates a socket object, binds it to a specific address and port, and listens for incoming connections. When a client connects, the server sends a message to the client and closes the connection.

The client program creates a socket object, connects to the server, and receives the message sent by the server. Finally, the client closes the connection.

This example demonstrates the basic principles of the server-client architecture in Python using sockets.

52. SMTP servers and email authentication

SMTP (Simple Mail Transfer Protocol) is the protocol used for sending email over the internet. When you send an email using Python's `smtplib` library, you need to specify the SMTP server and port number to use. You also need to provide your email account credentials (such as your email address and password) to log in to the SMTP server.

SMTP servers may require authentication to prevent unauthorized access. There are different types of email authentication, such as SMTP authentication, DKIM (DomainKeys Identified Mail), and SPF (Sender Policy Framework). These methods help to verify the sender's identity and prevent email spoofing and spam.

When using the `smtplib` library to send email, it's important to configure your email account and SMTP server settings correctly to ensure successful delivery and prevent email rejection or blocking.

53. Socket programming using the socket module

Socket programming allows you to create network connections and exchange data between computers over a network. Python provides a built-in `socket` module that allows you to create sockets and use them to communicate over a network. Here's an example:

```python
import socket

# Create a socket object
s = socket.socket(socket.AF_INET, socket.SOCK_STREAM)

# Get local machine name host = socket.gethostname()

# Define port number
port = 12345

# Bind the socket to a specific address and port
s.bind((host, port))

# Listen for incoming connections
s.listen(5)

# Wait for a client connection
client_socket, client_address = s.accept()
print('Got connection from', client_address)

# Send a message to the client
message = 'Thank you for connecting'
client_socket.send(message.encode())

# Close the client connection
client_socket.close()

# Close the server socket
s.close()
```

In this example, we first create a socket object using the `socket.socket()` function. We then get the local machine name and define a port number to use. We bind the socket to the address and port using the `bind()` method, and then start listening for incoming connections using the `listen()` method.

When a client connects to our server, we accept the connection using the `accept()` method, which returns a client socket and the client's address. We then send a message to the client using the `send()` method and close the client socket.

Finally, we close the server socket. This is a simple example, but you can use socket programming to create more complex network applications.

54. String manipulation

String manipulation refers to the process of modifying strings in various ways. Python provides many built-in string methods that allow you to do this. Here are some examples:

```python
# Get the length of a string
s = 'Hello, world!'
length = len(s)

# Convert a string to uppercase
s = 'Hello, world!' uppercase = s.upper()

# Split a string into a list of substrings
s = 'Hello, world!' substrings = s.split()

# Replace a substring with another string
s = 'Hello, world!'
new_s = s.replace('world', 'Python')
```

55. Symmetric and asymmetric encryption

Symmetric encryption is a type of encryption where the same key is used for both encrypting and decrypting data. In symmetric encryption, the sender and the receiver of the data share a common secret key that is used to encrypt and decrypt the data.

Asymmetric encryption, also known as public-key encryption, is a type of encryption where two different keys are used for encrypting and decrypting data. In asymmetric encryption, each party has a public key and a private key. The public key can be shared with anyone, while the private key must be kept secret. Data encrypted with a public key can only be decrypted with the corresponding private key.

Both symmetric and asymmetric encryption have their own strengths and weaknesses, and are used in different contexts depending on the security requirements and performance constraints.

56. Tokenization, stemming, and POS tagging

Tokenization, stemming, and POS (part-of-speech) tagging are common techniques used in natural language processing (NLP) to preprocess text data for analysis. Python's NLTK (Natural Language Toolkit) library provides a comprehensive set of tools and resources for NLP, such as text preprocessing, part-of-speech tagging, named entity recognition, sentiment analysis, and machine learning algorithms.

Here's an example of using NLTK to perform tokenization, stemming, and POS tagging on a piece of text:

```python
import nltk
from nltk.tokenize import word_tokenize
from nltk.stem import SnowballStemmer
from nltk import pos_tag

# Download and install required resources
nltk.download('punkt')
nltk.download('averaged_perceptron_tagger')

# Define some text to preprocess
text = 'The quick brown foxes jumped over the lazy dogs.'

# Tokenize the text into words
tokens = word_tokenize(text)

# Perform stemming on the tokens
stemmer = SnowballStemmer('english')
stemmed_tokens = [stemmer.stem(word) for word in tokens]
# Perform POS tagging on the tokens
pos_tags = pos_tag(tokens)

# Print the results
print('Original text:', text)
print('Tokenized text:', tokens)
print('Stemmed text:', stemmed_tokens)
print('POS tags:', pos_tags)
```

In this example, we use various functions and resources provided by NLTK to preprocess a piece of text. We tokenize the text into words using the word_tokenize() function, perform stemming on the tokens using the SnowballStemmer class, and perform POS tagging on the tokens using the pos_tag() function. The POS tags represent the syntactic category of each word in the text, such as noun, verb, adjective, etc. Finally, we print the results of each step to the console.

57. Web API integration using the requests library

Python's `requests` library provides a simple and flexible way to send HTTP requests and integrate with web APIs. Here's an example:

```python
import requests

response = requests.get('https://api.example.com/resource', params={'param1': 'value1'})
data = response.json()

response = requests.post('https://api.example.com/resource', json={'key1': 'value1'})
data = response.json()

response = requests.put('https://api.example.com/resource/123', json={'key1': 'value1'})
data = response.json()

response = requests.delete('https://api.example.com/resource/123')
```

In this example, we use the `requests.get()`, `requests.post()`, `requests.put()`, and `requests.delete()` functions to send HTTP requests to different URLs and with different HTTP methods. We use the `params` and `json` parameters to include query parameters and request data in the requests, respectively.

We extract the response data in JSON format using the `response.json()` method. The `requests` library also provides many other features, such as request headers, cookies, timeouts, and authentication, to make it easy to integrate with web APIs.

58. Web APIs with Flask

Web APIs are a popular way of providing access to data and services over the internet. Python's `Flask` micro-framework provides a lightweight and flexible framework for building web APIs using HTTP requests and responses. Flask allows you to define routes and handlers for incoming requests, and to return JSON data or other types of content in response.

Here's an example of using `Flask` to define a simple web API:

```
from flask import Flask, jsonify

# Define the Flask app
app = Flask(__name__)

# Define a route and a handler for the root endpoint
@app.route('/')
def hello():
    return 'Hello, world!'

# Define a route and a handler for a JSON API endpoint
@app.route('/api/data')
def data():
    data = {'name': 'John', 'age': 30, 'city': 'New York'}
    return jsonify(data)

# Run the Flask app
if __name__ == '__main__':
    app.run()
```

In this example, we define a `Flask` app using the `Flask()` class, and define two routes using the `route()` decorator and the appropriate HTTP method (GET by default). We define a handler for the root endpoint that returns a simple text message, and a handler for a JSON API endpoint that returns a dictionary of data as JSON using the `jsonify()` function. Finally, we run the `Flask` app using the `run()` method. When the app is running, it will listen for incoming requests on the specified port (by default, port 5000) and route them to the appropriate handler based on the URL and HTTP method. This example demonstrates the basic structure of a Flask web API, and how to define routes and handlers for different endpoints.

59. Web development using the Flask framework

Flask is a micro web framework for Python that allows you to build web applications quickly and easily. Here's an example:

```
from flask import Flask, render_template

app = Flask(__name__)

@app.route('/')
def hello_world():
    return 'Hello, World!'
```

```python
@app.route('/about')
def about():
    return render_template('about.html')

if __name__ == '__main__':
    app.run()
```

In this example, we import the Flask module and create a Flask application object. We define two routes using the `@app.route()` decorator: one for the root URL (`/`) that returns a string, and one for an about page (`/about`) that renders an HTML template.

We then start the Flask development server using the `app.run()` method. This is a simple example, but Flask provides many features for handling HTTP requests, routing, templates, and more.

60. Web scraping using BeautifulSoup

Web scraping is the process of extracting data from websites using automated scripts or programs. Python's `BeautifulSoup` library provides a simple and easy-to-use interface for parsing HTML and XML documents and extracting data from them.

Here's an example of using `BeautifulSoup` to scrape data from a website:

```python
import requests
from bs4 import BeautifulSoup

# Send an HTTP request to the website
response = requests.get('https://www.example.com')

# Parse the HTML content using BeautifulSoup
soup = BeautifulSoup(response.content, 'html.parser')

# Find all the links on the page
links = soup.find_all('a')

# Print the links
for link in links:
    print(link.get('href'))
```

In this example, we use the `requests` library to send an HTTP request to the website `https://www.example.com` and retrieve its HTML content. We use the `BeautifulSoup` library to parse the HTML content and extract all the links on the page using the `find_all()` method. We then iterate over the links and print their `href` attributes.

`BeautifulSoup` provides many other functions and options for web scraping, such as filtering and searching for specific tags and attributes, handling different encodings and document types, and navigating the HTML tree structure. It's important to respect website policies and legal regulations when scraping data from websites.

61. Web scraping with Beautiful Soup and Requests

Web scraping is the process of extracting data from websites using automated software tools, and is a common technique used for data mining, research, and analysis. Beautiful Soup and Requests are two popular Python libraries for web scraping, which provide a simple and powerful API for navigating HTML and XML documents, and fetching data from web pages.

Here's an example of using Beautiful Soup and Requests to scrape data from a web page:

```python
import requests
from bs4 import BeautifulSoup

# Fetch the HTML content of a web page
url = 'https://en.wikipedia.org/wiki/List_of_countries_by_GDP_(nominal)'
response = requests.get(url)
html = response.content

# Parse the HTML content using Beautiful Soup
soup = BeautifulSoup(html, 'html.parser')

# Extract the table data from the web page
table = soup.find('table', {'class': 'wikitable sortable'})
rows = table.findAll('tr')
for row in rows:
    cols = row.findAll('td')
    for col in cols:
        print(col.text.strip())
```

In this example, we use the `requests` library to fetch the HTML content of a Wikipedia page, and use Beautiful Soup to parse the HTML content and extract the table data from the page. We use the `find()` and `findAll()` methods of the `soup` object to navigate the HTML document and select the desired elements, and use the `text` attribute to extract the text content of the selected elements. This example demonstrates the basic principles of web scraping using Beautiful Soup and Requests.

62. Web scraping with Selenium

Web scraping is the process of extracting data from websites using automated scripts or tools. Python's `Selenium` library provides a powerful and flexible framework for automating web browsers and performing web scraping tasks.

Here's an example of using `Selenium` to scrape data from a website:

```python
from selenium import webdriver

# Create a webdriver instance and load a website  driver = webdriver.Chrome()
driver.get('https://www.example.com')

# Find an element on the page using a CSS selector and print its text content
element = driver.find_element_by_css_selector('#header')  print(element.text)

# Click a button on the page to load more data
button = driver.find_element_by_css_selector('#load-more')
button.click()

# Wait for some time to let the new data load
driver.implicitly_wait(10)

# Find a list of elements on the page and print their text content
elements = driver.find_elements_by_css_selector('.item')
for element in elements:
    print(element.text)

# Close the browser window
driver.quit()
```

In this example, we create a `webdriver` instance using the Chrome browser driver, and load a website named `https://www.example.com`. We use various methods provided by `Selenium` to find and interact with elements on the page, such as finding an element by its CSS selector, clicking a button, and waiting for some time to let new data load. We then find a list of elements on the page and print their text content. Finally, we close the browser window using the `quit()` method.

63. Widgets and event handling

In GUI programming, widgets are the visual elements that users interact with, such as buttons, text boxes, and menus. Tkinter provides many built-in widgets that you can use to create GUI applications. Widgets have different properties and options that you can configure, such as size, color, font, and layout.

Event handling is the process of responding to user actions or events, such as button clicks, mouse movements, or key presses. Tkinter provides a built-in event loop that constantly checks for user events and triggers event handlers when events occur. You can bind event handlers to widgets using the bind() method, which takes an event type and a callback function as arguments.

Here's an example of using Tkinter widgets and event handling:

```python
import tkinter as tk

# Define the event handler function
def on_button_click():
    label.config(text='Button clicked!')

# Create a new window
window = tk.Tk()

# Create a label
label = tk.Label(window, text='Hello, Tkinter!')

# Add the label to the window
label.pack()

# Create a button
button = tk.Button(window, text='Click me!', command=on_button_click)

# Add the button to the window
button.pack()

# Start the main event loop
window.mainloop()
```

In this example, we define an event handler function on_button_click() that changes the label text when the button is clicked. We create a label and a button using the tk.Label() and tk.Button() functions, respectively, and add them to the window using the pack() method. We bind the on_button_click() function to the button using the command parameter. Finally, we start the main event loop using the mainloop() method.

40 INTERMEDIATE LEVEL EXERCISES

The exercises in this book, and this section, are not arranged in any particular order according to the difficulty level. This may seem unorganized, but in fact, it grants readers the flexibility to skip ahead and find the information that they need at that particular moment. Furthermore, this is especially beneficial for students or readers who are more advanced in their studies as they may not need to cover the basics.

In this way, you can focus on the more challenging areas of the subject matter and progress at your own pace, which can be very rewarding. Ultimately, the lack of a prescribed order can be an advantage rather than a disadvantage, offering you the ability to customize your learning experience and make the most of your time and effort.

You can follow the order if you want, but you can also go directly to the exercise that you need to focus on.

The best way to learn is to enjoy yourself, so have fun coding your future.

LET'S START.

Intermediate Level Exercises

Exercise 1: Web Scraping

Concepts:

- HTTP requests using the requests module

- HTML parsing using BeautifulSoup

Description: Web scraping is a common task for many Python programmers. In this exercise, you'll write a script that scrapes data from a website.

Solution:

```python
import requests
from bs4 import BeautifulSoup

url = 'https://www.example.com'
response = requests.get(url)
soup = BeautifulSoup(response.text, 'html.parser')

# Find all links on the page
links = soup.find_all('a')
for link in links:
    print(link.get('href'))
```

Exercise 2: File I/O

Concepts:

- Reading and writing files using Python's built-in open() function

- String manipulation

Description: Working with files is an essential part of any programming language. In this exercise, you'll write a script that reads data from a file and writes data to a file.

Solution:

```python
# Read data from a file
with open('input.txt', 'r') as f:
```

```
    data = f.read()

# Manipulate the data
data = data.upper()

# Write data to a file
with open('output.txt', 'w') as f:
    f.write(data)
```

Exercise 3: Data Analysis

Concepts:

- Reading data from a CSV file using Pandas

- Data manipulation using Pandas

- Basic data analysis using Pandas

Description: Python has a vast ecosystem of libraries for data analysis. In this exercise, you'll use the Pandas library to read data from a CSV file and perform some basic data analysis.

Solution:

```
import pandas as pd

# Read data from a CSV file
data = pd.read_csv('data.csv')

# Display the first 5 rows of the data
print(data.head())

# Calculate some basic statistics
print(data.describe())
```

Exercise 4: Command-Line Interface

Concepts:

- Command-line arguments using the argparse module

- String manipulation

Description: Python can be used to create command-line tools. In this exercise, you'll write a script that accepts command-line arguments and performs a task based on those arguments.

Solution:

```python
import argparse

# Create an argument parser
parser = argparse.ArgumentParser()
parser.add_argument('name', help='Your name')
parser.add_argument('age', type=int, help='Your age')
args = parser.parse_args()

# Print a greeting
greeting = f'Hello, {args.name}! You are {args.age} years old.'
print(greeting)
```

Exercise 5: API Integration

Concepts:

- HTTP requests using the requests module

- JSON parsing

Description: Many modern applications have APIs that can be accessed programmatically. In this exercise, you'll write a script that interacts with a RESTful API.

Solution:

```python
import requests

# Make a GET request to an API
url = 'https://api.example.com/users'
response = requests.get(url)

# Parse the response as JSON
data = response.json()

# Display the data
for user in data:
    print(user['name'], user['email'])
```

Exercise 6: Regular Expressions

Concepts:

- Regular expressions using the re module
- User input validation

Description: Regular expressions are powerful tools for pattern matching and data validation. In this exercise, you'll write a script that uses regular expressions to validate user input.

Solution:

```python
import re

# Define a regular expression pattern for email validation
pattern = r'^[a-zA-Z0-9._%+-]+@[a-zA-Z0-9.-]+\.[a-zA-Z]{2,}$'

# Get user input
email = input('Enter your email address: ')

# Validate the input using the regular expression
if re.match(pattern, email):
    print('Valid email address')
else:
    print('Invalid email address')
```

Exercise 7: Object-Oriented Programming

Concepts:

- Classes and objects
- Encapsulation
- Inheritance

Description: Object-oriented programming is a fundamental concept in Python. In this exercise, you'll write a simple class that demonstrates the principles of object-oriented programming.

Solution:

```python
class Person:
    def __init__(self, name, age):
        self.name = name
        self.age = age

    def greet(self):
        print(f'Hello, my name is {self.name} and I am {self.age} years old.')

class Student(Person):
    def __init__(self, name, age, major):
        super().__init__(name, age)
        self.major = major

    def describe(self):
        print(f'I am a student majoring in {self.major}.')

# Create objects and call methods
person = Person('Alice', 25)
person.greet()

student = Student('Bob', 20, 'Computer Science')
student.greet()
student.describe()
```

Exercise 8: Concurrency

Concepts:

- Threading using the threading module

- Synchronization using locks

Description: Python has powerful concurrency features that allow you to write concurrent and parallel programs. In this exercise, you'll write a script that demonstrates concurrent programming using threads.

Solution:

```python
import threading

counter = 0
lock = threading.Lock()

def increment():
    global counter
```

life_rule_2 = 'ENJOY THE WAY, HAVE FUN WHILE "CODE" YOUR FUTURE' |

```python
    with lock:
        counter += 1

threads = []
for i in range(10):
    t = threading.Thread(target=increment)
    threads.append(t)
    t.start()

for t in threads:
    t.join()

print(f'The counter is {counter}.')
```

Exercise 9: Testing

Concepts:

- Unit testing using the unittest module

- Test-driven development

Description: Testing is a crucial part of software development. In this exercise, you'll write unit tests for a simple function.

Solution:

```python
import unittest

def is_palindrome(s):
    return s == s[::-1]

class TestPalindrome(unittest.TestCase):
    def test_is_palindrome(self):
        self.assertTrue(is_palindrome('racecar'))
        self.assertFalse(is_palindrome('hello'))

if __name__ == '__main__':
    unittest.main()
```

Exercise 10: Data Visualization

Concepts:

- Data visualization using Matplotlib

- Line charts

Description: Data visualization is an essential part of data analysis. In this exercise, you'll use the Matplotlib library to create a simple line chart.

Solution:

```python
import matplotlib.pyplot as plt

# Create some data
x = [1, 2, 3, 4, 5]
y = [2, 4, 6, 8, 10]

# Create a line chart
plt.plot(x, y)

# Add labels and a title
plt.xlabel('X values')
plt.ylabel('Y values')
plt.title('Line chart')

# Display the chart
plt.show()
```

Exercise 11: Database Operations

Concepts:

- Connecting to a database using the SQLite3 module

- Creating tables and inserting data

- Querying data using SQL

Description: Python has a wide variety of libraries for working with databases. In this exercise, you'll write a script that performs some common database operations.

Solution:

```python
import sqlite3

# Connect to the database
conn = sqlite3.connect('example.db')

# Create a table
```

```
conn.execute('''CREATE TABLE IF NOT EXISTS users
               (id INTEGER PRIMARY KEY,
                name TEXT,
                email TEXT)''')

# Insert some data
conn.execute("INSERT INTO users (name, email) VALUES (?, ?)", ('Alice', 'alice@example.co
m'))
conn.execute("INSERT INTO users (name, email) VALUES (?, ?)", ('Bob', 'bob@example.com'))

# Query the data
cursor = conn.execute("SELECT id, name, email FROM users")
for row in cursor:
    print(f'{row[0]} - {row[1]} ({row[2]})')

# Close the database connection
conn.close()
```

Exercise 12: Networking

Concepts:

- Socket programming using the socket module

- Server-client architecture

Description: Python has excellent networking capabilities, allowing you to build network applications. In this exercise, you'll write a script that implements a simple server and client.

Solution:

```
scssCopy code
# Server code
import socket

server_socket = socket.socket(socket.AF_INET, socket.SOCK_STREAM)
server_socket.bind(('localhost', 8000))
server_socket.listen(1)

while True:
    client_socket, address = server_socket.accept()
    data = client_socket.recv(1024)
    response = data.upper()
    client_socket.sendall(response)
    client_socket.close()

# Client code
import socket
```

```
client_socket = socket.socket(socket.AF_INET, socket.SOCK_STREAM)
client_socket.connect(('localhost', 8000))
client_socket.sendall(b'Hello, server!')
response = client_socket.recv(1024)
print(response)
client_socket.close()
```

Exercise 13: Data Science

Concepts:

- Data manipulation using NumPy and Pandas

- Data analysis using Pandas

Description: Python is a popular language for data science due to its powerful libraries. In this exercise, you'll use the NumPy and Pandas libraries to perform some data analysis.

Solution:

```
import numpy as np
import pandas as pd

# Create some data
data = {'x': np.arange(10),
        'y': np.random.randn(10)}

# Create a DataFrame from the data
df = pd.DataFrame(data)

# Calculate some statistics
print(df.mean())
print(df.std())

# Create a new column based on a calculation
df['z'] = df['x'] * df['y']

# Display the DataFrame
print(df)
```

Exercise 14: Web Development

Concepts:

- Web development using the Flask framework

- HTTP methods and routing

Description: Python can be used to build web applications using a variety of web frameworks. In this exercise, you'll write a simple Flask web application.

Solution:

```python
from flask import Flask, request

app = Flask(__name__)

@app.route('/', methods=['GET'])
def home():
    return 'Hello, world!'

@app.route('/greet', methods=['POST'])
def greet():
    name = request.form.get('name')
    return f'Hello, {name}!'

if __name__ == '__main__':
    app.run()
```

Exercise 15: Asynchronous Programming

Concepts:

- Asynchronous programming using asyncio

- Coroutines

Description: Python has powerful features for asynchronous programming, allowing you to write efficient and scalable programs. In this exercise, you'll write a script that demonstrates asynchronous programming using asyncio.

Solution:

```python
import asyncio

async def coroutine():
    print('Coroutine started')
    await asyncio.sleep(1)
```

```
    print('Coroutine ended')

loop = asyncio.get_event_loop()
loop.run_until_complete(coroutine())
loop.close()
```

This script defines a coroutine using the `async` keyword. The coroutine sleeps for one second using the `asyncio.sleep()` function. The `asyncio.get_event_loop()` function is used to create an event loop, and the `loop.run_until_complete()` method is used to run the coroutine until it completes. Finally, the event loop is closed using the `loop.close()` method.

Note that the above code demonstrates only the basic concepts of asynchronous programming with asyncio. More complex programs may require additional concepts and techniques, such as event loops, futures, and callbacks.

Exercise 16: Image Processing

Concepts:

- Image processing using the Pillow library

- Image manipulation and conversion

Description: Python has many libraries for working with images. In this exercise, you'll use the Pillow library to perform some basic image processing tasks.

Solution:

```
from PIL import Image

# Open an image file
image = Image.open('image.jpg')

# Display information about the image
print(image.format)
print(image.size)
print(image.mode)

# Convert the image to grayscale
grayscale_image = image.convert('L')
grayscale_image.show()

# Resize the image
resized_image = image.resize((300, 300))
```

```
resized_image.show()

# Save the image in a different format
resized_image.save('image.png')
```

Exercise 17: Email Sending

Concepts:

- Email sending using the smtplib library

- SMTP servers and email authentication

Description: Python has libraries for sending email programmatically. In this exercise, you'll write a script that sends an email using the smtplib library.

Solution:

```
import smtplib

sender_email = 'your_email@example.com'
sender_password = 'your_password'
receiver_email = 'recipient_email@example.com'
message = 'Hello, world!'

with smtplib.SMTP('smtp.gmail.com', 587) as server:
    server.starttls()
    server.login(sender_email, sender_password)
    server.sendmail(sender_email, receiver_email, message)
```

Exercise 18: Web API Integration

Concepts:

- RESTful APIs and HTTP requests

- Web API integration using the requests library

Description: Python can be used to integrate with many different web APIs. In this exercise, you'll write a script that interacts with a RESTful API using the requests library.

Solution:

```python
import requests

response = requests.get('https://api.example.com/users')
data = response.json()

for user in data:
    print(user['name'], user['email'])
```

Exercise 19: Data Encryption

Concepts:

- Data encryption using the cryptography library

- Symmetric and asymmetric encryption

Description: Python has built-in libraries for encrypting and decrypting data. In this exercise, you'll write a script that encrypts and decrypts some data using the cryptography library.

Solution:

```python
from cryptography.fernet import Fernet
from cryptography.hazmat.primitives import hashes
from cryptography.hazmat.primitives.asymmetric import rsa, padding
from cryptography.hazmat.primitives.serialization import load_pem_private_key, load_pem_pu
blic_key

# Symmetric encryption
key = Fernet.generate_key()
fernet = Fernet(key)
plaintext = b'This is a secret message'
ciphertext = fernet.encrypt(plaintext)
decrypted_plaintext = fernet.decrypt(ciphertext)
print(decrypted_plaintext)

# Asymmetric encryption
private_key = rsa.generate_private_key(
    public_exponent=65537,
    key_size=2048
)
public_key = private_key.public_key()

plaintext = b'This is a secret message'
ciphertext = public_key.encrypt(
```

```
    plaintext,
    padding.OAEP(
        mgf=padding.MGF1(algorithm=hashes.SHA256()),
        algorithm=hashes.SHA256(),
        label=None
    )
)

decrypted_plaintext = private_key.decrypt(
    ciphertext,
    padding.OAEP(
        mgf=padding.MGF1(algorithm=hashes.SHA256()),
        algorithm=hashes.SHA256(),
        label=None
    )
)
print(decrypted_plaintext)
```

Exercise 20: GUI Programming

Concepts:

- GUI programming using the Tkinter library

- Widgets and event handling

Description: Python has libraries for building graphical user interfaces (GUIs). In this exercise, you'll write a script that uses the Tkinter library to create a simple GUI.

Solution:

```
import tkinter as tk

def button_clicked():
    label.config(text='Hello, world!')

root = tk.Tk()

label = tk.Label(root, text='Welcome to my GUI')
label.pack()

button = tk.Button(root, text='Click me!', command=button_clicked)
button.pack()

root.mainloop()
```

This script creates a window using the `tkinter.Tk()` method. It then creates a `Label` widget and a `Button` widget and packs them into the window using the `pack()` method. Finally, it enters the main event loop using the `mainloop()` method.

When the button is clicked, the `button_clicked()` function is called, which updates the text of the label widget using the `config()` method.

Exercise 21: File I/O

Concepts:

- File I/O in Python

- Reading and writing files

Description: Python has built-in support for reading and writing files. In this exercise, you'll write a script that reads from and writes to a file.

Solution:

```python
# Write to a file
with open('example.txt', 'w') as file:
    file.write('Hello, world!\n')
    file.write('How are you today?\n')

# Read from a file
with open('example.txt', 'r') as file:
    for line in file:
        print(line.strip())
```

Exercise 22: Logging

Concepts:

- Logging in Python

- Log levels and handlers

Description: Python has built-in support for logging. In this exercise, you'll write a script that logs some messages to a file.

Solution:

```
import logging

logging.basicConfig(filename='example.log', level=logging.DEBUG)

logging.debug('This is a debug message')
logging.info('This is an info message')
logging.warning('This is a warning message')
logging.error('This is an error message')
logging.critical('This is a critical message')
```

Exercise 23: Web Scraping

Concepts:

- Web scraping using BeautifulSoup

- HTML parsing and navigation

Description: Python can be used for web scraping, which involves extracting data from websites. In this exercise, you'll use the BeautifulSoup library to scrape data from a website.

Solution:

```
import requests
from bs4 import BeautifulSoup

response = requests.get('https://en.wikipedia.org/wiki/Python_(programming_language)')
soup = BeautifulSoup(response.text, 'html.parser')
print(soup.title.string)

links = soup.find_all('a')
for link in links:
    print(link.get('href'))
```

Exercise 24: Concurrency with asyncio

Concepts:

- Asynchronous programming using asyncio

- Coroutines and event loops

Description: Python has powerful support for asynchronous programming using the asyncio library. In this exercise, you'll write a script that demonstrates the use of asyncio for concurrent programming.

Solution:

```python
import asyncio

async def coroutine(id):
    print(f'Coroutine {id} started')
    await asyncio.sleep(1)
    print(f'Coroutine {id} ended')

async def main():
    tasks = []
    for i in range(10):
        tasks.append(asyncio.create_task(coroutine(i)))
    await asyncio.gather(*tasks)

asyncio.run(main())
```

Exercise 25: Data Analysis with Pandas

Concepts:

- Data analysis with Pandas

- Loading and manipulating data with DataFrames

Description: Pandas is a powerful library for data analysis and manipulation in Python. In this exercise, you'll use Pandas to perform some data analysis tasks.

Solution:

```python
import pandas as pd

# Load data from a CSV file
data = pd.read_csv('example.csv')

# Print the first five rows of the data
print(data.head())

# Calculate some statistics on the data
print(data.describe())
```

```
# Group the data by a column and calculate some statistics
grouped_data = data.groupby('category')
print(grouped_data.mean())
```

In this script, we load data from a CSV file into a Pandas DataFrame. We then print the first five rows of the data using the `head()` method, and calculate some statistics on the data using the `describe()` method.

Finally, we group the data by the `category` column using the `groupby()` method and calculate some statistics on each group using the `mean()` method.

Exercise 26: Regular Expressions

Concepts:

- Regular expressions in Python

- Pattern matching and substitution

Description: Regular expressions are a powerful tool for searching and manipulating text. In this exercise, you'll write a script that uses regular expressions to search for patterns in text.

Solution:

```python
import re

text = 'The quick brown fox jumps over the lazy dog'

# Search for a pattern in the text
pattern = r'\b\w{4}\b'
matches = re.findall(pattern, text)
print(matches)

# Substitute a pattern in the text
pattern = r'\bthe\b'
replaced_text = re.sub(pattern, 'a', text, flags=re.IGNORECASE)
print(replaced_text)
```

Exercise 27: Database ORM

Concepts:

- Object-relational mapping using SQLAlchemy

- Creating tables and querying data

Description: Python has many object-relational mapping (ORM) libraries for working with databases. In this exercise, you'll write a script that uses the SQLAlchemy ORM to interact with a database.

Solution:

```python
from sqlalchemy import create_engine, Column, Integer, String
from sqlalchemy.orm import sessionmaker
from sqlalchemy.ext.declarative import declarative_base

# Define a database engine
engine = create_engine('sqlite:///example.db')

# Define a session factory
Session = sessionmaker(bind=engine)

# Define a declarative base
Base = declarative_base()

# Define a model class
class User(Base):
    __tablename__ = 'users'

    id = Column(Integer, primary_key=True)
    name = Column(String)
    email = Column(String)

# Create the table
Base.metadata.create_all(engine)

# Add some data
session = Session()
session.add(User(name='Alice', email='alice@example.com'))
session.add(User(name='Bob', email='bob@example.com'))
session.commit()

# Query the data
users = session.query(User).all()
for user in users:
    print(user.name, user.email)
```

Exercise 28: Web Scraping with Selenium

Concepts:

- Web scraping with Selenium

- Browser automation and DOM manipulation

Description: Selenium is a popular library for web scraping that allows you to control a web browser programmatically. In this exercise, you'll write a script that uses Selenium to scrape data from a website.

Solution:

```python
from selenium import webdriver

driver = webdriver.Chrome()

driver.get('https://en.wikipedia.org/wiki/Python_(programming_language)')

heading = driver.find_element_by_tag_name('h1')
print(heading.text)

links = driver.find_elements_by_tag_name('a')
for link in links:
    print(link.get_attribute('href'))

driver.close()
```

Exercise 29: Natural Language Processing

Concepts:

- Natural language processing using the NLTK library

- Tokenization, stemming, and POS tagging

Description: Python has many libraries for natural language processing (NLP). In this exercise, you'll use the NLTK library to perform some basic NLP tasks.

Solution:

```python
import nltk
from nltk.tokenize import word_tokenize
from nltk.stem import PorterStemmer
from nltk import pos_tag
```

```
nltk.download('punkt')
nltk.download('averaged_perceptron_tagger')

text = 'The quick brown fox jumped over the lazy dogs'

# Tokenize the text
tokens = word_tokenize(text)
print(tokens)

# Stem the tokens
stemmer = PorterStemmer()
stemmed_tokens = [stemmer.stem(token) for token in tokens]
print(stemmed_tokens)

# Perform part-of-speech tagging on the tokens
pos_tags = pos_tag(tokens)
print(pos_tags)
```

Exercise 30: Machine Learning

Concepts:

- Machine learning using scikit-learn

- Data preparation, model training, and prediction

Description: Python has many libraries for machine learning, including scikit-learn. In this exercise, you'll use scikit-learn to train a simple machine learning model.

Solution:

```
import pandas as pd
from sklearn.model_selection import train_test_split
from sklearn.linear_model import LinearRegression

# Load data from a CSV file
data = pd.read_csv('example.csv')

# Prepare the data
X = data['x'].values.reshape(-1, 1)
y = data['y'].values.reshape(-1, 1)

# Split the data into training and testing sets
X_train, X_test, y_train, y_test = train_test_split(X, y, test_size=0.2, random_state=0)

# Train the model
model = LinearRegression()
```

```
model.fit(X_train, y_train)

# Make predictions on the test set
y_pred = model.predict(X_test)

# Evaluate the model
score = model.score(X_test, y_test)
print(score)
```

In this script, we load data from a CSV file into a Pandas DataFrame. We then prepare the data by splitting it into input (X) and output (y) variables, and splitting it into training and testing sets using the `train_test_split()` method.

We then train a linear regression model using the training data, and make predictions on the testing data using the `predict()` method. Finally, we evaluate the performance of the model using the `score()` method, which calculates the coefficient of determination (R^2) for the model.

Exercise 31: Image Recognition with Deep Learning

Concepts:

- Deep learning with Keras

- Convolutional neural networks and image recognition

Description: Deep learning is a powerful technique for image recognition. In this exercise, you'll use the Keras library to train a deep learning model to recognize images.

Solution:

```
import numpy as np
from keras.datasets import mnist
from keras.models import Sequential
from keras.layers import Dense, Flatten, Conv2D, MaxPooling2D
from keras.utils import to_categorical

# Load the MNIST dataset
(X_train, y_train), (X_test, y_test) = mnist.load_data()

# Preprocess the data
X_train = X_train.reshape(-1, 28, 28, 1) / 255.0
X_test = X_test.reshape(-1, 28, 28, 1) / 255.0
y_train = to_categorical(y_train)
y_test = to_categorical(y_test)
```

```python
# Define the model architecture
model = Sequential()
model.add(Conv2D(32, (3, 3), activation='relu', input_shape=(28, 28, 1)))
model.add(MaxPooling2D((2, 2)))
model.add(Conv2D(64, (3, 3), activation='relu'))
model.add(MaxPooling2D((2, 2)))
model.add(Conv2D(64, (3, 3), activation='relu'))
model.add(Flatten())
model.add(Dense(64, activation='relu'))
model.add(Dense(10, activation='softmax'))

# Compile the model
model.compile(optimizer='adam', loss='categorical_crossentropy', metrics=['accuracy'])

# Train the model
model.fit(X_train, y_train, epochs=5, batch_size=64)

# Evaluate the model
loss, accuracy = model.evaluate(X_test, y_test)
print(accuracy)
```

Exercise 32: Web APIs with Flask

Concepts:

- Web APIs with Flask

- RESTful architecture and HTTP methods

Description: Flask is a lightweight web framework for Python. In this exercise, you'll write a simple Flask application that exposes a web API.

Solution:

```python
from flask import Flask, request

app = Flask(__name__)

@app.route('/hello', methods=['GET'])
def hello():
    name = request.args.get('name')
    if name:
        return f'Hello, {name}!'
    else:
        return 'Hello, world!'
```

```
if __name__ == '__main__':
    app.run()
```

Exercise 33: GUI Programming with PyQt

Concepts:

- GUI programming with PyQt

- Widgets and event handling

Description: PyQt is a powerful library for building graphical user interfaces (GUIs) with Python. In this exercise, you'll write a script that uses PyQt to create a simple GUI.

Solution:

```
import sys
from PyQt5.QtWidgets import QApplication, QWidget, QLabel, QLineEdit, QPushButton

class MyWindow(QWidget):
    def __init__(self):
        super().__init__()

        self.label = QLabel('Enter your name:', self)
        self.label.move(50, 50)

        self.textbox = QLineEdit(self)
        self.textbox.move(50, 80)

        self.button = QPushButton('Say hello', self)
        self.button.move(50, 110)
        self.button.clicked.connect(self.button_clicked)

        self.setWindowTitle('Hello, world!')
        self.setGeometry(100, 100, 200, 150)

    def button_clicked(self):
        name = self.textbox.text()
        self.label.setText(f'Hello, {name}!')

app = QApplication(sys.argv)
window = MyWindow()
window.show()
sys.exit(app.exec_())
```

Exercise 34: Web Scraping with Beautiful Soup and Requests

Concepts:

- Web scraping with Beautiful Soup and Requests

- HTML parsing and navigation

Description: Beautiful Soup and Requests are popular libraries for web scraping. In this exercise, you'll write a script that uses these libraries to scrape data from a website.

Solution:

```python
import requests
from bs4 import BeautifulSoup

url = 'https://en.wikipedia.org/wiki/Python_(programming_language)'

response = requests.get(url)
soup = BeautifulSoup(response.text, 'html.parser')

title = soup.find('h1', {'id': 'firstHeading'}).text
print(title)

content = soup.find('div', {'id': 'mw-content-text'}).text
print(content[:100])
```

Exercise 35: Data Visualization with Matplotlib

Concepts:

- Data visualization with Matplotlib

- Line plots and labels

Description: Matplotlib is a popular library for data visualization in Python. In this exercise, you'll write a script that uses Matplotlib to create a simple line plot.

Solution:

```python
import matplotlib.pyplot as plt

x = [1, 2, 3, 4, 5]
```

```
y = [1, 4, 9, 16, 25]

plt.plot(x, y)
plt.xlabel('x')
plt.ylabel('y')
plt.title('A Simple Line Plot')
plt.show()
```

Exercise 36: Data Analysis with NumPy

Concepts:

- Data analysis with NumPy

- Creating and manipulating arrays

Description: NumPy is a powerful library for numerical computing in Python. In this exercise, you'll write a script that uses NumPy to perform some basic data analysis tasks.

Solution:

```
import numpy as np

# Create a 2D array
data = np.array([[1, 2, 3], [4, 5, 6], [7, 8, 9]])

# Print the array
print(data)

# Calculate some statistics on the array
print(np.mean(data))
print(np.median(data))
print(np.std(data))

# Reshape the array
reshaped_data = data.reshape(1, 9)
print(reshaped_data)
```

Exercise 37: Object-Oriented Programming

Concepts:

- Object-oriented programming in Python

- Classes, objects, and inheritance

Description: Python is an object-oriented programming language. In this exercise, you'll write a script that demonstrates the use of object-oriented programming in Python.

Solution:

```python
class Shape:
    def __init__(self, x, y):
        self.x = x
        self.y = y

    def move(self, dx, dy):
        self.x += dx
        self.y += dy

class Rectangle(Shape):
    def __init__(self, x, y, width, height):
        super().__init__(x, y)
        self.width = width
        self.height = height

    def area(self):
        return self.width * self.height

class Circle(Shape):
    def __init__(self, x, y, radius):
        super().__init__(x, y)
        self.radius = radius

    def area(self):
        return 3.14159 * self.radius ** 2

rect = Rectangle(0, 0, 10, 5)
print(rect.area())
rect.move(1, 1)
print(rect.x, rect.y)

circ = Circle(0, 0, 5)
print(circ.area())
circ.move(2, 2)
print(circ.x, circ.y)
```

In this script, we define a `Shape` class that has an `x` and `y` coordinate, and a `move()` method that moves the shape by a specified amount in the x and y directions.

We then define a `Rectangle` class that inherits from `Shape`, and adds a `width` and `height` attribute, as well as an `area()` method that calculates the area of the rectangle.

We also define a `Circle` class that inherits from `Shape`, and adds a `radius` attribute, as well as an `area()` method that calculates the area of the circle.

Finally, we create instances of the `Rectangle` and `Circle` classes, and call their `area()` and `move()` methods.

Exercise 38: Regular Expressions

Concepts:

- Regular expressions in Python

- Searching for patterns in text

Description: Regular expressions are a powerful tool for text processing in Python. In this exercise, you'll write a script that uses regular expressions to search for patterns in a text file.

Solution:

```python
import re

with open('example.txt', 'r') as f:
    data = f.read()

pattern = r'\d{3}-\d{2}-\d{4}'
matches = re.findall(pattern, data)

for match in matches:
    print(match)
```

In this script, we open a text file and read its contents into a variable. We then define a regular expression pattern that matches a social security number in the format XXX-XX-XXXX.

We use the `findall()` function from the `re` module to find all occurrences of the pattern in the text, and print them out.

Exercise 39: File I/O

Concepts:

- File I/O in Python

- Reading and writing text files

Description: File I/O is a common task in Python programming. In this exercise, you'll write a script that reads data from a file, performs some processing, and writes the results to another file.

Solution:

```python
with open('input.txt', 'r') as f:
    data = f.readlines()

# Process the data
output = []
for line in data:
    line = line.strip()
    words = line.split()
    words.reverse()
    output.append(' '.join(words))

# Write the results to a file
with open('output.txt', 'w') as f:
    for line in output:
        f.write(line + '\n')
```

In this script, we open an input file and read its contents into a list of strings. We then process the data by splitting each line into words, reversing the order of the words, and joining them back together into a single string.

We write the resulting strings to an output file, with each string on a separate line.

Exercise 40: Data Manipulation with Pandas

Concepts:

- Data manipulation with Pandas

- Reading and filtering data

Description: Pandas is a powerful library for data manipulation in Python. In this exercise, you'll write a script that uses Pandas to load, process, and analyze a dataset.

Solution:

```python
import pandas as pd

# Load the data from a CSV file
data = pd.read_csv('example.csv')

# Filter the data to include only rows where the value is greater than 5
filtered_data = data[data['value'] > 5]

# Calculate the mean and standard deviation of the filtered data
mean = filtered_data['value'].mean()
std = filtered_data['value'].std()

print(f'Mean: {mean}')
print(f'Standard deviation: {std}')
```

In this script, we load a dataset from a CSV file into a Pandas DataFrame. We then filter the data to include only rows where the value is greater than 5.

We calculate the mean and standard deviation of the filtered data using the `mean()` and `std()` methods of the DataFrame, and print out the results.

ADVANCED LEVEL
CHAPTER 3

ADVANCED LEVEL CONCEPTS

In this last chapter you will practice **135 advanced level python concepts** during the next **50 advanced level exercises**. These exercises will guide you through each concept, providing detailed explanations and examples so that you can gain a solid understanding of each one. By the end of the 50 exercises, you will have not only practice 135 (maybe new) concepts, but you will also have developed the skills to apply them in real-world situations. This will give you a strong foundation on which to build as you continue to advance your knowledge and abilities in this field.

The following concepts are organized alphabetically.

Concepts List:

1. Aggregation 157
2. ARIMA model 158
3. AWS 159
4. Bar Chart 159
5. Beautiful Soup library 160
6. Big Data 161
7. Big Data Processing 161
8. Boto3 library 162
9. Candlestick Charts 162
10. Client-Server Architecture 163
11. Cloud Computing 165
12. Collaborative Filtering 165
13. Computer Networking 166
14. Computer Vision 167
15. Convolutional Neural Network 168
16. CPU-bound tasks 169
17. Cross-Validation 169
18. CSV file handling 170
19. CSV File I/O 170
20. Cybersecurity 171

21. Data Analysis 172
22. Data Cleaning 172
23. Data Engineering 173
24. Data Extraction 174
25. Data Integration 175
26. Apache Spark 175
27. Data Manipulation 176
28. Data Preprocessing 177
29. Data Processing 178
30. Data Retrieval 178
31. Data Science 179
32. Data Streaming 180
33. Data Transformations 181
34. Data Visualization 181
35. Database Interaction 182
36. Database Programming ... 183
37. Decision Tree Classifier 184
38. Deep Learning 185
39. DevOps 186
40. Distributed Systems 187
41. Fabric library 188
42. Feature Engineering 188
43. File Uploads 189
44. Flask framework 190
45. Form handling 191
46. Gensim library 192
47. Grid Search 193
48. Heatmap 193
49. Heroku 194
50. HTML Parsing 195
51. HTML templates 196
52. HTTP methods 197
53. Image Filtering 197
54. Image Loading 198
55. Image Manipulation 199
56. Image Processing 199
57. Image Segmentation 200
58. Kafka 201

59. Keras library 202
60. Latent Dirichlet Allocation 203
61. Line Chart 204
62. Machine Learning 205
63. MapReduce 206
64. Markov Chains 207
65. Matplotlib library 208
66. MNIST dataset 209
67. Model Evaluation 209
68. Model Training 210
69. Multiprocessing 211
70. Multithreading 212
71. Named Entity Recognition 213
72. Natural Language Generation 214
73. Natural Language Processing 215
74. Network Analysis 216
75. Network Programming 217
76. NLTK library 218
77. NumPy library 218
78. Object Detection 219
79. OpenAI Gym library 220
80. OpenCV library 221
81. Packet Sniffing 222
82. Pandas library 223
83. Parallel Processing 223
84. Parquet file format 224
85. Part-of-Speech Tagging 225
86. PDF Report Generation 226
87. Pillow library 227
88. Plotly library 227
89. Pre-trained models 228
90. Process Pool 229
91. Protocol Implementation 230
92. PyKafka library 231
93. Pyro library 232
94. PySpark 233
95. Q-Learning 233
96. Recommendation Systems 235

97. Regular expressions 236
98. Reinforcement Learning 237
99. Remote Method Invocation 238
100. ReportLab library 241
101. Requests library 241
102. Routing 242
103. Scapy library 243
104. Scatter Chart 243
105. Scikit-Learn library 244
106. Sentiment Analysis 244
107. Socket library 245
108. Socket Programming 245
109. spaCy library 246
110. SQL 247
111. SQL queries 248
112. SQLite 249
113. SQLite database 249
114. SQLite library 250
115. SQLite3 module 250
116. Statsmodels library 251
117. Stemming 251
118. Stop Words Removal 252
119. Stream Processing 252
120. Subplots 253
121. Support Vector Machines 254
122. Surprise library 255
123. TCP/IP Protocol 256
124. TensorFlow library 256
125. Text Corpus 257
126. Text Preprocessing 258
127. Text Processing 258
128. Text Representation 259
129. Threading library 259
130. Time Series Analysis 260
131. Tokenization 261
132. Topic Modeling 262
133. Web Application Deployment ... 263
134. Web Development 264
135. Web scraping 265

Advanced Level Concepts

1. Aggregation:

In programming, aggregation refers to the process of collecting and summarizing data from multiple sources or objects. It is a useful technique for analyzing large amounts of data and gaining insights into complex systems.

For example, suppose you have a list of sales data for a company that includes information about each sale, such as the customer, the product sold, the date of the sale, and the price. To analyze this data, you might want to aggregate it by product or by customer, to see which products are selling the most or which customers are generating the most revenue.

In Python, you can use aggregation functions like sum(), count(), and mean() to perform this type of analysis on your data.

Here's an example of how to use aggregation in Python:

```python
sales_data = [
    {'customer': 'Alice', 'product': 'Widget', 'date': '2022-01-01', 'price': 100},
    {'customer': 'Bob', 'product': 'Gizmo', 'date': '2022-01-02', 'price': 200},
    {'customer': 'Charlie', 'product': 'Widget', 'date': '2022-01-03', 'price': 150},
    {'customer': 'Alice', 'product': 'Thingamajig', 'date': '2022-01-04', 'price': 75},
    {'customer': 'Bob', 'product': 'Widget', 'date': '2022-01-05', 'price': 125},
    {'customer': 'Charlie', 'product': 'Gizmo', 'date': '2022-01-06', 'price': 250},
]

# Aggregate by product
product_sales = {}
for sale in sales_data:
    product = sale['product']
    if product not in product_sales:
        product_sales[product] = []
    product_sales[product].append(sale['price'])

for product, sales in product_sales.items():
    print(f"{product}: total sales = {sum(sales)}, avg. sale price = {sum(sales) / len(sales)}")

# Output:
# Widget: total sales = 225, avg. sale price = 112.5
# Gizmo: total sales = 450, avg. sale price = 225.0
```

```python
# Thingamajig: total sales = 75, avg. sale price = 75.0

# Aggregate by customer
customer_sales = {}
for sale in sales_data:
    customer = sale['customer']
    if customer not in customer_sales:
        customer_sales[customer] = []
    customer_sales[customer].append(sale['price'])

for customer, sales in customer_sales.items():
    print(f"{customer}: total sales = {sum(sales)}, avg. sale price = {sum(sales) / len(sa
les)}")

# Output:
# Alice: total sales = 175, avg. sale price = 87.5
# Bob: total sales = 325, avg. sale price = 162.5
# Charlie: total sales = 400, avg. sale price = 200.0
```

2. ARIMA model (continued):

The ARIMA model consists of three components: the autoregressive (AR) component, the integrated (I) component, and the moving average (MA) component. The AR component refers to the regression of the variable on its own past values, the MA component refers to the regression of the variable on past forecast errors, and the I component refers to the differencing of the series to make it stationary.

Here's an example of how to use the ARIMA model in Python:

```python
import pandas as pd
import numpy as np
import matplotlib.pyplot as plt
from statsmodels.tsa.arima.model import ARIMA

# Load the data
data = pd.read_csv("sales.csv", parse_dates=['date'], index_col='date')

# Create the ARIMA model
model = ARIMA(data, order=(1, 1, 1))

# Fit the model
result = model.fit()

# Make a forecast
forecast = result.forecast(steps=30)

# Plot the results
```

```
plt.plot(data.index, data.values)
plt.plot(forecast.index, forecast.values)
plt.show()
```

3. AWS:

AWS (Amazon Web Services) is a cloud computing platform that provides a wide range of services for building, deploying, and managing applications and infrastructure in the cloud. Some of the key services offered by AWS include virtual servers (EC2), storage (S3), databases (RDS), and machine learning (SageMaker).

AWS is a popular choice for many companies and developers because it offers a scalable and cost-effective way to build and deploy applications. With AWS, you can easily spin up new servers or resources as your application grows, and only pay for what you use.

Here's an example of how to use AWS in Python:

```
import boto3

# Create an S3 client
s3 = boto3.client('s3')

# Upload a file to S3
with open('test.txt', 'rb') as f:
    s3.upload_fileobj(f, 'my-bucket', 'test.txt')

# Download a file from S3
with open('test.txt', 'wb') as f:
    s3.download_fileobj('my-bucket', 'test.txt', f)
```

4. Bar Chart:

A bar chart is a graphical representation of data that uses rectangular bars to show the size or frequency of a variable. Bar charts are commonly used to compare the values of different categories or groups, and can be easily created in Python using libraries like Matplotlib or Seaborn.

Here's an example of how to create a bar chart in Python:

```python
import matplotlib.pyplot as plt

# Create some data
x = ['A', 'B', 'C', 'D']
y = [10, 20, 30, 40]

# Create a bar chart
plt.bar(x, y)

# Add labels and title
plt.xlabel('Category')
plt.ylabel('Value')
plt.title('My Bar Chart')

# Show the chart
plt.show()
```

5. Beautiful Soup library:

Beautiful Soup is a Python library used for web scraping and parsing HTML and XML documents. It provides a simple and intuitive interface for navigating and manipulating complex HTML and XML data, making it easy to extract the information you need from websites.

Here's an example of how to use Beautiful Soup in Python:

```python
from bs4 import BeautifulSoup
import requests

# Load a webpage
response = requests.get("https://www.example.com")
html = response.content

# Parse the HTML with Beautiful Soup
soup = BeautifulSoup(html, 'html.parser')

# Extract the title of the webpage
title = soup.title.text

# Print the title
print(title)
```

Output:

```
Copy code
Example Domain
```

In this example, we first use the requests library to retrieve the HTML content of a webpage, then we pass the HTML content to the BeautifulSoup constructor to create a BeautifulSoup object. Finally, we extract the title of the webpage using the `title` attribute of the `soup` object.

6. Big Data:

Big Data refers to extremely large and complex data sets that are difficult to process using traditional data processing methods. Big Data is characterized by the four Vs: Volume (the amount of data), Velocity (the speed at which data is generated), Variety (the different types of data), and Veracity (the quality and accuracy of the data).

Examples of Big Data include social media data, sensor data, and transaction data. Big Data is typically processed using distributed computing technologies such as Hadoop and Spark, which allow for parallel processing of large data sets across multiple nodes.

7. Big Data Processing:

Big Data Processing is the process of analyzing and processing large and complex data sets using distributed computing technologies. Big Data Processing is typically done using tools like Hadoop and Spark, which provide a framework for distributed processing of large data sets across multiple nodes.

The main advantage of Big Data Processing is the ability to process and analyze large data sets quickly and efficiently, which can lead to insights and discoveries that would not be possible using traditional data processing methods.

Here's an example of how to do Big Data Processing in Python using the PySpark library:

```
from pyspark import SparkContext, SparkConf

# Configure the Spark context
conf = SparkConf().setAppName("MyApp")
sc = SparkContext(conf=conf)
```

```
# Load the data
data = sc.textFile("mydata.txt")

# Perform some processing
result = data.filter(lambda x: x.startswith("A")).count()

# Print the result
print(result)
```

8. Boto3 library:

Boto3 is a Python library used for interacting with Amazon Web Services (AWS) using Python code. Boto3 provides an easy-to-use API for working with AWS services, such as EC2, S3, and RDS.

Here's an example of how to use Boto3 to interact with AWS in Python:

```
import boto3

# Create an EC2 client
ec2 = boto3.client('ec2')

# Start a new EC2 instance
response = ec2.run_instances(
    ImageId='ami-0c55b159cbfafe1f0',
    InstanceType='t2.micro',
    KeyName='my-key-pair',
    MinCount=1,
    MaxCount=1
)

# Get the ID of the new instance
instance_id = response['Instances'][0]['InstanceId']

# Stop the instance
ec2.stop_instances(InstanceIds=[instance_id])
```

9. Candlestick Charts:

A candlestick chart is a type of financial chart used to represent the movement of stock prices over time. It is a useful tool for visualizing patterns and trends in stock prices, and is commonly used by traders and analysts.

A candlestick chart consists of a series of bars or "candles" that represent the opening, closing, high, and low prices of a stock over a given period of time. The length and color of the candles can be used to indicate whether the stock price increased or decreased over that period.

Here's an example of how to create a candlestick chart in Python using the Matplotlib library:

```python
import matplotlib.pyplot as plt
from mpl_finance import candlestick_ohlc
import pandas as pd
import numpy as np
import matplotlib.dates as mpl_dates

# Load the data
data = pd.read_csv('stock_prices.csv', parse_dates=['date'])

# Convert the data to OHLC format
ohlc = data[['date', 'open', 'high', 'low', 'close']]
ohlc['date'] = ohlc['date'].apply(lambda x: mpl_dates.date2num(x))
ohlc = ohlc.astype(float).values.tolist()

# Create the candlestick chart
fig, ax = plt.subplots()
candlestick_ohlc(ax, ohlc)

# Set the x-axis labels
date_format = mpl_dates.DateFormatter('%d %b %Y')
ax.xaxis.set_major_formatter(date_format)
fig.autofmt_xdate()

# Set the chart title
plt.title('Stock Prices')

# Show the chart
plt.show()
```

In this example, we first load the stock price data from a CSV file, convert it to OHLC (Open-High-Low-Close) format, and then create a candlestick chart using the Matplotlib library. We also format the x-axis labels and set the chart title before displaying the chart.

10. Client-Server Architecture:

Client-Server Architecture is a computing architecture where a client program sends requests to a server program over a network, and the server program responds to those requests. This architecture is used in many different types of applications, such as web applications, database management systems, and file servers.

In a client-server architecture, the client program is typically a user interface that allows users to interact with the application, while the server program is responsible for processing the requests and returning the results. The server program may be running on a remote machine, which allows multiple clients to access the same application at the same time.

Here's an example of how to implement a simple client-server architecture in Python:

```python
# Server code
import socket

# Create a TCP/IP socket
sock = socket.socket(socket.AF_INET, socket.SOCK_STREAM)

# Bind the socket to a specific address and port
server_address = ('localhost', 12345)
sock.bind(server_address)

# Listen for incoming connections
sock.listen(1)

while True:
    # Wait for a connection
    connection, client_address = sock.accept()

    try:
        # Receive the data from the client
        data = connection.recv(1024)

        # Process the data
        result = process_data(data)

        # Send the result back to the client
        connection.sendall(result)
    finally:
        # Clean up the connection
        connection.close()

# Client code
import socket

# Create a TCP/IP socket
```

```python
sock = socket.socket(socket.AF_INET, socket.SOCK_STREAM)

# Connect the socket to the server's address and port
server_address = ('localhost', 12345)
sock.connect(server_address)

try:
    # Send some data to the server
    data = b'Hello, server!'
    sock.sendall(data)

    # Receive the response from the server
    result = sock.recv(1024)
finally:
    # Clean up the socket
    sock.close()
```

In this example, we create a simple client-server architecture using sockets. The server program listens for incoming connections, receives data from the client, processes the data, and sends the result back to the client. The client program connects to the server, sends data to the server, receives the result, processes the result, and closes the connection.

In a real-world client-server architecture, the client program would typically be a web browser or mobile app, while the server program would be a web server or application server. The server program would handle multiple simultaneous connections from clients, and may also communicate with other servers and services as needed.

11. Cloud Computing:

Cloud Computing is the delivery of computing services, including servers, storage, databases, and software, over the internet. Cloud Computing allows businesses and individuals to access computing resources on demand, without the need for physical infrastructure, and pay only for what they use.

Examples of Cloud Computing services include Amazon Web Services (AWS), Microsoft Azure, and Google Cloud Platform (GCP). Cloud Computing has revolutionized the way businesses and individuals access and use computing resources, enabling rapid innovation and scalability.

12. Collaborative Filtering:

Collaborative Filtering is a technique used in recommender systems to predict a user's interests based on the preferences of similar users. Collaborative Filtering works by analyzing the historical data of users and their interactions with products or services, and identifying patterns and similarities between users.

There are two main types of Collaborative Filtering: User-Based Collaborative Filtering and Item-Based Collaborative Filtering. User-Based Collaborative Filtering recommends products or services to a user based on the preferences of similar users, while Item-Based Collaborative Filtering recommends similar products or services to a user based on their preferences.

Here's an example of how to implement Collaborative Filtering in Python using the Surprise library:

```python
from surprise import Dataset
from surprise import Reader
from surprise import KNNWithMeans

# Load the data
reader = Reader(line_format='user item rating', sep=',', rating_scale=(1, 5))
data = Dataset.load_from_file('ratings.csv', reader=reader)

# Train the model
sim_options = {'name': 'pearson_baseline', 'user_based': False}
algo = KNNWithMeans(sim_options=sim_options)
trainset = data.build_full_trainset()
algo.fit(trainset)

# Get the top recommendations for a user
user_id = 123
n_recommendations = 10
user_items = trainset.ur[user_id]
candidate_items = [item_id for (item_id, _) in trainset.all_items() if item_id not in user
_items]
predictions = [algo.predict(user_id, item_id) for item_id in candidate_items]
top_recommendations = sorted(predictions, key=lambda x: x.est, reverse=True)[:n_recommenda
tions]
```

13. Computer Networking:

Computer Networking is the field of study that focuses on the design, implementation, and maintenance of computer networks. A computer network is a collection of devices, such as computers, printers, and servers, that are connected together to share resources and information.

Computer Networking is essential for enabling communication and collaboration between devices and users across different locations and environments. Computer networks can be designed and implemented using a variety of technologies and protocols, such as TCP/IP, DNS, and HTTP.

14. Computer Vision:

Computer Vision is the field of study that focuses on enabling computers to interpret and understand visual data from the world around them, such as images and videos. Computer Vision is used in a wide range of applications, such as autonomous vehicles, facial recognition, and object detection.

Computer Vision involves the use of techniques such as image processing, pattern recognition, and machine learning to enable computers to interpret and understand visual data. Some of the key challenges in Computer Vision include object recognition, object tracking, and scene reconstruction.

Here's an example of how to implement Computer Vision in Python using the OpenCV library:

```python
import cv2

# Load an image
img = cv2.imread('example.jpg')

# Convert the image to grayscale
gray = cv2.cvtColor(img, cv2.COLOR_BGR2GRAY)

# Apply edge detection
edges = cv2.Canny(gray, 100, 200)

# Display the results
cv2.imshow('Original Image', img)
cv2.imshow('Grayscale Image', gray)
cv2.imshow('Edges', edges)
cv2.waitKey(0)
cv2.destroyAllWindows()
```

In this example, we load an image, convert it to grayscale, and apply edge detection using the Canny algorithm. We then display the original image, the grayscale image, and the edges detected in the image.

15. Convolutional Neural Network:

A Convolutional Neural Network (CNN) is a type of deep neural network that is commonly used for image recognition and classification tasks. A CNN consists of multiple layers, including convolutional layers, pooling layers, and fully connected layers.

In a CNN, the convolutional layers apply filters to the input image to extract features, such as edges and textures. The pooling layers downsample the feature maps to reduce the size of the input, while preserving the important features. The fully connected layers use the output of the previous layers to classify the image.

Here's an example of how to implement a CNN in Python using the Keras library:

```python
from keras.models import Sequential
from keras.layers import Conv2D, MaxPooling2D, Flatten, Dense

# Create the CNN model
model = Sequential()
model.add(Conv2D(32, (3, 3), activation='relu', input_shape=(28, 28, 1)))
model.add(MaxPooling2D((2, 2)))
model.add(Conv2D(64, (3, 3), activation='relu'))
model.add(MaxPooling2D((2, 2)))
model.add(Conv2D(64, (3, 3), activation='relu'))
model.add(Flatten())
model.add(Dense(64, activation='relu'))
model.add(Dense(10, activation='softmax'))

# Compile the model
model.compile(optimizer='adam', loss='categorical_crossentropy', metrics=['accuracy'])

# Train the model
model.fit(x_train, y_train, epochs=5, validation_data=(x_test, y_test))
```

In this example, we create a CNN model using the Keras library, which consists of multiple convolutional layers, pooling layers, and fully connected layers. We then compile the model using the Adam optimizer and categorical cross-entropy loss, and train the model on a dataset of images. The output of the model is a probability distribution over the possible classes of the image.

16. CPU-bound tasks:

CPU-bound tasks are tasks that primarily require processing power from the CPU (Central Processing Unit) to complete. These tasks typically involve mathematical computations, data processing, or other operations that require the CPU to perform intensive calculations or data manipulation.

Examples of CPU-bound tasks include video encoding, scientific simulations, and machine learning algorithms. CPU-bound tasks can benefit from multi-threading or parallel processing to improve performance and reduce the time required to complete the task.

17. Cross-Validation:

Cross-Validation is a technique used in machine learning to evaluate the performance of a model on a dataset. Cross-Validation involves dividing the dataset into multiple subsets or "folds," training the model on a subset of the data, and evaluating the performance of the model on the remaining data.

The most common type of Cross-Validation is k-Fold Cross-Validation, where the dataset is divided into k equal-sized folds, and the model is trained k times, each time using a different fold as the validation set and the remaining folds as the training set. The performance of the model is then averaged across the k runs.

Here's an example of how to implement Cross-Validation in Python using the scikit-learn library:

```python
from sklearn.model_selection import cross_val_score
from sklearn.linear_model import LogisticRegression
from sklearn.datasets import load_iris

# Load the dataset
iris = load_iris()

# Create the model
model = LogisticRegression()

# Evaluate the model using k-Fold Cross-Validation
scores = cross_val_score(model, iris.data, iris.target, cv=5)

# Print the average score
print('Average Score:', scores.mean())
```

In this example, we load the Iris dataset, create a logistic regression model, and evaluate the performance of the model using k-Fold Cross-Validation with k=5. We then print the average score across the k runs.

18. CSV file handling:

CSV (Comma-Separated Values) file handling is a technique used in programming to read and write data from and to CSV files. CSV files are commonly used to store tabular data, such as spreadsheets or databases, in a plain-text format that can be easily read and manipulated by humans and machines.

CSV files typically have a header row that defines the names of the columns, and one or more data rows that contain the values for each column. CSV files can be easily created and edited using spreadsheet software, such as Microsoft Excel or Google Sheets.

Here's an example of how to read a CSV file in Python using the Pandas library:

```python
import pandas as pd

# Load the CSV file
data = pd.read_csv('data.csv')

# Print the data
print(data)
```

In this example, we load a CSV file called "data.csv" using the Pandas library, and print the contents of the file.

19. CSV File I/O:

CSV (Comma-Separated Values) File I/O (Input/Output) is a technique used in programming to read and write data from and to CSV files. CSV files are commonly used to store tabular data, such as spreadsheets or databases, in a plain-text format that can be easily read and manipulated by humans and machines.

CSV files typically have a header row that defines the names of the columns, and one or more data rows that contain the values for each column. CSV files can be easily created and edited using spreadsheet software, such as Microsoft Excel or Google Sheets.

Here's an example of how to write data to a CSV file in Python using the csv module:

```
import csv

# Define the data
data = [
    ['Name', 'Age', 'Gender'],
    ['John', 30, 'Male'],
    ['Jane', 25, 'Female'],
    ['Bob', 40, 'Male']
]

# Write the data to a CSV file
with open('data.csv', 'w', newline='') as file:
    writer = csv.writer(file)
    writer.writerows(data)
```

In this example, we define a list of data that represents a table with three columns: Name, Age, and Gender. We then use the csv module to write the data to a CSV file called "data.csv".

20. Cybersecurity:

Cybersecurity is the practice of protecting computer systems and networks from theft, damage, or unauthorized access. Cybersecurity is an important field of study and practice, as more and more business operations and personal information are conducted online and stored in digital form.

Cybersecurity involves a variety of techniques and technologies, including firewalls, encryption, malware detection, and vulnerability assessments. Cybersecurity professionals work to identify and mitigate security risks, as well as to respond to and recover from security incidents.

Some common cybersecurity threats include phishing attacks, malware infections, and data breaches. It's important for individuals and organizations to take steps to protect themselves from these threats, such as using strong passwords, keeping software up to date, and using anti-virus software.

21. Data Analysis:

Data Analysis is the process of inspecting, cleaning, transforming, and modeling data to extract useful information and draw conclusions. Data Analysis is used in a wide range of fields, including business, science, and social sciences, to make informed decisions and gain insights from data.

Data Analysis involves a variety of techniques and tools, including statistical analysis, data mining, and machine learning. Data Analysis can be performed using a variety of software and programming languages, such as Excel, R, and Python.

Here's an example of how to perform Data Analysis in Python using the Pandas library:

```python
import pandas as pd

# Load the data
data = pd.read_csv('data.csv')

# Perform Data Analysis
mean_age = data['Age'].mean()
median_income = data['Income'].median()

# Print the results
print('Mean Age:', mean_age)
print('Median Income:', median_income)
```

In this example, we load a CSV file called "data.csv" using the Pandas library, and perform Data Analysis on the data by calculating the mean age and median income of the dataset.

22. Data Cleaning:

Data Cleaning is the process of identifying and correcting errors, inconsistencies, and inaccuracies in data. Data Cleaning is an important step in the Data Analysis process, as it ensures that the data is accurate, reliable, and consistent.

Data Cleaning involves a variety of techniques and tools, including removing duplicates, filling in missing values, and correcting spelling errors. Data Cleaning can be performed using a variety of software and programming languages, such as Excel, R, and Python.

Here's an example of how to perform Data Cleaning in Python using the Pandas library:

```python
import pandas as pd

# Load the data
data = pd.read_csv('data.csv')

# Perform Data Cleaning
data.drop_duplicates(inplace=True)
data.fillna(value=0, inplace=True)

# Print the cleaned data
print(data)
```

In this example, we load a CSV file called "data.csv" using the Pandas library, and perform Data Cleaning on the data by removing duplicates and filling in missing values with 0.

23. Data Engineering:

Data Engineering is the process of designing, building, and maintaining the systems and infrastructure that enable the processing, storage, and analysis of data. Data Engineering is an important field of study and practice, as more and more data is generated and collected in digital form.

Data Engineering involves a variety of techniques and technologies, including database design, data warehousing, and ETL (Extract, Transform, Load) processes. Data Engineering professionals work to ensure that data is stored and processed in a way that is efficient, secure, and scalable.

Here's an example of how to perform Data Engineering in Python using the Apache Spark framework:

```python
from pyspark.sql import SparkSession

# Create a SparkSession
spark = SparkSession.builder.appName('Data Engineering Example').getOrCreate()

# Load the data
data = spark.read.csv('data.csv', header=True, inferSchema=True)

# Perform Data Engineering
data.write.format('parquet').mode('overwrite').save('data.parquet')
```

```
# Print the results
print('Data Engineering Complete')
```

In this example, we use the Apache Spark framework to perform Data Engineering on a CSV file called "data.csv". We load the data into a Spark DataFrame, and then use the DataFrame API to write the data to a Parquet file format, which is a columnar storage format that is optimized for querying and processing large datasets.

24. Data Extraction:

Data Extraction is the process of retrieving data from various sources, such as databases, web pages, or files, and transforming it into a format that can be used for analysis or other purposes. Data Extraction is an important step in the Data Analysis process, as it allows us to gather data from various sources and combine it into a single dataset.

Data Extraction involves a variety of techniques and tools, including web scraping, database querying, and file parsing. Data Extraction can be performed using a variety of software and programming languages, such as Python, SQL, and R.

Here's an example of how to perform Data Extraction in Python using the BeautifulSoup library:

```
import requests
from bs4 import BeautifulSoup

# Send a GET request to the web page
response = requests.get('https://www.example.com')

# Parse the HTML content using BeautifulSoup
soup = BeautifulSoup(response.content, 'html.parser')

# Extract the desired data
links = []
for link in soup.find_all('a'):
    links.append(link.get('href'))

# Print the results
print(links)
```

In this example, we use the requests library to send a GET request to a web page, and the BeautifulSoup library to parse the HTML content of the page. We then extract all of the links on the page and print the results.

25. Data Integration:

Data Integration is the process of combining data from multiple sources into a single, unified dataset. Data Integration is an important step in the Data Analysis process, as it allows us to combine data from various sources and perform analysis on the combined dataset.

Data Integration involves a variety of techniques and tools, including data warehousing, ETL (Extract, Transform, Load) processes, and data federation. Data Integration can be performed using a variety of software and programming languages, such as SQL, Python, and R.

Here's an example of how to perform Data Integration in Python using the Pandas library:

```python
import pandas as pd

# Load the data from multiple sources
data1 = pd.read_csv('data1.csv')
data2 = pd.read_csv('data2.csv')
data3 = pd.read_csv('data3.csv')

# Combine the data into a single dataset
combined_data = pd.concat([data1, data2, data3])

# Print the combined data
print(combined_data)
```

In this example, we load data from three different CSV files using the Pandas library, and then combine the data into a single dataset using the concat function. We then print the combined dataset.

26. Apache Spark:

Apache Spark is an open-source distributed computing system that is designed to process large amounts of data in parallel across a cluster of computers. Apache Spark is commonly used for big data processing, machine learning, and data analysis.

Apache Spark provides a variety of programming interfaces, including Python, Java, and Scala, as well as a set of libraries for data processing, machine learning, and graph processing. Apache Spark can be run on a variety of platforms, including on-premise clusters, cloud platforms, and standalone machines.

Here's an example of how to use Apache Spark in Python to perform data processing:

```python
from pyspark.sql import SparkSession

# Create a SparkSession
spark = SparkSession.builder.appName('Data Processing Example').getOrCreate()

# Load the data
data = spark.read.csv('data.csv', header=True, inferSchema=True)

# Perform Data Processing
processed_data = data.filter(data['Age'] > 30)

# Print the processed data
processed_data.show()
```

In this example, we use Apache Spark to perform data processing on a CSV file called "data.csv". We load the data into a Spark DataFrame, and then use the DataFrame API to filter the data to only include rows where the age is greater than 30.

27. Data Manipulation:

Data Manipulation is the process of modifying or transforming data in order to prepare it for analysis or other purposes. Data Manipulation is an important step in the Data Analysis process, as it allows us to transform the data into a format that is suitable for analysis.

Data Manipulation involves a variety of techniques and tools, including filtering, sorting, grouping, and joining. Data Manipulation can be performed using a variety of software and programming languages, such as Excel, SQL, and Python.

Here's an example of how to perform Data Manipulation in Python using the Pandas library:

```python
import pandas as pd

# Load the data
data = pd.read_csv('data.csv')

# Perform Data Manipulation
processed_data = data[data['Age'] > 30]

# Print the processed data
print(processed_data)
```

In this example, we use the Pandas library to perform data manipulation on a CSV file called "data.csv". We load the data into a Pandas DataFrame, and then use boolean indexing to filter the data to only include rows where the age is greater than 30.

28. Data Preprocessing:

Data Preprocessing is the process of preparing data for analysis or other purposes by cleaning, transforming, and organizing the data. Data Preprocessing is an important step in the Data Analysis process, as it ensures that the data is accurate, complete, and in a format that is suitable for analysis.

Data Preprocessing involves a variety of techniques and tools, including data cleaning, data transformation, and data normalization. Data Preprocessing can be performed using a variety of software and programming languages, such as Excel, R, and Python.

Here's an example of how to perform Data Preprocessing in Python using the scikit-learn library:

```python
from sklearn.preprocessing import StandardScaler
import pandas as pd

# Load the data
data = pd.read_csv('data.csv')

# Perform Data Preprocessing
scaler = StandardScaler()
scaled_data = scaler.fit_transform(data)

# Print the processed data
print(scaled_data)
```

In this example, we use the scikit-learn library to perform Data Preprocessing on a CSV file called "data.csv". We load the data into a Pandas DataFrame, and then use the StandardScaler class to normalize the data by scaling it to have zero mean and unit variance.

29. Data Processing:

Data Processing is the process of transforming raw data into a format that is suitable for analysis or other purposes. Data Processing is an important step in the Data Analysis process, as it allows us to transform the data into a format that is suitable for analysis.

Data Processing involves a variety of techniques and tools, including data cleaning, data transformation, and data normalization. Data Processing can be performed using a variety of software and programming languages, such as Excel, R, and Python.

Here's an example of how to perform Data Processing in Python using the Pandas library:

```python
import pandas as pd

# Load the data
data = pd.read_csv('data.csv')

# Perform Data Processing
processed_data = data.drop_duplicates().fillna(0)

# Print the processed data
print(processed_data)
```

In this example, we use the Pandas library to perform Data Processing on a CSV file called "data.csv". We load the data into a Pandas DataFrame, and then use the drop_duplicates and fillna functions to remove duplicates and fill in missing values with 0.

30. Data Retrieval:

Data Retrieval is the process of retrieving data from a data source, such as a database, web service, or file, and extracting the desired data for further processing or analysis. Data Retrieval is an important step in the Data Analysis process, as it allows us to gather data from various sources and combine it into a single dataset.

Data Retrieval involves a variety of techniques and tools, including database querying, web scraping, and file parsing. Data Retrieval can be performed using a variety of software and programming languages, such as SQL, Python, and R.

Here's an example of how to perform Data Retrieval in Python using the Pandas library and SQL:

```python
import pandas as pd
import sqlite3

# Connect to the database
conn = sqlite3.connect('data.db')

# Load the data using SQL
data = pd.read_sql_query('SELECT * FROM customers', conn)

# Print the data
print(data)
```

In this example, we connect to a SQLite database called "data.db", and then use SQL to retrieve data from the "customers" table. We load the data into a Pandas DataFrame using the read_sql_query function, and then print the data.

31. Data Science:

Data Science is a field of study that involves the use of statistical and computational methods to extract knowledge and insights from data. Data Science is an interdisciplinary field that combines elements of mathematics, statistics, computer science, and domain expertise.

Data Science involves a variety of techniques and tools, including statistical analysis, machine learning, and data visualization. Data Science can be used in a wide range of fields, including business, healthcare, and social sciences.

Here's an example of how to perform Data Science in Python using the scikit-learn library:

```python
from sklearn.linear_model import LinearRegression
import pandas as pd
```

```
# Load the data
data = pd.read_csv('data.csv')

# Perform Data Science
model = LinearRegression()
X = data[['Age', 'Income']]
y = data['Spending']
model.fit(X, y)

# Print the results
print('Coefficients:', model.coef_)
print('Intercept:', model.intercept_)
```

In this example, we use the scikit-learn library to perform Data Science on a CSV file called "data.csv". We load the data into a Pandas DataFrame, and then use the LinearRegression class to fit a linear regression model to the data.

32. Data Streaming:

Data Streaming is the process of processing and analyzing data in real-time as it is generated or received. Data Streaming is an important technology for applications that require fast and continuous data processing, such as real-time analytics, fraud detection, and monitoring.

Data Streaming involves a variety of techniques and tools, including message brokers, stream processing engines, and real-time databases. Data Streaming can be performed using a variety of software and programming languages, such as Apache Kafka, Apache Flink, and Python.

Here's an example of how to perform Data Streaming in Python using the Apache Kafka library:

```
from kafka import KafkaConsumer

# Create a KafkaConsumer
consumer = KafkaConsumer('topic', bootstrap_servers=['localhost:9092'])

# Process the data
for message in consumer:
    print(message.value)
```

In this example, we use the Apache Kafka library to create a KafkaConsumer that subscribes to a topic and reads messages from it in real-time. We then process the data by printing the value of each message.

33. Data Transformations:

Data Transformations are the processes of modifying or transforming data in order to prepare it for analysis or other purposes. Data Transformations are an important step in the Data Analysis process, as they allow us to transform the data into a format that is suitable for analysis.

Data Transformations involve a variety of techniques and tools, including data cleaning, data normalization, and data aggregation. Data Transformations can be performed using a variety of software and programming languages, such as Excel, R, and Python.

Here's an example of how to perform Data Transformations in Python using the Pandas library:

```python
import pandas as pd

# Load the data
data = pd.read_csv('data.csv')

# Perform Data Transformations
transformed_data = data.groupby('Age')['Income'].mean()

# Print the transformed data
print(transformed_data)
```

In this example, we use the Pandas library to perform Data Transformations on a CSV file called "data.csv". We load the data into a Pandas DataFrame, and then use the groupby function to group the data by age and calculate the mean income for each age group.

34. Data Visualization:

Data Visualization is the process of presenting data in a visual format, such as a chart, graph, or map, in order to make it easier to understand and analyze. Data Visualization is an important step in the Data Analysis process, as it allows us to identify patterns and trends in the data and communicate the results to others.

Data Visualization involves a variety of techniques and tools, including charts, graphs, maps, and interactive visualizations. Data Visualization can be performed using a variety of software and programming languages, such as Excel, R, Python, and Tableau.

Here's an example of how to perform Data Visualization in Python using the Matplotlib library:

```python
import pandas as pd
import matplotlib.pyplot as plt

# Load the data
data = pd.read_csv('data.csv')

# Perform Data Visualization
plt.scatter(data['Age'], data['Income'])
plt.xlabel('Age')
plt.ylabel('Income')
plt.show()
```

In this example, we use the Matplotlib library to perform Data Visualization on a CSV file called "data.csv". We load the data into a Pandas DataFrame, and then use the scatter plot to visualize the relationship between age and income.

35. Database Interaction:

Database Interaction is the process of connecting to a database, retrieving data from the database, and performing operations on the data. Database Interaction is an important step in the Data Analysis process, as it allows us to store and retrieve data from a database, which can be a more efficient and scalable way to manage large datasets.

Database Interaction involves a variety of techniques and tools, including SQL, Python database libraries such as SQLite and psycopg2, and cloud-based databases such as Amazon RDS and Google Cloud SQL.

Here's an example of how to perform Database Interaction in Python using the SQLite database:

```python
import sqlite3

# Connect to the database
conn = sqlite3.connect('data.db')

# Retrieve data from the database
cursor = conn.execute('SELECT * FROM customers')

# Print the data
for row in cursor:
    print(row)
```

In this example, we use the SQLite database to perform Database Interaction. We connect to the "data.db" database using the connect function, and then retrieve data from the "customers" table using a SQL query. We then print the data using a loop.

36. Database Programming:

Database Programming is the process of writing code to interact with a database, such as retrieving data, modifying data, or creating tables. Database Programming is an important skill for working with databases and is used in a wide range of applications, such as web development, data analysis, and software engineering.

Database Programming involves a variety of techniques and tools, including SQL, Python database libraries such as SQLite and psycopg2, and Object-Relational Mapping (ORM) frameworks such as SQLAlchemy.

Here's an example of how to perform Database Programming in Python using the SQLAlchemy ORM framework:

```python
from sqlalchemy import create_engine, Column, Integer, String
from sqlalchemy.ext.declarative import declarative_base
from sqlalchemy.orm import sessionmaker

# Connect to the database
engine = create_engine('sqlite:///data.db')
Base = declarative_base()
Session = sessionmaker(bind=engine)

# Define the data model
class Customer(Base):
    __tablename__ = 'customers'
```

```
    id = Column(Integer, primary_key=True)
    name = Column(String)
    age = Column(Integer)
    email = Column(String)

# Create a new customer
session = Session()
new_customer = Customer(name='John Doe', age=35, email='johndoe@example.com')
session.add(new_customer)
session.commit()

# Retrieve data from the database
customers = session.query(Customer).all()
for customer in customers:
    print(customer.name, customer.age, customer.email)
```

In this example, we use the SQLAlchemy ORM framework to perform Database Programming in Python. We define a data model for the "customers" table, and then create a new customer and insert it into the database using a session. We then retrieve data from the database using a query and print the results.

37. Decision Tree Classifier:

The Decision Tree Classifier is a machine learning algorithm that is used for classification tasks. The Decision Tree Classifier works by constructing a tree-like model of decisions and their possible consequences. The tree is constructed by recursively splitting the data into subsets based on the value of a specific attribute, with the goal of maximizing the purity of the subsets.

The Decision Tree Classifier is commonly used in applications such as fraud detection, medical diagnosis, and customer segmentation.

Here's an example of how to use the Decision Tree Classifier in Python using the scikit-learn library:

```
from sklearn.tree import DecisionTreeClassifier
from sklearn.datasets import load_iris

# Load the data
iris = load_iris()
X, y = iris.data, iris.target

# Train the model
model = DecisionTreeClassifier()
```

```
model.fit(X, y)

# Make predictions
predictions = model.predict(X)
print(predictions)
```

In this example, we use the scikit-learn library to train a Decision Tree Classifier on the Iris dataset, which is a classic dataset used for classification tasks. We load the data into the X and y variables, and then use the fit function to train the model. We then use the predict function to make predictions on the data and print the results.

38. Deep Learning:

Deep Learning is a subset of machine learning that involves the use of neural networks with many layers. The term "deep" refers to the fact that the networks have multiple layers, allowing them to learn increasingly complex representations of the data.

Deep Learning is used for a wide range of applications, such as image recognition, natural language processing, and speech recognition. Deep Learning has achieved state-of-the-art performance on many tasks and is a rapidly advancing field.

Deep Learning involves a variety of techniques and tools, including convolutional neural networks, recurrent neural networks, and deep belief networks. Deep Learning can be performed using a variety of software and programming languages, such as Python and TensorFlow.

Here's an example of how to perform Deep Learning in Python using the TensorFlow library:

```
import tensorflow as tf
from tensorflow import keras
from tensorflow.keras import layers

# Load the data
(x_train, y_train), (x_test, y_test) = keras.datasets.mnist.load_data()

# Perform Data Preprocessing
x_train = x_train.reshape(-1, 28 * 28).astype("float32") / 255.0
x_test = x_test.reshape(-1, 28 * 28).astype("float32") / 255.0
y_train = keras.utils.to_categorical(y_train)
y_test = keras.utils.to_categorical(y_test)

# Train the model
```

```python
model = keras.Sequential(
    [
        layers.Dense(512, activation="relu"),
        layers.Dense(256, activation="relu"),
        layers.Dense(10, activation="softmax"),
    ]
)
model.compile(optimizer='adam', loss='categorical_crossentropy', metrics=['accuracy'])
model.fit(x_train, y_train, epochs=10, batch_size=32, validation_split=0.2)

# Evaluate the model
test_loss, test_acc = model.evaluate(x_test, y_test)
print("Test Accuracy:", test_acc)
```

In this example, we use the TensorFlow library to perform Deep Learning on the MNIST dataset, which is a dataset of handwritten digits. We load the data into the x_train, y_train, x_test, and y_test variables, and then perform Data Preprocessing to prepare the data for training. We then train a neural network model with two hidden layers and evaluate the model on the test data.

39. DevOps:

DevOps is a set of practices and tools that combine software development and IT operations to improve the speed and quality of software delivery. DevOps involves a culture of collaboration between development and operations teams, and a focus on automation, monitoring, and continuous improvement.

DevOps involves a variety of techniques and tools, including version control systems, continuous integration and continuous delivery (CI/CD) pipelines, containerization, and monitoring tools. DevOps can be used in a wide range of applications, from web development to cloud infrastructure management.

Here's an example of a DevOps pipeline:

```
1. Developers write code and commit changes to a version control system (VCS) such as Git.
2. The VCS triggers a continuous integration (CI) server to build the code, run automated
   tests, and generate reports.
3. If the build and tests pass, the code is automatically deployed to a staging environmen
   t for further testing and review.
4. If the staging tests pass, the code is automatically deployed to a production environme
   nt.
5. Monitoring tools are used to monitor the production environment and alert the operation
   s team to any issues.
6. The operations team uses automation tools to deploy patches and updates as needed, and
```

```
   to perform other tasks such as scaling the infrastructure.
   7. The cycle repeats, with new changes being committed to the VCS and automatically deploy
   ed to production as they are approved and tested.
```

40. Distributed Systems:

A Distributed System is a system in which multiple computers work together to achieve a common goal. Distributed Systems are used in a wide range of applications, such as web applications, cloud computing, and scientific computing.

Distributed Systems involve a variety of techniques and tools, including distributed file systems, distributed databases, message passing, and coordination protocols. Distributed Systems can be implemented using a variety of software and programming languages, such as Apache Hadoop, Apache Kafka, and Python.

Here's an example of a Distributed System architecture:

```
   1. Clients send requests to a load balancer, which distributes the requests to multiple se
   rvers.
   2. Each server processes the request and retrieves or updates data from a distributed data
   base.
   3. The servers communicate with each other using a message passing protocol such as Apache
   Kafka.
   4. Coordination protocols such as ZooKeeper are used to manage the distributed system and
    ensure consistency.
   5. Monitoring tools are used to monitor the performance and health of the system, and to a
   lert the operations team to any issues.
   6. The system can be scaled horizontally by adding more servers to the cluster as needed.
   7. The cycle repeats, with new requests being processed by the servers and updates being m
   ade to the distributed database.
```

In a Distributed System, each computer (or node) has its own CPU, memory, and storage. The nodes work together to perform a task or set of tasks. Distributed Systems offer several advantages over centralized systems, such as increased fault tolerance, scalability, and performance.

However, Distributed Systems also present several challenges, such as ensuring data consistency, managing network communication, and dealing with failures. As a result, Distributed Systems often require specialized software and expertise to design and manage effectively.

41. Fabric library:

Fabric is a Python library that simplifies the process of remote system administration and deployment. Fabric provides a set of tools and functions for executing commands on remote machines over SSH.

Fabric is commonly used for automating repetitive tasks, such as deploying web applications or managing servers. Fabric allows users to define tasks in Python scripts and execute them across multiple machines simultaneously.

Here's an example of using Fabric to deploy a web application to a remote server:

```python
from fabric import Connection

def deploy():
    with Connection('user@host'):
        run('git pull')
        run('docker-compose up -d')
```

In this example, the `deploy` function connects to a remote server using SSH and executes two commands: `git pull` to update the application code from a Git repository, and `docker-compose up -d` to start the application using Docker.

42. Feature Engineering:

Feature Engineering is the process of selecting and transforming raw data into features that can be used for machine learning models. Feature Engineering is a critical step in the machine learning pipeline, as the quality of the features can have a significant impact on the performance of the model.

Feature Engineering involves a variety of techniques, such as data cleaning, data normalization, feature selection, and feature transformation. Feature Engineering requires a deep understanding of the data and the problem domain, and often involves iterative experimentation and testing to find the best set of features for the model.

Here's an example of Feature Engineering for a text classification problem:

```python
import pandas as pd
import spacy
```

```
nlp = spacy.load('en_core_web_sm')

def preprocess_text(text):
    doc = nlp(text)
    lemmas = [token.lemma_ for token in doc if not token.is_stop and token.is_alpha]
    return ' '.join(lemmas)

data = pd.read_csv('data.csv')
data['clean_text'] = data['text'].apply(preprocess_text)
```

In this example, we use the Spacy library to preprocess a dataset of text documents for a text classification problem. We apply tokenization, stop word removal, and lemmatization to each document, and store the cleaned text in a new column called `clean_text`. The cleaned text can then be used as input features for a machine learning model.

43. File Uploads:

File Uploads refer to the process of transferring files from a client machine to a server machine over a network. File Uploads are commonly used in web applications for allowing users to upload files, such as images or documents, to a server.

File Uploads typically involve a form on a web page that allows users to select one or more files and submit the form to a server. The server then receives the file(s) and stores them on disk or in a database.

Here's an example of handling File Uploads in a Python web application using the Flask framework:

```
from flask import Flask, request, redirect, url_for
import os

app = Flask(__name__)
app.config['UPLOAD_FOLDER'] = '/path/to/uploads'

@app.route('/upload', methods=['GET', 'POST'])
def upload_file():
    if request.method == 'POST':
        file = request.files['file']
        filename = file.filename
        file.save(os.path.join(app.config['UPLOAD_FOLDER'], filename))
        return redirect(url_for('success'))
    return '''
        <!doctype html>
```

```
        <title>Upload new File</title>
        <h1>Upload new File</h1>
        <form method=post enctype=multipart/form-data>
          <input type=file name=file>
          <input type=submit value=Upload>
        </form>
    '''

@app.route('/success')
def success():
    return 'File uploaded successfully'
```

In this example, we define a Flask web application with two routes: `/upload` for handling
File Uploads, and `/success` for displaying a success message. The `/upload` route
accepts both GET and POST requests, and processes POST requests that contain a
file upload. The uploaded file is saved to disk in the `UPLOAD_FOLDER` directory and a
redirect is returned to the `/success` route. The `/success` route simply displays a success
message to the user.

44. Flask framework:

Flask is a popular web framework for building web applications in Python. Flask is
known for its simplicity and flexibility, and is often used for building small to medium-
sized web applications.

Flask provides a set of tools and libraries for handling common web development tasks,
such as routing, request handling, form processing, and template rendering. Flask is
also highly extensible, with a large number of third-party extensions available for adding
functionality such as database integration, user authentication, and API development.

Here's an example of a simple Flask web application:

```
from flask import Flask

app = Flask(__name__)

@app.route('/')
def hello():
    return 'Hello, World!'
```

In this example, we define a Flask application with a single route (/) that returns a simple greeting message. When the application is run, it listens for incoming HTTP requests and responds with the appropriate content.

Form handling:

Form handling refers to the process of processing data submitted through a web form on a website. Forms are a common way for users to provide data to web applications, such as contact forms, registration forms, and search forms.

When a user submits a form, the data is typically sent as an HTTP POST request to the web server. The server then processes the data and responds with an appropriate message or takes some action based on the data.

In Python web applications, form handling can be implemented using a variety of libraries and frameworks, such as Flask, Django, and Pyramid. These frameworks provide tools for handling form submissions, validating user input, and storing data in a database.

Here's an example of handling form submissions in a Flask web application:

```python
from flask import Flask, request

app = Flask(__name__)

@app.route('/contact', methods=['GET', 'POST'])
def contact():
    if request.method == 'POST':
        name = request.form['name']
        email = request.form['email']
        message = request.form['message']
        # process the data, e.g. send an email
        return 'Thank you for your message!'
    return '''
        <form method="post">
            <label>Name:</label>
            <input type="text" name="name"><br>
            <label>Email:</label>
            <input type="email" name="email"><br>
            <label>Message:</label>
            <textarea name="message"></textarea><br>
            <input type="submit" value="Send">
        </form>
    '''
```

In this example, we define a Flask route (`/contact`) that handles both GET and POST requests. When a POST request is received, the form data is extracted using the `request.form` object and processed as needed. The server responds with a thank you message. When a GET request is received, the form HTML is returned to the user for filling out. The user submits the form by clicking the "Send" button.

46. Gensim library:

Gensim is a Python library for topic modeling, document indexing, and similarity retrieval with large corpora. Gensim provides tools for building and training topic models, such as Latent Dirichlet Allocation (LDA), and for transforming text data into numerical representations, such as bag-of-words and tf-idf.

Gensim is widely used in natural language processing and information retrieval applications, such as document classification, clustering, and recommendation systems.

Here's an example of using Gensim to build and train an LDA topic model:

```python
from gensim import corpora, models

# Define a corpus of documents
corpus = [
    'The quick brown fox jumps over the lazy dog',
    'A stitch in time saves nine',
    'A penny saved is a penny earned'
]

# Tokenize the documents and create a dictionary
tokenized_docs = [doc.lower().split() for doc in corpus]
dictionary = corpora.Dictionary(tokenized_docs)

# Create a bag-of-words representation of the documents
bow_corpus = [dictionary.doc2bow(doc) for doc in tokenized_docs]

# Train an LDA topic model
lda_model = models.LdaModel(bow_corpus, num_topics=2, id2word=dictionary, passes=10)
```

In this example, we define a corpus of three documents, tokenize the documents and create a dictionary of unique tokens, create a bag-of-words representation of the documents using the dictionary, and train an LDA topic model with two topics and ten passes over the corpus.

47. Grid Search:

Grid Search is a technique for tuning the hyperparameters of a machine learning model by exhaustively searching over a range of parameter values and selecting the best combination of parameters that yields the highest performance on a validation set.

Grid Search is commonly used in machine learning to find the optimal values of hyperparameters, such as learning rate, regularization strength, and number of hidden layers, for a given model architecture.

Here's an example of using Grid Search to tune the hyperparameters of a Support Vector Machine (SVM) classifier:

```python
from sklearn.model_selection import GridSearchCV
from sklearn.svm import SVC
from sklearn.datasets import load_iris

iris = load_iris()

# Define the parameter grid
param_grid = {
    'C': [0.1, 1, 10],
    'kernel': ['linear', 'rbf'],
    'gamma': [0.1, 1, 10]
}

# Define the SVM classifier
svc = SVC()

# Perform Grid Search
grid_search = GridSearchCV(svc, param_grid, cv=5)
grid_search.fit(iris.data, iris.target)

# Print the best parameters and score
print(grid_search.best_params_)
print(grid_search.best_score_)
```

In this example, we define a parameter grid consisting of three values for `C`, two kernel types, and three values for `gamma`. We define an SVM classifier, and perform Grid Search with five-fold cross-validation to find the best combination of hyperparameters that maximizes the mean validation score.

48. Heatmap:

A Heatmap is a graphical representation of data that uses color to show the relative values of a matrix of numbers. Heatmaps are commonly used in data visualization to identify patterns and trends in large datasets.

In Python, Heatmaps can be created using a variety of libraries, such as Matplotlib, Seaborn, and Plotly. These libraries provide tools for creating Heatmaps from data in a variety of formats, such as lists, arrays, and dataframes.

Here's an example of creating a Heatmap with the Seaborn library:

```python
import seaborn as sns
import numpy as np

# Create a matrix of random numbers
data = np.random.rand(10, 10)

# Create a Heatmap using Seaborn
sns.heatmap(data, cmap='coolwarm')
```

In this example, we create a 10x10 matrix of random numbers and create a Heatmap using the Seaborn library. The `cmap` argument specifies the color map to use for the Heatmap. Seaborn provides a range of built-in color maps, such as `coolwarm`, `viridis`, and `magma`, that can be used to customize the appearance of the Heatmap.

49. Heroku:

Heroku is a cloud platform that enables developers to deploy, manage, and scale web applications. Heroku supports a wide range of programming languages and frameworks, including Python, Ruby, Node.js, and Java, and provides tools for managing application deployments, database integration, and add-on services.

Heroku is widely used by small to medium-sized businesses and startups as a platform for deploying and scaling web applications. Heroku offers a free tier for developers to test and deploy their applications, as well as paid plans for larger-scale deployments and enterprise-level features.

Here's an example of deploying a Flask web application to Heroku:

```
# Install the Heroku CLI
```

```
curl https://cli-assets.heroku.com/install.sh | sh

# Login to Heroku
heroku login

# Create a new Heroku app
heroku create myapp

# Deploy the Flask app to Heroku
git push heroku master

# Start the Heroku app
heroku ps:scale web=1
```

In this example, we use the Heroku CLI to create a new Heroku app and deploy a Flask web application to the Heroku platform. We use Git to push the application code to the Heroku remote repository and scale the app to one dyno using the `ps:scale` command.

50. HTML Parsing:

HTML Parsing is the process of extracting data from HTML documents using parsing libraries and tools. HTML is the standard markup language used for creating web pages, and contains a hierarchical structure of elements and attributes that define the content and structure of a web page.

In Python, HTML Parsing can be performed using a variety of libraries, such as BeautifulSoup, lxml, and html5lib. These libraries provide tools for parsing HTML documents and extracting data from specific elements, such as tables, lists, and forms.

Here's an example of using BeautifulSoup to extract data from an HTML table:

```python
from bs4 import BeautifulSoup
import requests

# Fetch the HTML content
url = 'https://en.wikipedia.org/wiki/List_of_countries_by_population_(United_Nations)'
response = requests.get(url)
html = response.content

# Parse the HTML content with BeautifulSoup
soup = BeautifulSoup(html, 'html.parser')

# Find the table element
table = soup.find('table', {'class': 'wikitable sortable'})
```

```
# Extract the table data
data = []
rows = table.find_all('tr')
for row in rows:
    cols = row.find_all('td')
    cols = [col.text.strip() for col in cols]
    data.append(cols)

# Print the table data
for row in data:
    print(row)
```

In this example, we fetch the HTML content of a Wikipedia page and use BeautifulSoup to parse the HTML and extract data from a specific table element. We iterate over the rows and columns of the table and extract the text content of each cell. Finally, we print the extracted data to the console.

51. HTML templates:

HTML Templates are pre-designed HTML files that can be used to create web pages with consistent design and layout. HTML templates typically include placeholders for dynamic content, such as text, images, and data, that can be filled in at runtime using server-side code or client-side scripting.

In Python web development, HTML templates are commonly used with web frameworks such as Flask, Django, and Pyramid to create dynamic web pages that display data from a database or user input.

Here's an example of using HTML templates with Flask:

```
from flask import Flask, render_template

app = Flask(__name__)

# Define a route that renders an HTML template
@app.route('/')
def index():
    return render_template('index.html', title='Home')

if __name__ == '__main__':
    app.run()
```

In this example, we define a Flask web application with a single route that renders an HTML template using the `render_template` function. The function takes the name of the HTML template file and any variables that should be passed to the template for rendering.

52. HTTP Methods:

HTTP Methods are the standardized ways that clients and servers communicate with each other over the Hypertext Transfer Protocol (HTTP). HTTP defines several methods, or verbs, that can be used to perform actions on a resource, such as retrieving, updating, creating, or deleting data.

In Python web development, HTTP methods are commonly used with web frameworks such as Flask, Django, and Pyramid to create RESTful APIs that expose resources and allow clients to interact with them using HTTP requests.

Here's an example of defining HTTP methods in Flask:

```python
from flask import Flask, request

app = Flask(__name__)

# Define a route that accepts GET and POST requests
@app.route('/', methods=['GET', 'POST'])
def index():
    if request.method == 'GET':
        # Return a response for GET requests
        return 'Hello, World!'
    elif request.method == 'POST':
        # Handle POST requests and return a response
        return 'Received a POST request'

if __name__ == '__main__':
    app.run()
```

In this example, we define a Flask web application with a single route that accepts both GET and POST requests. We use the `request` object to check the method of the incoming request and return a response based on the method type.

53. Image Filtering:

Image Filtering is the process of manipulating the colors and values of pixels in an image to achieve a desired effect or enhancement. Image Filtering techniques include blurring, sharpening, edge detection, and noise reduction, among others.

In Python, Image Filtering can be performed using a variety of libraries, such as Pillow, OpenCV, and Scikit-Image. These libraries provide tools for reading, manipulating, and saving image data in a variety of formats, such as JPEG, PNG, and BMP.

Here's an example of using the Pillow library to apply a Gaussian blur filter to an image:

```python
from PIL import Image, ImageFilter

# Open an image file
img = Image.open('image.jpg')

# Apply a Gaussian blur filter
blur_img = img.filter(ImageFilter.GaussianBlur(radius=5))

# Save the filtered image
blur_img.save('blur_image.jpg')
```

In this example, we use the Pillow library to open an image file, apply a Gaussian blur filter with a radius of 5 pixels, and save the filtered image to a new file.

54. Image Loading:

Image Loading is the process of reading image data from a file or a stream and converting it into a format that can be manipulated and displayed. Image Loading libraries provide tools for reading and decoding image data from a variety of formats, such as JPEG, PNG, and BMP.

In Python, Image Loading can be performed using a variety of libraries, such as Pillow, OpenCV, and Scikit-Image. These libraries provide tools for reading, manipulating, and saving image data in a variety of formats.

Here's an example of using the Pillow library to load an image from a file:

```python
from PIL import Image

# Open an image file
img = Image.open('image.jpg')
```

```
# Display the image
img.show()
```

In this example, we use the Pillow library to open an image file and display the image using the `show()` method.

55. Image Manipulation:

Image Manipulation is the process of modifying the colors and values of pixels in an image to achieve a desired effect or enhancement. Image Manipulation techniques include resizing, cropping, rotating, flipping, and color adjustment, among others.

In Python, Image Manipulation can be performed using a variety of libraries, such as Pillow, OpenCV, and Scikit-Image. These libraries provide tools for reading, manipulating, and saving image data in a variety of formats.

Here's an example of using the Pillow library to resize an image:

```
from PIL import Image

# Open an image file
img = Image.open('image.jpg')

# Resize the image to 50% of its original size
resized_img = img.resize((int(img.size[0]*0.5), int(img.size[1]*0.5)))

# Save the resized image
resized_img.save('resized_image.jpg')
```

In this example, we use the Pillow library to open an image file, resize the image to 50% of its original size, and save the resized image to a new file.

56. Image Processing:

Image Processing is the manipulation of digital images using algorithms and techniques to extract information, enhance or modify the images, or extract features for machine learning applications. Image Processing techniques include image filtering, edge detection, segmentation, feature extraction, and restoration, among others.

In Python, Image Processing can be performed using a variety of libraries, such as Pillow, OpenCV, and Scikit-Image. These libraries provide tools for reading, manipulating, and saving image data in a variety of formats, and for performing various image processing techniques.

Here's an example of using the OpenCV library to perform image processing:

```python
import cv2

# Read an image file
img = cv2.imread('image.jpg')

# Convert the image to grayscale
gray_img = cv2.cvtColor(img, cv2.COLOR_BGR2GRAY)

# Apply a Canny edge detection filter
edge_img = cv2.Canny(gray_img, 100, 200)

# Display the processed image
cv2.imshow('Processed Image', edge_img)
cv2.waitKey(0)
cv2.destroyAllWindows()
```

In this example, we use the OpenCV library to read an image file, convert the image to grayscale, and apply a Canny edge detection filter to detect the edges in the image. We then display the processed image using the `imshow()` function.

57. Image Segmentation:

Image Segmentation is the process of dividing an image into multiple segments or regions that represent different parts of the image. Image Segmentation techniques are commonly used in computer vision applications to identify and extract objects from an image, or to separate different regions of an image based on their properties.

In Python, Image Segmentation can be performed using a variety of libraries, such as Pillow, OpenCV, and Scikit-Image. These libraries provide tools for performing various Image Segmentation techniques, such as thresholding, clustering, and region-growing.

Here's an example of using the Scikit-Image library to perform Image Segmentation using thresholding:

```python
from skimage import io, filters

# Read an image file
img = io.imread('image.jpg')

# Apply a thresholding filter to segment the image
thresh_img = img > filters.threshold_otsu(img)

# Display the segmented image
io.imshow(thresh_img)
io.show()
```

In this example, we use the Scikit-Image library to read an image file and apply a thresholding filter to segment the image. We then display the segmented image using the `imshow()` function.

58. Kafka:

Apache Kafka is a distributed streaming platform that is used to build real-time data pipelines and streaming applications. Kafka is designed to handle large volumes of streaming data and provides features for scalability, fault-tolerance, and data processing.

In Python, Kafka can be used with the Kafka-Python library, which provides a Python API for interacting with Kafka clusters. Kafka can be used to build real-time data processing systems, data pipelines, and streaming applications.

Here's an example of using Kafka-Python to publish and consume messages from a Kafka cluster:

```python
from kafka import KafkaProducer, KafkaConsumer

# Create a Kafka Producer
producer = KafkaProducer(bootstrap_servers='localhost:9092')

# Publish a message to a Kafka topic
producer.send('my-topic', b'Hello, World!')

# Create a Kafka Consumer
consumer = KafkaConsumer('my-topic', bootstrap_servers='localhost:9092')

# Consume messages from a Kafka topic
```

```
for message in consumer:
    print(message.value)
```

In this example, we use Kafka-Python to create a Kafka Producer that publishes a message to a Kafka topic, and a Kafka Consumer that consumes messages from the same topic.

59. Keras library:

Keras is a high-level neural networks API, written in Python and capable of running on top of TensorFlow, CNTK, or Theano. Keras provides a user-friendly interface for building and training deep neural networks, including convolutional neural networks (CNNs), recurrent neural networks (RNNs), and multi-layer perceptrons (MLPs).

In Keras, building a neural network involves defining the layers of the network, compiling the model with a loss function and an optimizer, and fitting the model to the training data. Keras provides a wide range of layers, including convolutional layers, pooling layers, recurrent layers, and dense layers, among others.

Here's an example of using Keras to build a simple MLP for binary classification:

```
from keras.models import Sequential
from keras.layers import Dense
from sklearn.datasets import make_classification
from sklearn.model_selection import train_test_split

# Generate a random binary classification dataset
X, y = make_classification(n_samples=1000, n_features=10, n_classes=2, random_state=42)

# Split the dataset into training and testing sets
X_train, X_test, y_train, y_test = train_test_split(X, y, test_size=0.2, random_state=42)

# Define the model architecture
model = Sequential()
model.add(Dense(10, input_dim=10, activation='relu'))
model.add(Dense(1, activation='sigmoid'))

# Compile the model with a binary cross-entropy loss and a gradient descent optimizer
model.compile(loss='binary_crossentropy', optimizer='adam', metrics=['accuracy'])

# Fit the model to the training data
model.fit(X_train, y_train, epochs=10, batch_size=32)

# Evaluate the model on the testing data
```

```
loss, accuracy = model.evaluate(X_test, y_test)
print('Test Accuracy:', accuracy)
```

In this example, we use Keras to build a simple MLP with one hidden layer for binary classification. We compile the model with a binary cross-entropy loss function and an Adam optimizer, and fit the model to the training data. We then evaluate the model on the testing data and print the test accuracy.

60. **Latent Dirichlet Allocation:**

Latent Dirichlet Allocation (LDA) is a statistical model used to identify topics in a collection of documents. LDA is a generative probabilistic model that assumes that each document is a mixture of topics, and each topic is a probability distribution over words in the vocabulary.

In Python, LDA can be performed using the Gensim library, which provides a simple and efficient API for training and using LDA models. To use LDA with Gensim, we first need to create a dictionary of the documents, which maps each word to a unique integer ID. We then convert the documents to bag-of-words representations, which count the occurrences of each word in each document. Finally, we train an LDA model on the bag-of-words representations using Gensim's `LdaModel` class.

Here's an example of using Gensim to train an LDA model on a collection of documents:

```
from gensim.corpora import Dictionary
from gensim.models.ldamodel import LdaModel
from sklearn.datasets import fetch_20newsgroups

# Load a collection of newsgroup documents
newsgroups = fetch_20newsgroups(subset='train')

# Create a dictionary of the documents
dictionary = Dictionary(newsgroups.data)

# Convert the documents to bag-of-words representations
corpus = [dictionary.doc2bow(doc) for doc in newsgroups.data]

# Train an LDA model on the bag-of-words representations
lda_model = LdaModel(corpus, num_topics=10, id2word=dictionary, passes=10)

# Print the top words for each topic
for topic in lda_model.show_topics(num_topics=10, num_words=10, formatted=False):
    print('Topic {}: {}'.format(topic[0], ' '.join([w[0] for w in topic[1]])))
```

In this example, we use Gensim to train an LDA model on a collection of newsgroup documents. We create a dictionary of the documents, convert them to bag-of-words representations, and train an LDA model with 10 topics using Gensim's `LdaModel` class. We then print the top words for each topic using the `show_topics()` method of the trained model.

61. Line Chart:

A line chart, also known as a line graph, is a type of chart used to display data as a series of points connected by straight lines. Line charts are commonly used to visualize trends in data over time, such as stock prices, weather patterns, or website traffic.

In Python, line charts can be created using the Matplotlib library, which provides a variety of functions for creating different types of charts. To create a line chart in Matplotlib, we can use the `plot()` function, which takes a set of x and y coordinates and plots them as a line. We can also customize the appearance of the chart by adding labels, titles, and legends.

Here's an example of creating a simple line chart in Matplotlib:

```python
import matplotlib.pyplot as plt

# Define the x and y coordinates for the line chart
x = [1, 2, 3, 4, 5]
y = [1, 4, 9, 16, 25]

# Create the line chart
plt.plot(x, y)

# Add labels, title, and legend
plt.xlabel('X Label')
plt.ylabel('Y Label')
plt.title('My Line Chart')
plt.legend(['My Line'])

# Display the chart
plt.show()
```

In this example, we define the x and y coordinates for the line chart, and create the chart using Matplotlib's `plot()` function. We then add labels, a title, and a legend to the chart, and display it using the `show()` function.

62. Machine Learning:

Machine learning is a branch of artificial intelligence (AI) that involves the development of algorithms and models that can learn patterns and relationships in data, and use them to make predictions or decisions. Machine learning is used in a wide range of applications, such as image recognition, natural language processing, fraud detection, and recommendation systems.

In Python, machine learning can be implemented using a variety of libraries, such as Scikit-learn, TensorFlow, Keras, and PyTorch. These libraries provide a variety of machine learning models and algorithms, such as linear regression, logistic regression, decision trees, random forests, support vector machines, neural networks, and deep learning models.

Here's an example of using Scikit-learn to train a linear regression model on a dataset:

```python
from sklearn.linear_model import LinearRegression
from sklearn.datasets import make_regression
from sklearn.model_selection import train_test_split

# Generate a random regression dataset
X, y = make_regression(n_samples=1000, n_features=10, noise=0.1, random_state=42)

# Split the dataset into training and testing sets
X_train, X_test, y_train, y_test = train_test_split(X, y, test_size=0.2, random_state=42)

# Train a linear regression model on the training data
model = LinearRegression()
model.fit(X_train, y_train)

# Evaluate the model on the testing data
score = model.score(X_test, y_test)
print('Test R^2 Score:', score)
```

In this example, we use Scikit-learn to train a linear regression model on a randomly generated dataset. We split the dataset into training and testing sets, train the model on the training data using the `LinearRegression()` class, and evaluate the model on the testing data using the `score()` method.

63. MapReduce:

MapReduce is a programming model and framework used for processing large datasets in a distributed and parallel manner. MapReduce was originally developed by Google for processing web pages and building search indexes, and has since been adopted by a wide range of companies and organizations for big data processing.

In Python, MapReduce can be implemented using the Hadoop Distributed File System (HDFS) and the Pydoop library. The MapReduce programming model consists of two main functions: a Map function that processes the data and generates intermediate key-value pairs, and a Reduce function that aggregates the intermediate results and produces the final output.

Here's an example of using Pydoop to implement a simple MapReduce program:

```python
import pydoop.hdfs as hdfs

# Define the Map function
def mapper(key, value):
    words = value.strip().split()
    for word in words:
        yield (word, 1)

# Define the Reduce function
def reducer(key, values):
    yield (key, sum(values))

# Open the input file on HDFS
with hdfs.open('/input.txt') as infile:
    data = infile.read()

# Split the data into lines
lines = data.strip().split('\n')

# Map the lines to intermediate key-value pairs
intermediate = [pair for line in lines for pair in mapper(None, line)]

# Group the intermediate key-value pairs by key
groups = {}
for key, value in intermediate:
    if key not in groups:
        groups[key] = []
    groups[key].append(value)

# Reduce the groups to produce the final output
output = [pair for key, values in groups.items() for pair in reducer(key, values)]
```

```
# Write the output to a file on HDFS
with hdfs.open('/output.txt', 'w') as outfile:
    for key, value in output:
        outfile.write('{}\t{}\n'.format(key, value))
```

In this example, we define the Map and Reduce functions and use Pydoop to process a text file stored on HDFS. We map the lines of the file to intermediate key-value pairs using the `mapper()` function, group the intermediate results by key, and reduce the groups to produce the final output using the `reducer()` function. Finally, we write the output to a file on HDFS.

64. Markov Chains:

Markov chains are mathematical models used to describe the probability of transitioning from one state to another in a sequence of events. Markov chains are often used in natural language processing, speech recognition, and other applications where the probability of a particular event depends on the previous events in the sequence.

In Python, Markov chains can be implemented using the Markovify library, which provides a simple API for creating and using Markov models based on text corpora. To use Markovify, we first create a corpus of text data, such as a collection of books or articles. We then use the `Text()` class to parse the text and create a Markov model, which can be used to generate new text that has a similar style and structure to the original corpus.

Here's an example of using Markovify to generate new sentences based on a corpus of text:

```
import markovify

# Load a text corpus
with open('corpus.txt') as f:
    text = f.read()

# Create a Markov model from the corpus
model = markovify.Text(text)

# Generate a new sentence
sentence = model.make_sentence()

print(sentence)
```

In this example, we use Markovify to create a Markov model from a text corpus stored in a file. We then generate a new sentence using the `make_sentence()` method of the Markov model.

65. Matplotlib library:

Matplotlib is a data visualization library for Python that provides a variety of functions and tools for creating charts and plots. Matplotlib can be used to create a wide range of chart types, including line charts, bar charts, scatter plots, and histograms.

To use Matplotlib, we first need to import the library and create a new figure and axis object. We can then use a variety of functions to create different types of charts, such as `plot()` for line charts, `bar()` for bar charts, and `scatter()` for scatter plots. We can also customize the appearance of the chart by adding labels, titles, and legends.

Here's an example of creating a simple line chart in Matplotlib:

```python
import matplotlib.pyplot as plt

# Define the x and y coordinates for the line chart
x = [1, 2, 3, 4, 5]
y = [1, 4, 9, 16, 25]

# Create a new figure and axis object
fig, ax = plt.subplots()

# Create the line chart
ax.plot(x, y)

# Add labels, title, and legend
ax.set_xlabel('X Label')
ax.set_ylabel('Y Label')
ax.set_title('My Line Chart')
ax.legend(['My Line'])

# Display the chart
plt.show()
```

In this example, we define the x and y coordinates for the line chart, create a new figure and axis object using Matplotlib's `subplots()` function, and create the chart using the `plot()` method of the axis object. We then add labels, a title, and a legend to the chart using the `set_xlabel()`, `set_ylabel()`, `set_title()`, and `legend()` methods of the axis object, and display the chart using the `show()` function.

66. MNIST dataset:

The MNIST dataset is a widely-used benchmark dataset for machine learning and computer vision tasks, particularly for image classification. It consists of a set of 70,000 grayscale images of handwritten digits, each of size 28x28 pixels. The images are divided into a training set of 60,000 images and a test set of 10,000 images.

In Python, the MNIST dataset can be downloaded and loaded using the TensorFlow or Keras libraries, which provide a convenient API for working with the dataset. Once the dataset is loaded, it can be used to train and evaluate machine learning models for image classification tasks.

Here's an example of loading the MNIST dataset using Keras:

```python
from keras.datasets import mnist

# Load the MNIST dataset
(X_train, y_train), (X_test, y_test) = mnist.load_data()

# Print the shape of the training and test sets
print('Training set:', X_train.shape, y_train.shape)
print('Test set:', X_test.shape, y_test.shape)
```

In this example, we use Keras to load the MNIST dataset and print the shapes of the training and test sets.

67. Model Evaluation:

Model evaluation is the process of assessing the performance of a machine learning model on a test dataset. The goal of model evaluation is to determine how well the model is able to generalize to new, unseen data, and to identify any areas where the model may be overfitting or underfitting the training data.

In Python, model evaluation can be performed using a variety of metrics and techniques, such as accuracy, precision, recall, F1 score, and confusion matrices. These metrics can be calculated using the scikit-learn library, which provides a range of tools for model evaluation and validation.

Here's an example of using scikit-learn to evaluate the performance of a machine learning model:

```
from sklearn.metrics import accuracy_score, precision_score, recall_score, f1_score, confu
sion_matrix

# Load the test data and model predictions
y_true = [0, 1, 1, 0, 1, 0, 0, 1]
y_pred = [0, 1, 0, 0, 1, 1, 0, 1]

# Calculate the accuracy, precision, recall, and F1 score
accuracy = accuracy_score(y_true, y_pred)
precision = precision_score(y_true, y_pred)
recall = recall_score(y_true, y_pred)
f1 = f1_score(y_true, y_pred)

# Calculate the confusion matrix
confusion = confusion_matrix(y_true, y_pred)

# Print the evaluation metrics and confusion matrix
print('Accuracy:', accuracy)
print('Precision:', precision)
print('Recall:', recall)
print('F1 score:', f1)
print('Confusion matrix:\n', confusion)
```

In this example, we load the true labels and predicted labels for a binary classification problem and use scikit-learn to calculate the accuracy, precision, recall, and F1 score. We also calculate the confusion matrix, which shows the number of true positives, true negatives, false positives, and false negatives for the predictions.

68. Model Training:

Model training is the process of using a machine learning algorithm to learn the patterns and relationships in a dataset and generate a predictive model. In Python, model training can be performed using a variety of machine learning libraries, such as scikit-learn, TensorFlow, and Keras.

The process of model training typically involves the following steps:

1. Load and preprocess the training data

2. Define the machine learning model and its parameters

3. Train the model using the training data

4. Evaluate the performance of the trained model on a test dataset

5. Fine-tune the model parameters and repeat steps 3-4 until the desired level of performance is achieved

Here's an example of training a simple linear regression model using scikit-learn:

```python
from sklearn.linear_model import LinearRegression
from sklearn.datasets import load_boston
from sklearn.model_selection import train_test_split
from sklearn.metrics import mean_squared_error

# Load the Boston housing dataset
data = load_boston()

# Split the data into training and test sets
X_train, X_test, y_train, y_test = train_test_split(data.data, data.target, test_size=0.2)

# Create and train a linear regression model
model = LinearRegression()
model.fit(X_train, y_train)

# Evaluate the performance of the model on the test set
y_pred = model.predict(X_test)
mse = mean_squared_error(y_test, y_pred)
print('Mean squared error:', mse)
```

In this example, we load the Boston housing dataset and split it into training and test sets using scikit-learn's `train_test_split()` function. We then create and train a linear regression model using the training data, and evaluate the performance of the model on the test set using the mean squared error metric.

69. Multiprocessing:

Multiprocessing is a technique for parallel computing in Python that allows multiple processes to run concurrently on a multi-core processor or a distributed cluster. In Python, multiprocessing can be implemented using the `multiprocessing` module, which provides a simple API for spawning and managing child processes.

The `multiprocessing` module provides several classes and functions for creating and managing processes, such as `Process`, `Pool`, and `Queue`. Processes can communicate with each other using shared memory and inter-process communication (IPC) mechanisms, such as pipes and sockets.

Here's an example of using multiprocessing to perform a CPU-bound task in parallel:

```
import multiprocessing

# Define a function to perform a CPU-bound task
def my_task(x):
    return x**2

# Create a pool of worker processes
pool = multiprocessing.Pool()

# Generate a list of inputs
inputs = range(10)

# Map the inputs to the worker function in parallel
results = pool.map(my_task, inputs)

# Print the results
print(results)
```

In this example, we define a simple function `my_task()` to perform a CPU-bound task, and use the `Pool` class from the `multiprocessing` module to create a pool of worker processes. We then generate a list of inputs and map them to the worker function in parallel using the `map()` method of the pool object. Finally, we print the results of the parallel computation.

70. Multithreading:

Multithreading is a technique for concurrent programming in Python that allows multiple threads to run concurrently within a single process. In Python, multithreading can be implemented using the `threading` module, which provides a simple API for creating and managing threads.

The `threading` module provides several classes and functions for creating and managing threads, such as `Thread`, `Lock`, and `Condition`. Threads can communicate with each other using shared memory and synchronization primitives, such as locks and conditions.

Here's an example of using multithreading to perform a simple task in parallel:

```
import threading

# Define a function to perform a simple task
```

```
def my_task():
    print('Hello, world!')

# Create a thread object and start the thread
thread = threading.Thread(target=my_task)
thread.start()

# Wait for the thread to finish
thread.join()
```

In this example, we define a simple function `my_task()` to print a message, and create a `Thread` object to run the function in a separate thread. We start the thread using the `start()` method, and wait for the thread to finish using the `join()` method. The output of the program should be "Hello, world!".

71. Named Entity Recognition:

Named Entity Recognition (NER) is a subtask of Natural Language Processing (NLP) that involves identifying and classifying named entities in text into predefined categories such as person names, organization names, locations, and dates. In Python, NER can be performed using a variety of NLP libraries, such as spaCy, NLTK, and Stanford CoreNLP.

The process of NER typically involves the following steps:

1. Tokenize the text into words or phrases

2. Part-of-speech (POS) tag each token to identify its grammatical role in the sentence

3. Apply NER algorithms to identify and classify named entities based on their context and surrounding words

Here's an example of performing NER using spaCy:

```
import spacy

# Load the spaCy English model
nlp = spacy.load('en_core_web_sm')

# Define a sample text
text = 'John Smith is a software engineer at Google in New York.'

# Process the text using spaCy
doc = nlp(text)
```

```
# Print the named entities and their categories
for ent in doc.ents:
    print(ent.text, ent.label_)
```

In this example, we load the spaCy English model and define a sample text. We then process the text using spaCy's `nlp()` function and print the named entities and their categories using the `ents` attribute of the parsed document.

72. Natural Language Generation:

Natural Language Generation (NLG) is a subfield of Artificial Intelligence (AI) that involves generating natural language text from structured data or machine-readable instructions. In Python, NLG can be performed using a variety of NLG libraries, such as NLTK, GPT-3, and OpenAI's GPT-2.

The process of NLG typically involves the following steps:

1. Extract and preprocess the data or instructions

2. Define a template or model for generating natural language text

3. Apply text generation algorithms to produce natural language text based on the input data or instructions

Here's an example of using GPT-2 to generate natural language text:

```
import openai

# Set up the OpenAI API key
openai.api_key = 'YOUR_API_KEY'

# Define the prompt for text generation
prompt = 'Once upon a time, there was a magical forest'

# Generate text using GPT-2
response = openai.Completion.create(
    engine='text-davinci-002',
    prompt=prompt,
    max_tokens=50
)

# Print the generated text
print(response.choices[0].text)
```

In this example, we use OpenAI's GPT-2 model to generate natural language text based on a given prompt. We first set up the OpenAI API key, define the prompt, and use the `Completion.create()` method to generate text using the specified GPT-2 engine and parameters. Finally, we print the generated text.

73. Natural Language Processing:

Natural Language Processing (NLP) is a subfield of Artificial Intelligence (AI) that involves analyzing and processing human language data, such as text and speech. In Python, NLP can be performed using a variety of NLP libraries, such as NLTK, spaCy, and TextBlob.

The process of NLP typically involves the following steps:

1. Tokenization: Breaking down text into individual words or tokens

2. Part-of-speech (POS) tagging: Labeling each word with its grammatical part of speech, such as noun, verb, or adjective

3. Named Entity Recognition (NER): Identifying and categorizing named entities, such as people, organizations, and locations, in the text

4. Sentiment analysis: Analyzing the sentiment or opinion expressed in the text, such as positive, negative, or neutral

5. Topic modeling: Identifying and extracting topics or themes from a collection of text documents

Here's an example of performing NLP tasks using the spaCy library:

```python
import spacy

# Load the English language model
nlp = spacy.load('en_core_web_sm')

# Define a text document for NLP processing
text = 'Apple is looking at buying U.K. startup for $1 billion'

# Perform NLP tasks on the text document
doc = nlp(text)
for token in doc:
    print(f'{token.text}: {token.pos_}, {token.dep_}')
```

```
for ent in doc.ents:
    print(f'{ent.text}: {ent.label_}')
```

In this example, we load the English language model in spaCy and define a text document for NLP processing. We then perform tokenization and POS tagging on the text document using spaCy's `nlp()` method and loop over each token to print its text, POS tag, and dependency relation. We also perform NER using spaCy's `ents` property and loop over each named entity to print its text and entity label.

74. Network Analysis:

Network Analysis is a branch of data science that involves analyzing and modeling complex networks, such as social networks, communication networks, and biological networks. In Python, network analysis can be performed using a variety of libraries, such as NetworkX, igraph, and graph-tool.

The process of network analysis typically involves the following steps:

1. Define the network structure and data

2. Analyze the network topology and properties, such as degree distribution, centrality measures, and clustering coefficients

3. Model the network using graph theory and machine learning techniques

4. Visualize the network using graph drawing algorithms and software

Here's an example of network analysis using NetworkX:

```
import networkx as nx

# Define a social network graph
G = nx.Graph()
G.add_edge('Alice', 'Bob')
G.add_edge('Bob', 'Charlie')
G.add_edge('Charlie', 'David')
G.add_edge('David', 'Eva')

# Calculate the degree centrality of the nodes
centrality = nx.degree_centrality(G)

# Print the centrality measures
for node, centrality in centrality.items():
    print(f'{node}: {centrality}')
```

In this example, we define a simple social network graph using NetworkX and calculate the degree centrality of the nodes using the `degree_centrality()` function. We then print the centrality measures for each node in the graph.

75. Network Programming:

Network Programming is a branch of computer programming that involves developing applications and services that communicate over computer networks, such as the Internet. In Python, network programming can be performed using a variety of libraries and frameworks, such as socket, asyncio, Twisted, and Django.

The process of network programming typically involves the following tasks:

1. Establishing network connections and sockets

2. Sending and receiving data over the network using protocols such as TCP/IP and UDP

3. Implementing network services, such as web servers, chat clients, and file transfer protocols

4. Securing network communications using encryption and authentication techniques

Here's an example of network programming using the socket library:

```python
import socket

# Define the host and port for the server
HOST = 'localhost'
PORT = 8000

# Create a socket object and bind it to the host and port
server_socket = socket.socket(socket.AF_INET, socket.SOCK_STREAM)
server_socket.bind((HOST, PORT))

# Listen for incoming client connections
server_socket.listen()

# Accept client connections and handle incoming data
while True:
    client_socket, client_address = server_socket.accept()
    print(f'Client connected from {client_address}')
    data = client_socket.recv(1024)
    print(f'Received data: {data}')
```

```
response = b'Thank you for connecting!'
client_socket.sendall(response)
client_socket.close()
```

In this example, we create a simple server using the socket library that listens for incoming client connections on a specified host and port. We then accept client connections and handle incoming data by printing the received data and sending a response back to the client. Finally, we close the client socket connection.

76. NLTK library:

The Natural Language Toolkit (NLTK) is a Python library for working with human language data. NLTK provides a suite of tools and methods for NLP tasks such as tokenization, POS tagging, NER, sentiment analysis, and more. It also includes a wide range of corpora and datasets for training and testing NLP models.

Here's an example of using NLTK for tokenization and POS tagging:

```
import nltk

# Download the necessary NLTK data
nltk.download('punkt')
nltk.download('averaged_perceptron_tagger')

# Define a text document for NLP processing
text = "John likes to play soccer in the park with his friends"

# Perform tokenization and POS tagging
tokens = nltk.word_tokenize(text)
pos_tags = nltk.pos_tag(tokens)

# Print the tokens and POS tags
print(tokens)
print(pos_tags)
```

In this example, we first download the necessary NLTK data using the `nltk.download()` function. We then define a text document for NLP processing and perform tokenization and POS tagging using NLTK's `word_tokenize()` and `pos_tag()` functions. Finally, we print the resulting tokens and POS tags.

77. NumPy library:

NumPy is a Python library for working with arrays and numerical data. NumPy provides a powerful set of functions and methods for performing mathematical operations on arrays, such as addition, subtraction, multiplication, division, and more. It also includes tools for linear algebra, Fourier analysis, and random number generation.

Here's an example of using NumPy for array manipulation:

```python
import numpy as np

# Define two arrays for addition
a = np.array([1, 2, 3])
b = np.array([4, 5, 6])

# Perform array addition
c = a + b

# Print the result
print(c)
```

In this example, we define two arrays using NumPy's `array()` function and perform array addition using the `+` operator. Finally, we print the resulting array.

78. Object Detection:

Object detection is a computer vision task that involves identifying and localizing objects in an image or video. In Python, object detection can be performed using a variety of deep learning frameworks and libraries, such as TensorFlow, Keras, and OpenCV.

The process of object detection typically involves the following steps:

1. Image preprocessing: Preparing the image for object detection, such as resizing or normalization

2. Object detection: Identifying and localizing objects in the image using a pre-trained deep learning model

3. Post-processing: Refining the object detection results, such as filtering out false positives or grouping overlapping objects

Here's an example of object detection using the TensorFlow Object Detection API:

```
import tensorflow as tf
import cv2

# Load the pre-trained TensorFlow Object Detection API model
model = tf.saved_model.load('path/to/saved/model')

# Load and preprocess the input image
image = cv2.imread('path/to/image')
image = cv2.cvtColor(image, cv2.COLOR_BGR2RGB)
image = cv2.resize(image, (800, 600))

# Perform object detection on the input image
detections = model(image)

# Post-process the object detection results
# ...
```

In this example, we load a pre-trained TensorFlow Object Detection API model and perform object detection on an input image using the model's `__call__()` method. We then need to perform post-processing to refine the object detection results, such as filtering out low-confidence detections or grouping overlapping objects.

79. OpenAI Gym library:

OpenAI Gym is a Python library for developing and comparing reinforcement learning algorithms. It provides a variety of environments for testing and evaluating reinforcement learning algorithms, such as Atari games, robotics simulations, and control tasks.

Here's an example of using OpenAI Gym to train a reinforcement learning agent on the CartPole environment:

```
import gym

# Create the CartPole environment
env = gym.make('CartPole-v1')

# Reset the environment
state = env.reset()

# Perform random actions for 1000 steps
for i in range(1000):
    # Choose a random action
```

```
    action = env.action_space.sample()

    # Perform the action and observe the next state and reward
    next_state, reward, done, info = env.step(action)

    # Render the environment
    env.render()

    # Update the current state
    state = next_state

    # Terminate the episode if the pole falls over
    if done:
        break

# Close the environment
env.close()
```

In this example, we create the CartPole environment using OpenAI Gym's `make()` function and reset the environment using its `reset()` function. We then perform random actions on the environment for a specified number of steps, observing the resulting state, reward, and done flag at each step. Finally, we render the environment using its `render()` function and close the environment using its `close()` function.

80. OpenCV library:

OpenCV (Open Source Computer Vision) is a Python library for computer vision and image processing. OpenCV provides a wide range of tools and methods for tasks such as image loading, filtering, transformation, feature detection, and object recognition.

Here's an example of using OpenCV for image processing:

```
import cv2

# Load the input image
image = cv2.imread('path/to/image')

# Convert the image to grayscale
gray = cv2.cvtColor(image, cv2.COLOR_BGR2GRAY)

# Apply Gaussian blur to the image
blur = cv2.GaussianBlur(gray, (5, 5), 0)

# Detect edges in the image using Canny edge detection
edges = cv2.Canny(blur, 100, 200)
```

```
# Display the resulting image
cv2.imshow('Edges', edges)
cv2.waitKey(0)
cv2.destroyAllWindows()
```

In this example, we load an input image using OpenCV's `imread()` function and convert it to grayscale using OpenCV's `cvtColor()` function. We then apply Gaussian blur to the grayscale image using OpenCV's `GaussianBlur()` function and detect edges in the resulting image using OpenCV's `Canny()` function. Finally, we display the resulting image using OpenCV's `imshow()` function and wait for a key press before closing the window.

81.Packet Sniffing:

Packet sniffing is the process of capturing and analyzing network traffic to extract useful information. In Python, packet sniffing can be performed using libraries such as Scapy and PyShark. These libraries allow you to capture network traffic, analyze packets, and extract data such as source and destination IP addresses, port numbers, and protocol types.

Here's an example of using Scapy to capture and analyze network traffic:

```
from scapy.all import *

# Define a packet handling function
def handle_packet(packet):
    # Extract the source and destination IP addresses and protocol type
    src_ip = packet[IP].src
    dst_ip = packet[IP].dst
    proto = packet[IP].proto

    # Print the extracted data
    print(f'Source IP: {src_ip}, Destination IP: {dst_ip}, Protocol: {proto}')

# Start capturing network traffic
sniff(filter='ip', prn=handle_packet)
```

In this example, we define a packet handling function that extracts the source and destination IP addresses and protocol type from captured packets and prints the data to the console. We then use Scapy's `sniff()` function to start capturing network traffic that matches the specified filter (in this case, IP packets) and call the packet handling function for each captured packet.

82. Pandas library:

Pandas is a Python library for data manipulation and analysis. It provides powerful tools for working with structured data, such as data frames and series, and supports a wide range of operations such as filtering, grouping, joining, and aggregation.

Here's an example of using Pandas to read a CSV file and perform some basic data analysis:

```python
import pandas as pd

# Read the CSV file into a data frame
data = pd.read_csv('path/to/file.csv')

# Display the first 5 rows of the data frame
print(data.head())

# Calculate some basic statistics on the data
print(data.describe())

# Group the data by a column and calculate the mean value of another column
print(data.groupby('column1')['column2'].mean())
```

In this example, we use Pandas' `read_csv()` function to read a CSV file into a data frame and display the first 5 rows of the data using the `head()` function. We then use the `describe()` function to calculate some basic statistics on the data, such as the mean, standard deviation, and quartiles. Finally, we use the `groupby()` function to group the data by a column and calculate the mean value of another column for each group.

83. Parallel Processing:

Parallel processing is the execution of multiple tasks simultaneously, typically using multiple processing units such as CPU cores or GPUs. In Python, parallel processing can be performed using libraries such as multiprocessing and concurrent.futures. These libraries allow you to distribute tasks across multiple processing units and synchronize their execution.

Here's an example of using the multiprocessing library to perform parallel processing:

```python
import multiprocessing

# Define a function to perform some task
def worker(input):
    # Do some work with the input
    result = input ** 2

    # Return the result
    return result

if __name__ == '__main__':
    # Define a list of inputs
    inputs = [1, 2, 3, 4, 5]

    # Create a pool of worker processes
    with multiprocessing.Pool(processes=4) as pool:
        # Map the inputs to the worker function using the pool
        results = pool.map(worker, inputs)

    # Print the results
    print(results)
```

In this example, we define a worker function that performs some task on an input and returns a result. We then use the multiprocessing library to create a pool of worker processes and map the inputs to the worker function using the `map()` function. The library handles the distribution of the inputs and synchronization of the worker processes, and returns the results as a list.

84. Parquet file format:

Parquet is a file format for storing structured data in a column-oriented format, optimized for efficient querying and processing. It is designed to work with big data technologies such as Hadoop and Spark, and supports compression and encoding techniques to reduce storage and processing costs.

In Python, the Parquet file format can be read and written using libraries such as PyArrow and fastparquet. These libraries provide high-performance I/O operations and support for data manipulation and analysis.

Here's an example of using PyArrow to read and write Parquet files:

```python
import pandas as pd
```

```python
import pyarrow as pa
import pyarrow.parquet as pq

# Create a Pandas data frame
data = pd.DataFrame({
    'column1': [1, 2, 3],
    'column2': ['a', 'b', 'c']
})

# Convert the data frame to an Arrow table
table = pa.Table.from_pandas(data)

# Write the table to a Parquet file
pq.write_table(table, 'path/to/file.parquet')

# Read the Parquet file into an Arrow table
table = pq.read_table('path/to/file.parquet')

# Convert the table to a Pandas data frame
data = table.to_pandas()

# Display the data frame
print(data)
```

In this example, we create a Pandas data frame and convert it to an Arrow table using the `Table.from_pandas()` function. We then write the table to a Parquet file using the `write_table()` function, and read the file into an Arrow table using the `read_table()` function. Finally, we convert the table back to a Pandas data frame using the `to_pandas()` function and display the data.

85. Part-of-Speech Tagging:

Part-of-speech tagging is the process of assigning grammatical tags to words in a sentence, such as noun, verb, adjective, or adverb. In Python, part-of-speech tagging can be performed using libraries such as NLTK and spaCy. These libraries provide pre-trained models for part-of-speech tagging, as well as tools for training custom models on specific domains or languages.

Here's an example of using NLTK to perform part-of-speech tagging:

```python
import nltk

# Download the NLTK data
nltk.download('averaged_perceptron_tagger')
```

```
# Define a sentence
sentence = 'The quick brown fox jumps over the lazy dog'

# Tokenize the sentence
tokens = nltk.word_tokenize(sentence)

# Perform part-of-speech tagging
tags = nltk.pos_tag(tokens)

# Print the tags
print(tags)
```

In this example, we first download the NLTK data for part-of-speech tagging using the `download()` function. We then define a sentence and tokenize it into individual words using the `word_tokenize()` function. Finally, we perform part-of-speech tagging using the `pos_tag()` function, which assigns grammatical tags to each word in the sentence, and print the results.

86. PDF Report Generation:

PDF report generation refers to the process of creating PDF documents that contain formatted text, images, and other elements, typically used for sharing information or presenting data. In Python, PDF report generation can be performed using libraries such as ReportLab and PyFPDF. These libraries provide tools for creating PDF documents from scratch or from existing templates, as well as for adding text, images, tables, and other elements.

Here's an example of using ReportLab to create a PDF report:

```
from reportlab.pdfgen import canvas

# Create a new PDF document
pdf = canvas.Canvas('report.pdf')

# Add some text to the document
pdf.drawString(100, 750, 'Hello World!')

# Save the document
pdf.save()
```

In this example, we import the `canvas` class from the ReportLab library, which provides a high-level interface for creating PDF documents. We then create a new PDF document using the `Canvas()` function and add some text to it using the `drawString()` method. Finally, we save the document to a file using the `save()` method.

87. Pillow library:

Pillow is a Python library for working with images, providing tools for opening, manipulating, and saving image files in various formats. It is a fork of the Python Imaging Library (PIL), with added support for Python 3 and additional features and improvements.

In Pillow, images are represented as `Image` objects, which can be loaded from files, created from scratch, or manipulated using various methods and operations. The library supports a wide range of image formats, including JPEG, PNG, GIF, BMP, and TIFF.

Here's an example of using Pillow to open and manipulate an image:

```python
from PIL import Image

# Open an image file
image = Image.open('image.jpg')

# Resize the image
size = (200, 200)
image = image.resize(size)

# Convert the image to grayscale
image = image.convert('L')

# Save the image to a file
image.save('new_image.jpg')
```

In this example, we import the `Image` class from the Pillow library and open an image file using the `open()` function. We then resize the image to a smaller size using the `resize()` method, and convert it to grayscale using the `convert()` method. Finally, we save the modified image to a file using the `save()` method.

88. Plotly library:

Plotly is a Python library for creating interactive data visualizations, including charts, graphs, and maps. It provides a wide range of chart types and customization options, as well as tools for adding interactivity, annotations, and animations to visualizations.

In Plotly, visualizations are created using the `plotly.graph_objs` module, which provides classes for defining data and layout properties for charts. The library supports a wide range of chart types, including scatter plots, bar charts, line charts, and heatmaps.

Here's an example of using Plotly to create a simple line chart:

```
import plotly.graph_objs as go

# Define some data
x = [1, 2, 3, 4, 5]
y = [10, 8, 6, 4, 2]

# Create a line chart
fig = go.Figure(data=go.Scatter(x=x, y=y))

# Display the chart
fig.show()
```

In this example, we import the `graph_objs` module from Plotly and define some data for a line chart. We then create a new `Figure` object and add a `Scatter` trace with the data using the `data` argument. Finally, we display the chart using the `show()` method.

89. Pre-trained models:

Pre-trained models are machine learning models that have been trained on large datasets and made available for general use. They can be used as a starting point for developing new machine learning models, or as a solution for specific tasks that the model was trained on. Pre-trained models are available for a wide range of tasks, including image recognition, speech recognition, natural language processing, and more.

In Python, pre-trained models can be downloaded and used using libraries such as TensorFlow, Keras, PyTorch, and spaCy. These libraries provide pre-trained models for various tasks, as well as tools for fine-tuning and customizing the models.

Here's an example of using a pre-trained model for image recognition with TensorFlow:

```
import tensorflow as tf
from tensorflow import keras
```

```
# Load a pre-trained model
model = keras.applications.VGG16(weights='imagenet')

# Load an image file
image = keras.preprocessing.image.load_img('image.jpg', target_size=(224, 224))

# Preprocess the image
input_data = keras.applications.vgg16.preprocess_input(
    keras.preprocessing.image.img_to_array(image)
)

# Make a prediction
predictions = model.predict(tf.expand_dims(input_data, axis=0))

# Print the top predictions
decode_predictions = keras.applications.vgg16.decode_predictions(predictions, top=3)[0]
for _, name, score in decode_predictions:
    print(f'{name}: {score:.2%}')
```

In this example, we load a pre-trained VGG16 model for image recognition using the `keras.applications.VGG16()` function. We then load an image file and preprocess it using the `keras.preprocessing.image.load_img()` and `keras.applications.vgg16.preprocess_input()` functions, respectively. Finally, we make a prediction on the image using the `model.predict()` method and print the top predictions using the `keras.applications.vgg16.decode_predictions()` function.

90. Process Pool:

Process pool is a technique for parallelizing Python code by distributing work among multiple processes. It is similar to thread pool, but uses separate processes instead of threads, which can provide better performance and stability, especially for CPU-bound tasks.

In Python, process pool can be implemented using the `multiprocessing` module, which provides tools for creating and managing processes. The module provides a `Pool` class, which can be used to create a pool of worker processes and distribute tasks among them. The `Pool` class provides methods for submitting tasks, getting results, and managing the pool.

Here's an example of using a process pool to parallelize a CPU-bound task:

```
import multiprocessing
```

```
# Define a CPU-bound function
def cpu_bound_task(n):
    result = 0
    for i in range(1, n+1):
        result += i**2
    return result

# Create a process pool
pool = multiprocessing.Pool()

# Submit tasks to the pool
results = [pool.apply_async(cpu_bound_task, (i,)) for i in range(1, 6)]

# Get the results
output = [result.get() for result in results]

# Print the results
print(output)
```

In this example, we define a CPU-bound function `cpu_bound_task()` that performs a computation on a range of numbers. We then create a process pool using the `multiprocessing.Pool()` function and submit tasks to the pool using the `apply_async()` method. Finally, we get the results using the `get()` method and print them.

91. Protocol Implementation:

Protocol implementation refers to the process of implementing a communication protocol in software. A communication protocol is a set of rules and standards that govern the exchange of data between different systems. Implementing a protocol involves defining the structure and format of the data that will be exchanged, as well as the rules for transmitting and receiving the data.

In Python, protocol implementation can be done using the `socket` module, which provides low-level networking functionality. The module allows you to create and manipulate sockets, which are endpoints for sending and receiving data over a network. You can use the `socket` module to implement a wide range of protocols, including HTTP, FTP, SMTP, and more.

Here's an example of implementing a simple protocol using the `socket` module:

```
import socket
```

```python
# Create a server socket
server_socket = socket.socket(socket.AF_INET, socket.SOCK_STREAM)
server_socket.bind(('localhost', 8000))
server_socket.listen(1)

# Accept a client connection
client_socket, client_address = server_socket.accept()

# Receive data from the client
data = client_socket.recv(1024)

# Send a response back to the client
response = b'Hello, world!'
client_socket.sendall(response)

# Close the sockets
client_socket.close()
server_socket.close()
```

In this example, we create a server socket using the `socket.socket()` function and bind it to a local address and port. We then listen for incoming connections using the `listen()` method and accept a client connection using the `accept()` method. Once a client is connected, we receive data from the client using the `recv()` method and send a response back using the `sendall()` method. Finally, we close the client and server sockets using the `close()` method.

92. PyKafka library:

PyKafka is a Python library for interacting with Kafka, a distributed streaming platform that allows you to build real-time data pipelines and streaming applications. PyKafka provides a high-level API for producing and consuming messages, as well as low-level APIs for advanced use cases such as custom partitioning, message compression, and message delivery guarantees.

Here's an example of using PyKafka to produce messages:

```python
from pykafka import KafkaClient

# Create a Kafka client
client = KafkaClient(hosts='localhost:9092')

# Get a topic producer
topic = client.topics[b'my-topic']
producer = topic.get_producer()
```

```
# Produce a message
producer.produce(b'Hello, world!')

# Close the producer
producer.stop()
```

In this example, we create a Kafka client using the `KafkaClient()` function and get a producer for a topic using the `get_producer()` method. We then produce a message to the topic using the `produce()` method and close the producer using the `stop()` method.

93. Pyro library:

Pyro is a Python library for building distributed systems and applications using remote procedure calls (RPC). Pyro provides a way to invoke methods on objects that are located on remote machines as if they were local objects. This makes it easy to build distributed systems and applications that can scale across multiple machines.

Here's an example of using Pyro to call a method on a remote object:

```
import Pyro4

# Define a remote object
@Pyro4.expose
class MyObject:
    def hello(self, name):
        return f'Hello, {name}!'

# Create a Pyro daemon
daemon = Pyro4.Daemon()

# Register the remote object with the daemon
uri = daemon.register(MyObject)

# Print the object URI
print(uri)

# Start the daemon
daemon.requestLoop()
```

In this example, we define a remote object `MyObject` with a method `hello()` that takes a `name` parameter and returns a greeting message. We then create a Pyro daemon using the `Pyro4.Daemon()` function and register the remote object with the daemon using the `daemon.register()` method. We print the object URI using the `print()` function and start the daemon using the `daemon.requestLoop()` method.PySpark:

94. PySpark:

PySpark is a Python library for working with Spark, a fast and general-purpose cluster computing system that allows you to process large amounts of data in parallel. PySpark provides a Python API for working with Spark, allowing you to write Spark applications and run them on a cluster.

Here's an example of using PySpark to count the number of words in a text file:

```python
from pyspark import SparkContext

# Create a Spark context
sc = SparkContext('local', 'word_count')

# Load a text file into an RDD
lines = sc.textFile('/path/to/text/file.txt')

# Split the lines into words
words = lines.flatMap(lambda line: line.split())

# Count the number of words
word_counts = words.countByValue()

# Print the word counts
for word, count in word_counts.items():
    print(f'{word}: {count}')

# Stop the Spark context
sc.stop()
```

In this example, we create a Spark context using the `SparkContext()` function and load a text file into an RDD using the `textFile()` method. We then split the lines into words using the `flatMap()` method and count the number of words using the `countByValue()` method. Finally, we print the word counts using a `for` loop and stop the Spark context using the `stop()` method.

95. Q-Learning:

Q-learning is a reinforcement learning technique that can be used to learn an optimal policy for a Markov decision process (MDP). Q-learning is based on the idea of iteratively updating a Q-table, which stores the expected rewards for each action in each state. The Q-table is updated using the Bellman equation, which computes the expected reward for taking an action in a given state and then following the optimal policy thereafter.

Here's an example of using Q-learning to learn an optimal policy for a simple MDP:

```python
import numpy as np

# Define the MDP transition probabilities and rewards
P = np.array([
    [[0.5, 0.5], [0.9, 0.1]],
    [[0.1, 0.9], [0.5, 0.5]],
])
R = np.array([
    [[1, 1], [-1, -1]],
    [[-1, -1], [1, 1]],
])
gamma = 0.9

# Initialize the Q-table
Q = np.zeros((2, 2))

# Perform Q-learning for 100 episodes
for episode in range(100):
    # Reset the environment to a random state
    s = np.random.randint(2)

    # Play until the end of the episode
    while True:
        # Choose an action using an epsilon-greedy policy
        if np.random.rand() < 0.1:
            a = np.random.randint(2)
        else:
            a = np.argmax(Q[s])

        # Update the Q-table using the Bellman equation
        s_next = np.random.choice(2, p=P[s][a])
        reward = R[s][a][s_next]
        Q[s][a] += 0.1 * (reward + gamma * np.max(Q[s_next]) - Q[s][a])

        # Transition to the next state
        s = s_next

        # Check if the episode has ended
        if s == 0:
```

```
            break

# Print the final Q-table
print(Q)
```

In this example, we define a simple MDP with two states and two actions. We initialize the Q-table to all zeros and perform Q-learning for 100 episodes. In each episode, we start in a random state and play until the end of the episode, updating the Q-table using the Bellman equation. We use an epsilon-greedy policy to choose actions, with a random action chosen with probability 0.1 and the greedy action chosen with probability 0.9. Finally, we print the final Q-table.

96. Recommendation Systems:

Recommendation systems are algorithms that provide suggestions to users for items they may be interested in. These systems are widely used in e-commerce, social media, and online content platforms. There are two main types of recommendation systems: collaborative filtering and content-based filtering. Collaborative filtering recommends items based on the similarity of users' preferences, while content-based filtering recommends items based on their attributes.

Here's an example of using a collaborative filtering recommendation system to recommend movies to users:

```
import numpy as np

# Define the movie rating matrix
R = np.array([
    [5, 3, 0, 1],
    [4, 0, 0, 1],
    [1, 1, 0, 5],
    [0, 0, 4, 4],
    [0, 1, 5, 4],
])

# Compute the similarity matrix using cosine similarity
S = np.zeros((5, 5))
for i in range(5):
    for j in range(5):
        if i == j:
            continue
        S[i][j] = np.dot(R[i], R[j]) / (np.linalg.norm(R[i]) * np.linalg.norm(R[j]))
```

```python
# Make a recommendation for user 0
scores = np.zeros(4)
for j in range(4):
    if R[0][j] == 0:
        numerator = 0
        denominator = 0
        for i in range(5):
            if R[i][j] != 0:
                numerator += S[0][i] * R[i][j]
                denominator += S[0][i]
        scores[j] = numerator / denominator

# Print the recommended movie
print("Recommended movie:", np.argmax(scores))
```

In this example, we define a movie rating matrix, where each row represents a user and each column represents a movie. We compute the similarity matrix using cosine similarity and make a recommendation for user 0 based on the other users' ratings. We compute a score for each unrated movie by taking a weighted average of the ratings of the other users who rated that movie, where the weights are the cosine similarities between user 0 and the other users. Finally, we recommend the movie with the highest score.

97. Regular expressions:

Regular expressions, also known as regex or regexp, are a powerful tool for matching patterns in text. A regular expression is a sequence of characters that defines a search pattern. Regular expressions can be used to validate input, search for specific patterns in text, and extract data from text.

Here's an example of using regular expressions to extract email addresses from a string:

```python
import re

# Define a string that contains email addresses
s = "john.doe@example.com, jane.smith@example.com"

# Define a regular expression pattern for matching email addresses
pattern = r"\b[A-Za-z0-9._%+-]+@[A-Za-z0-9.-]+\.[A-Z|a-z]{2,}\b"

# Find all matches of the pattern in the string
matches = re.findall(pattern, s)
```

```
# Print the matches
print(matches)
```

In this example, we define a string that contains email addresses and a regular expression pattern for matching email addresses. We use the `re.findall()` function to find all matches of the pattern in the string. Finally, we print the matches.

98. Reinforcement Learning:

Reinforcement learning is a type of machine learning that involves learning by interacting with an environment. In reinforcement learning, an agent takes actions in an environment to maximize a reward signal. The agent learns by receiving feedback in the form of the reward signal, which indicates how good or bad the agent's actions were. Reinforcement learning has applications in robotics, game playing, and autonomous vehicles, among others.

Here's an example of using reinforcement learning to train an agent to play a simple game:

```
import numpy as np

# Define the game environment
n_states = 10
n_actions = 2
reward_table = np.zeros((n_states, n_actions))
reward_table[0][0] = 1
reward_table[0][1] = -1
reward_table[n_states-1][0] = -1
reward_table[n_states-1][1] = 1

# Define the Q-table
q_table = np.zeros((n_states, n_actions))

# Define the learning rate and discount factor
alpha = 0.1
gamma = 0.9

# Define the exploration rate
epsilon = 0.1

# Define the number of episodes
n_episodes = 1000

# Train the agent
for i in range(n_episodes):
```

```
    state = np.random.randint(n_states)
    while state != 0 and state != n_states-1:
        if np.random.uniform() < epsilon:
            action = np.random.randint(n_actions)
        else:
            action = np.argmax(q_table[state])
        next_state = state + 1 if action == 0 else state - 1
        reward = reward_table[state][action]
        q_table[state][action] = (1 - alpha) * q_table[state][action] + alpha * (reward +
 gamma * np.max(q_table[next_state]))
        state = next_state

# Test the agent
state = np.random.randint(n_states)
while state != 0 and state != n_states-1:
    action = np.argmax(q_table[state])
    next_state = state + 1 if action == 0 else state - 1
    state = next_state
print("Final state:", state)
```

In this example, we define a simple game environment where the agent starts at either the left or right end of a 10-state chain and has two possible actions: move left or move right. The reward for each state-action pair is predefined, with a positive reward for reaching the left end and a negative reward for reaching the right end. We initialize the Q-table to zeros and use the Q-learning algorithm to update the Q-values based on the rewards received. We train the agent for a fixed number of episodes and then test it on a randomly chosen starting state.

99. Remote Method Invocation:

Remote Method Invocation (RMI) is a Java-based technology that allows a Java object running in one virtual machine (VM) to invoke methods on a Java object running in another VM. RMI is used to build distributed applications and can be used to build client-server systems, distributed computing systems, and web services.

RMI uses a stub-skeleton mechanism to enable communication between remote objects. A stub is a client-side proxy object that represents the remote object, while a skeleton is a server-side object that dispatches method calls to the remote object.

To use RMI, you need to define a remote interface that specifies the methods that can be invoked remotely. You then implement the interface in a class that provides the actual implementation of the methods. Finally, you create a server that registers the remote object with the RMI registry, and a client that looks up the remote object in the RMI registry and invokes its methods.

Here's an example of using RMI to invoke a method on a remote object:

```java
// Remote interface
public interface Calculator extends Remote {
    int add(int a, int b) throws RemoteException;
}

// Implementation class
public class CalculatorImpl extends UnicastRemoteObject implements Calculator {
    public CalculatorImpl() throws RemoteException {
        super();
    }

    public int add(int a, int b) throws RemoteException {
        return a + b;
    }
}

// Server
public class Server {
    public static void main(String[] args) {
        try {
            Calculator calculator = new CalculatorImpl();
            Naming.rebind("Calculator", calculator);
            System.out.println("Server ready");
        } catch (Exception e) {
            System.err.println("Server exception: " + e.getMessage());
            e.printStackTrace();
        }
    }
}

// Client
public class Client {
    public static void main(String[] args) {
        try {
            Calculator calculator = (Calculator) Naming.lookup("Calculator");
            int result = calculator.add(3, 4);
            System.out.println("Result: " + result);
        } catch (Exception e) {
            System.err.println("Client exception: " + e.getMessage());
            e.printStackTrace();
        }
    }
}
```

In this example, we define a remote interface `Calculator` that contains a single method `add`. We then implement the interface in the class `CalculatorImpl`, which provides the implementation of the method. We create a server that instantiates the `CalculatorImpl` object and registers it with the RMI registry. Finally, we create a client that looks up the `Calculator` object in the RMI registry and invokes the `add` method on it.

Another example of using RMI is to invoke a remote method that returns a complex object:

```java
// Remote interface
public interface Account extends Remote {
    String getName() throws RemoteException;
    double getBalance() throws RemoteException;
}

// Implementation class
public class AccountImpl extends UnicastRemoteObject implements Account {
    private String name;
    private double balance;

    public AccountImpl(String name, double balance) throws RemoteException {
        super();
        this.name = name;
        this.balance = balance;
    }

    public String getName() throws RemoteException {
        return name;
    }

    public double getBalance() throws RemoteException {
        return balance;
    }
}

// Server
public class Server {
    public static void main(String[] args) {
        try {
            Account account = new AccountImpl("John Smith", 1000);
            Naming.rebind("Account", account);
            System.out.println("Server ready");
        } catch (Exception e) {
            System.err.println("Server exception: " + e.getMessage());
            e.printStackTrace();
        }
    }
}
```

```
// Client
```

100. ReportLab library:

ReportLab is a Python library for generating PDF documents. It provides a high-level API for creating and manipulating PDF documents, as well as a low-level API for more fine-grained control over the PDF file format.

With ReportLab, you can create PDF documents from scratch, or you can use pre-existing PDFs as templates and add your own content. The library provides a variety of tools for working with PDFs, including tools for creating and manipulating text, images, and vector graphics.

Here's an example of using ReportLab to generate a simple PDF document:

```
from reportlab.pdfgen import canvas

# Create a new PDF document
c = canvas.Canvas("example.pdf")

# Set the font and font size
c.setFont("Helvetica", 12)

# Draw some text on the page
c.drawString(100, 750, "Hello, world!")

# Save the PDF document
c.save()
```

In this example, we import the `canvas` module from ReportLab and use it to create a new PDF document called `example.pdf`. We set the font and font size using the `setFont` method, and then use the `drawString` method to draw the text "Hello, world!" on the page. Finally, we save the PDF document using the `save` method.

101. Requests library:

The Requests library is a popular Python library for making HTTP requests. It provides an easy-to-use API for sending HTTP requests and handling the response. With Requests, you can send GET, POST, PUT, DELETE, and other HTTP requests. You can also set headers, add parameters, and send data in different formats such as JSON and form-encoded data.

Here's an example of using the Requests library to send a GET request:

```
import requests

response = requests.get('https://api.github.com/repos/requests/requests')
print(response.status_code)
print(response.json())
```

In this example, we import the `requests` module and use the `get` method to send a GET request to the GitHub API to get information about the Requests library repository. We print the HTTP status code and the JSON response returned by the API.

102. Routing:

Routing is a mechanism used in web frameworks to match URLs to specific functions or methods that handle the request. In a web application, a request from a client is typically a URL that needs to be mapped to a specific function that generates the appropriate response.

Routing is usually done by defining URL patterns and associating them with functions or methods. The URL patterns can include variables that capture parts of the URL and pass them as arguments to the corresponding function or method.

Here's an example of using the Flask web framework to define a route:

```
from flask import Flask

app = Flask(__name__)

@app.route('/')
def hello_world():
    return 'Hello, World!'
```

In this example, we define a route for the root URL `/` and associate it with the `hello_world` function. When a client sends a request to the root URL, the Flask application calls the `hello_world` function and returns the response.

103. Scapy library:

Scapy is a Python library for packet manipulation and analysis. It allows you to capture, dissect, and forge network packets. Scapy supports a wide range of protocols and can be used to perform tasks such as network discovery, network scanning, and network testing.

Here's an example of using Scapy to send a ping request:

```python
from scapy.all import *

packet = IP(dst="google.com")/ICMP()
response = sr1(packet, timeout=2)
if response:
    print(response.summary())
else:
    print("No response")
```

In this example, we create an IP packet with the destination address set to `google.com` and an ICMP packet. We use the `sr1` function to send the packet and wait for a response with a timeout of 2 seconds. If we receive a response, we print a summary of the response.

104. Scatter Chart:

A scatter chart, also known as a scatter plot, is a graph that uses dots to represent data points. Each dot on the chart represents the value of two numeric variables. Scatter charts are useful for showing the relationship between two variables and identifying any patterns or trends in the data. For example, a scatter chart can be used to show the relationship between the price and the mileage of cars in a dataset.

Here's an example code for creating a scatter chart using Matplotlib:

```python
import matplotlib.pyplot as plt

# Sample data
x = [1, 2, 3, 4, 5]
y = [10, 20, 15, 25, 30]

# Create a scatter chart
plt.scatter(x, y)
```

```
# Set the chart title and axis labels
plt.title('Relationship between X and Y')
plt.xlabel('X')
plt.ylabel('Y')

# Show the chart
plt.show()
```

105. Scikit-Learn library:

Scikit-Learn is a popular open-source machine learning library for Python. It provides a range of machine learning algorithms for classification, regression, clustering, and dimensionality reduction, as well as tools for model selection and data preprocessing. Scikit-Learn is designed to work with NumPy and SciPy arrays, making it easy to integrate with other scientific Python libraries. The library includes many popular machine learning algorithms, such as linear regression, logistic regression, decision trees, and support vector machines.

Here's an example code for using Scikit-Learn's linear regression model to predict the price of a house based on its size:

```
from sklearn.linear_model import LinearRegression

# Sample data
X = [[100], [200], [300], [400], [500]]
y = [150, 250, 350, 450, 550]

# Create a linear regression model
model = LinearRegression()

# Fit the model to the data
model.fit(X, y)

# Predict the price of a house with a size of 250 square meters
predicted_price = model.predict([[250]])

print(predicted_price)  # Output: [300.]
```

106. Sentiment Analysis:

Sentiment analysis is the process of identifying and categorizing the emotions or opinions expressed in a piece of text. It uses natural language processing (NLP) techniques to analyze the sentiment of the text and assign it a positive, negative, or neutral label. Sentiment analysis is useful for a variety of applications, such as social media monitoring, customer feedback analysis, and brand reputation management.

For example, sentiment analysis can be used to analyze customer reviews of a product and identify the overall sentiment of the reviews as positive, negative, or neutral.

107. Socket library:

The socket library is a Python library used for low-level network programming. It provides a way for Python programs to access the underlying network protocols, such as TCP and UDP. The socket library allows programs to create and manipulate sockets, which are endpoints for communication between two processes over a network.

For example, the following code creates a TCP socket and connects to a web server to retrieve a web page:

```python
import socket

# Create a TCP socket
sock = socket.socket(socket.AF_INET, socket.SOCK_STREAM)

# Connect to a web server
server_address = ('www.example.com', 80)
sock.connect(server_address)

# Send a GET request for a web page
request = 'GET /index.html HTTP/1.1\r\nHost: www.example.com\r\n\r\n'
sock.sendall(request.encode())

# Receive the response data
response = sock.recv(1024)
print(response.decode())

# Close the socket
sock.close()
```

108. Socket Programming:

Socket programming is a type of network programming that uses sockets to enable communication between two processes over a network. Socket programming can be used for a variety of applications, such as client-server communication, file transfer, and remote procedure call. In Python, socket programming can be accomplished using the socket library.

For example, the following code creates a simple TCP server that listens for incoming client connections and sends a response:

```python
import socket

# Create a TCP socket
sock = socket.socket(socket.AF_INET, socket.SOCK_STREAM)

# Bind the socket to a port
server_address = ('localhost', 12345)
sock.bind(server_address)

# Listen for incoming connections
sock.listen(1)

while True:
    # Wait for a client connection
    client_sock, client_address = sock.accept()

    # Receive the client's data
    data = client_sock.recv(1024).decode()

    # Send a response back to the client
    response = 'Hello, ' + data
    client_sock.sendall(response.encode())

    # Close the client socket
    client_sock.close()
```

109. spaCy library:

spaCy is a Python library used for natural language processing (NLP). It provides tools for processing and analyzing text data, including tokenization, part-of-speech tagging, named entity recognition, and dependency parsing. spaCy is designed to be fast and efficient, and it includes pre-trained models for a variety of NLP tasks.

For example, the following code uses spaCy to tokenize and parse a sentence:

```python
import spacy

# Load the English language model
nlp = spacy.load('en_core_web_sm')

# Tokenize and parse a sentence
doc = nlp('The cat sat on the mat.')
for token in doc:
    print(token.text, token.pos_, token.dep_)
```

Output:

```
The DET det
cat NOUN nsubj
sat VERB ROOT
on ADP prep
the DET det
mat NOUN pobj
. PUNCT punct
```

110. SQL:

SQL (Structured Query Language) is a programming language used to manage and manipulate relational databases. It is used to store, modify, and retrieve data from a database. SQL can be used to create and delete databases, tables, and records. It is used by developers, data analysts, and data scientists to perform various database-related tasks.

Example:

Suppose you have a table in a database that contains customer information. You can use SQL to retrieve all customers who live in a specific city. The SQL query for this would look something like:

```sql
SELECT * FROM customers WHERE city = 'New York';
```

This query will retrieve all the customer records where the city is 'New York'. You can also use SQL to update, insert or delete records in the table. For example, to update a customer's phone number, you can use a query like:

```
UPDATE customers SET phone_number = '123-456-7890' WHERE customer_id = 1234;
```

This will update the phone number for the customer with ID 1234 in the 'customers' table.

111. SQL queries:

SQL queries are commands that are used to extract specific data from a database. These queries can be used to filter, sort, and group data as per specific requirements. SQL queries are written in SQL language, which is used to interact with a database. SQL queries can be simple or complex, depending on the complexity of the data that needs to be extracted.

Suppose you have a table called 'students' in a database that contains information about the students. You can use SQL queries to retrieve data from this table. For example, to retrieve the names of all the students in the table, you can use a query like:

```
SELECT name FROM students;
```

This query will retrieve the names of all the students in the 'students' table.

Here is an example of using SQL queries in Python using the SQLite library:

```python
import sqlite3

# Connect to a database
conn = sqlite3.connect('example.db')

# Create a cursor object
cur = conn.cursor()

# Execute an SQL query
cur.execute('SELECT * FROM users')

# Fetch the results
rows = cur.fetchall()
```

```
# Print the results
for row in rows:
    print(row)

# Close the connection
conn.close()
```

112. SQLite:

SQLite is a software library that provides a relational database management system. It is a lightweight database management system that is widely used in embedded systems and mobile devices due to its small size and low overhead. SQLite is an open-source project that is maintained by a team of developers.

Suppose you are developing a mobile application that requires a database to store data. You can use SQLite to create and manage the database for your application. SQLite provides a simple and efficient way to manage the database, which makes it an ideal choice for mobile applications.

Here is an example of creating an SQLite database in Python:

```
import sqlite3

# Connect to a database (if it doesn't exist, it will be created)
conn = sqlite3.connect('example.db')

# Close the connection
conn.close()
```

113. SQLite database:

An SQLite database is a file that contains a structured set of data. It is created and managed by the SQLite software library. SQLite databases are commonly used in small to medium-sized applications because of their simplicity and ease of use.

An SQLite database is as well, a file that contains tables and other database objects. Here is an example of creating an SQLite database and a table in Python:

```
import sqlite3
```

```
# Connect to a database (if it doesn't exist, it will be created)
conn = sqlite3.connect('example.db')

# Create a table
cur = conn.cursor()
cur.execute('CREATE TABLE users (id INTEGER PRIMARY KEY, name TEXT, age INTEGER)')

# Close the connection
conn.close()
```

114. SQLite library:

The SQLite library is a collection of functions and routines that are used to interact with an SQLite database. It provides a simple and efficient way to manage the database and perform various operations on it. The SQLite library is available in various programming languages like C, Python, Java, etc.

The SQLite library is a Python module that provides an interface to SQLite databases. Here is an example of inserting data into an SQLite database using the SQLite library:

```
import sqlite3

# Connect to a database
conn = sqlite3.connect('example.db')

# Insert data into the table
cur = conn.cursor()
cur.execute("INSERT INTO users VALUES (1, 'Alice', 25)")
cur.execute("INSERT INTO users VALUES (2, 'Bob', 30)")

# Commit the changes
conn.commit()

# Close the connection
conn.close()
```

115. SQLite3 module:

The SQLite3 module is a Python library that provides a simple way to interact with an SQLite database. It provides a set of functions that can be used to create, read, update, and delete data from the database. The SQLite3 module is included in the standard library of Python.

This is a Python module that provides an interface to SQLite databases. Here is an example of using the SQLite3 module to query an SQLite database:

```python
import sqlite3

# Connect to a database
conn = sqlite3.connect('example.db')

# Query the database
cur = conn.cursor()
cur.execute('SELECT * FROM users WHERE age > 25')
rows = cur.fetchall()

# Print the results
for row in rows:
    print(row)

# Close the connection
conn.close()
```

116. Statsmodels library:

Statsmodels is a Python library for performing statistical analysis, estimation, and modeling. It includes a wide range of statistical methods and models, such as regression analysis, time series analysis, and hypothesis testing. Here is an example of using Statsmodels to perform linear regression:

```python
import statsmodels.api as sm
import numpy as np

# Generate random data
x = np.random.randn(100)
y = 2 * x + np.random.randn(100)

# Perform linear regression
model = sm.OLS(y, sm.add_constant(x)).fit()

# Print model summary
print(model.summary())
```

117. Stemming:

Stemming is a process of reducing words to their root form, or stem, by removing prefixes and suffixes. It is commonly used in natural language processing to normalize text data. Here is an example of using the Porter stemming algorithm from the NLTK library:

```python
from nltk.stem import PorterStemmer

# Create a stemmer object
stemmer = PorterStemmer()

# Apply stemming to a word
word = "running"
stemmed_word = stemmer.stem(word)

print(stemmed_word)  # Output: run
```

118. Stop Words Removal:

Stop words are common words such as "the", "and", and "a" that are often removed from text data because they do not carry much meaning. Here is an example of using NLTK library to remove stop words from a sentence:

```python
import nltk
from nltk.corpus import stopwords

# Download the stop words corpus
nltk.download('stopwords')

# Get the list of stop words
stop_words = set(stopwords.words('english'))

# Remove stop words from a sentence
sentence = "This is a sample sentence with stop words"
words = sentence.split()
filtered_words = [word for word in words if word.lower() not in stop_words]

print(filtered_words)  # Output: ['sample', 'sentence', 'stop', 'words']
```

119. Stream Processing:

Stream processing is a method of processing data in real-time as it is generated, rather than storing it in a database or a file first. It is commonly used for processing large amounts of data that cannot fit into memory. Here is an example of using the PySpark library to perform stream processing:

```python
from pyspark.streaming import StreamingContext

# Create a Spark StreamingContext with batch interval of 1 second
ssc = StreamingContext(sparkContext, 1)

# Create a DStream from a TCP socket
lines = ssc.socketTextStream("localhost", 9999)

# Split each line into words
words = lines.flatMap(lambda line: line.split(" "))

# Count the occurrence of each word
word_counts = words.map(lambda word: (word, 1)).reduceByKey(lambda x, y: x + y)

# Print the word counts
word_counts.pprint()

# Start the streaming context
ssc.start()

# Wait for the streaming to finish
ssc.awaitTermination()
```

120. Subplots:

In data visualization, a subplot is a plot that is created within a larger plot. Subplots are useful for comparing and contrasting data or for showing multiple views of a dataset. In Python, subplots can be created using the `subplots()` method from the `matplotlib` library.

Here's an example of how to create a figure with multiple subplots in Python:

```python
import matplotlib.pyplot as plt
import numpy as np

# create a figure with two subplots
fig, axs = plt.subplots(2)
```

```
# create some data to plot
x = np.arange(0, 10, 0.1)
y1 = np.sin(x)
y2 = np.cos(x)

# plot the data on the subplots
axs[0].plot(x, y1)
axs[1].plot(x, y2)

# add a title and labels to the subplots
axs[0].set_title('Sin(x)')
axs[1].set_title('Cos(x)')
axs[0].set_xlabel('x')
axs[1].set_xlabel('x')
axs[0].set_ylabel('y')
axs[1].set_ylabel('y')

# display the subplots
plt.show()
```

In this example, we create a figure with two subplots using the `subplots()` method. We then create some data to plot and plot it on the subplots using the `plot()` method. Finally, we add a title and labels to the subplots and display them using the `show()` method.

121. Support Vector Machines:

Support Vector Machines (SVM) is a powerful machine learning algorithm used for classification and regression analysis. SVMs work by finding the best hyperplane that separates the different classes of data.

In Python, SVMs can be implemented using the `svm` module from the `sklearn` (Scikit-learn) library. Here's an example of how to use SVM for classification in Python:

```
from sklearn import svm
from sklearn.datasets import load_iris
from sklearn.model_selection import train_test_split

# load the iris dataset
iris = load_iris()

# split the data into training and testing sets
X_train, X_test, y_train, y_test = train_test_split(iris.data, iris.target, test_size=0.3)

# create a SVM classifier
clf = svm.SVC(kernel='linear', C=1)
```

```
# train the classifier using the training data
clf.fit(X_train, y_train)

# predict the classes of the test data
y_pred = clf.predict(X_test)

# print the accuracy of the classifier
print("Accuracy:", clf.score(X_test, y_test))
```

In this example, we load the iris dataset and split the data into training and testing sets using the `train_test_split()` method. We then create a SVM classifier with a linear kernel and train the classifier using the training data. Finally, we predict the classes of the test data using the `predict()` method and print the accuracy of the classifier using the `score()` method.

122. Surprise library:

Surprise is a Python library used for building and analyzing recommender systems. The library provides various algorithms for collaborative filtering, such as Singular Value Decomposition (SVD) and K-Nearest Neighbors (KNN).

Here's an example of how to use the Surprise library to build a recommender system:

```
from surprise import Dataset
from surprise import Reader
from surprise import SVD
from surprise.model_selection import cross_validate

# load the movielens-100k dataset
reader = Reader(line_format='user item rating timestamp', sep='\t')
data = Dataset.load_from_file('./ml-100k/u.data', reader=reader)

# use SVD algorithm for collaborative filtering
algo = SVD()

# evaluate the performance of the algorithm using cross-validation
results = cross_validate(algo, data, measures=['RMSE', 'MAE'], cv=5, verbose=True)

# print the average RMSE and MAE scores
print("RMSE:", sum(results['test_rmse'])/5)
print("MAE:", sum(results['test_mae'])/5)
```

In this example, we load the movielens-100k dataset and use the SVD algorithm for collaborative filtering. We then evaluate the performance of the algorithm using cross-validation and print the average RMSE and MAE scores.

123. TCP/IP Protocol:

The TCP/IP protocol is a set of communication protocols used for transmitting data over the internet. The protocol consists of several layers, including the application layer, transport layer, network layer, and link layer.

TCP/IP Protocol: The Transmission Control Protocol/Internet Protocol (TCP/IP) is a set of protocols that are used to connect devices to the Internet. The TCP part is responsible for reliable data delivery between applications on different devices, while the IP part is responsible for routing the data between different networks. Python provides support for TCP/IP protocols through the socket library, which allows you to create socket objects and connect them to other sockets to send and receive data.

In Python, TCP/IP communication can be implemented using the `socket` library. Here's an example of how to use the `socket` library to create a TCP client:

```python
import socket

# create a TCP client socket
client_socket = socket.socket(socket.AF_INET, socket.SOCK_STREAM)

# connect to the server
server_address = ('localhost', 8080)
client_socket.connect(server_address)

# send a message to the server
message = 'Hello, server!'
client_socket.send(message.encode())

# receive a response from the server
data = client_socket.recv(1024)
print("Received:", data.decode())

# close the socket
client
```

124. TensorFlow library

TensorFlow is a popular open-source library developed by Google for building and training machine learning models. It is primarily used for deep learning tasks such as image recognition and natural language processing. TensorFlow provides a high-level API that simplifies the process of building complex models, as well as a lower-level API for more advanced users. Here's an example of using TensorFlow to build a simple neural network:

```python
import tensorflow as tf

# Define the model architecture
model = tf.keras.Sequential([
    tf.keras.layers.Dense(64, activation='relu'),
    tf.keras.layers.Dense(10)
])

# Compile the model
model.compile(optimizer=tf.keras.optimizers.Adam(0.001),
              loss=tf.keras.losses.CategoricalCrossentropy(from_logits=True),
              metrics=[tf.keras.metrics.CategoricalAccuracy()])

# Train the model
model.fit(x_train, y_train, epochs=10, validation_data=(x_val, y_val))
```

125. Text Corpus

A text corpus is a large and structured set of texts that are used to study language patterns and analyze the frequency of words and phrases. Python provides several libraries for working with text corpora, including NLTK and spaCy. Here's an example of loading a text corpus using NLTK:

```python
import nltk
nltk.download('gutenberg')
from nltk.corpus import gutenberg

# Load the text corpus
corpus = gutenberg.words('shakespeare-macbeth.txt')

# Print the first 10 words
print(corpus[:10])
```

126. Text Preprocessing

Text preprocessing is the process of cleaning and preparing text data before it can be used for natural language processing tasks. This includes removing stop words, stemming, lemmatization, and removing punctuation, among other things. Here's an example of text preprocessing using NLTK library:

```python
import nltk
from nltk.corpus import stopwords
from nltk.stem import WordNetLemmatizer, PorterStemmer
from nltk.tokenize import word_tokenize

# Download stopwords and lemmatizer
nltk.download('stopwords')
nltk.download('wordnet')

# Define text and remove punctuation
text = "This is an example sentence! With some punctuation marks."
text = "".join([char for char in text if char.isalpha() or char.isspace()])

# Tokenize words and remove stop words
tokens = word_tokenize(text.lower())
stop_words = set(stopwords.words('english'))
tokens = [word for word in tokens if not word in stop_words]

# Apply lemmatization and stemming
lemmatizer = WordNetLemmatizer()
stemmer = PorterStemmer()
tokens = [lemmatizer.lemmatize(word) for word in tokens]
tokens = [stemmer.stem(word) for word in tokens]

print(tokens)
```

127. Text Processing

Text processing involves analyzing and manipulating text data for various natural language processing tasks, such as sentiment analysis, text classification, and named entity recognition. It can involve tasks such as tokenization, part-of-speech tagging, and syntactic parsing. Here's an example of text processing using NLTK library:

```python
import nltk
from nltk.tokenize import word_tokenize
from nltk.tag import pos_tag
```

```
# Define text
text = "I love to read books on natural language processing."

# Tokenize words and part-of-speech tagging
tokens = word_tokenize(text)
pos = pos_tag(tokens)

print(pos)
```

128. Text Representation

Text representation is the process of converting text data into a numerical format that can be used for machine learning algorithms. This can include methods such as bag-of-words, term frequency-inverse document frequency (TF-IDF), and word embeddings. Here's an example of text representation using the scikit-learn library:

```
from sklearn.feature_extraction.text import CountVectorizer, TfidfVectorizer
import pandas as pd

# Define text
text = ["I love to read books on natural language processing.",        "Text processing is
an important part of machine learning."]

# Convert text into bag-of-words representation
cv = CountVectorizer()
bow = cv.fit_transform(text)

# Convert text into TF-IDF representation
tfidf = TfidfVectorizer()
tfidf_matrix = tfidf.fit_transform(text)

# Print results
print(pd.DataFrame(bow.toarray(), columns=cv.get_feature_names()))
print(pd.DataFrame(tfidf_matrix.toarray(), columns=tfidf.get_feature_names()))
```

129. Threading library

The threading module in Python allows multiple threads to run simultaneously within the same program. This can be useful for tasks such as I/O operations or tasks that can be parallelized. Here's an example of using the threading module to run multiple tasks concurrently:

```python
import threading

# Define a function to run in a separate thread
def task():
    for i in range(10):
        print("Task running")

# Create and start a new thread
t = threading.Thread(target=task)
t.start()

# Main thread continues to run
for i in range(10):
    print("Main thread running")
```

130. Time Series Analysis

Time series analysis is the study of data points collected over time to identify patterns, trends, and seasonality to make predictions or draw insights. It is widely used in various fields, including finance, economics, weather forecasting, and more. In Python, the most popular libraries for time series analysis are Pandas, NumPy, and Statsmodels.

Example:

Let's say you have collected daily sales data for a retail store for the past year, and you want to analyze the data to forecast future sales. You can use time series analysis to identify trends, seasonality, and other patterns in the data. Here's some example code using Pandas library:

```python
import pandas as pd
import matplotlib.pyplot as plt

# Load the sales data into a Pandas DataFrame
sales_data = pd.read_csv('sales_data.csv', index_col=0, parse_dates=True)

# Visualize the time series data
plt.plot(sales_data)
plt.title('Daily Sales Data')
plt.xlabel('Date')
plt.ylabel('Sales')
plt.show()

# Identify the trend component using moving average
rolling_mean = sales_data.rolling(window=30).mean()
```

```
plt.plot(rolling_mean)
plt.title('Trend Component')
plt.xlabel('Date')
plt.ylabel('Sales')
plt.show()

# Decompose the time series into trend, seasonal, and residual components
from statsmodels.tsa.seasonal import seasonal_decompose
decomposition = seasonal_decompose(sales_data, model='additive')
trend = decomposition.trend
seasonal = decomposition.seasonal
residual = decomposition.resid

# Visualize the components
plt.subplot(411)
plt.plot(sales_data)
plt.title('Original Time Series')
plt.subplot(412)
plt.plot(trend)
plt.title('Trend Component')
plt.subplot(413)
plt.plot(seasonal)
plt.title('Seasonal Component')
plt.subplot(414)
plt.plot(residual)
plt.title('Residual Component')
plt.tight_layout()
plt.show()
```

This example demonstrates how you can use time series analysis techniques to identify the trend and seasonal components of the sales data and decompose the time series into its constituent parts. You can then use this information to make forecasts and predictions for future sales.

131. Tokenization:

Tokenization is the process of breaking down a text into individual words or phrases, known as tokens. This is an important step in many natural language processing tasks. Tokenization can be performed using a variety of methods, such as splitting the text by whitespace or punctuation. Let's look at an example:

```
import nltk
from nltk.tokenize import word_tokenize

text = "This is an example sentence."
```

```
tokens = word_tokenize(text)
print(tokens)
```

Output:

```
['This', 'is', 'an', 'example', 'sentence', '.']
```

132. Topic Modeling:

Topic modeling is a statistical method used to discover abstract topics that occur in a collection of documents. It is commonly used in natural language processing to analyze large collections of text data. One popular algorithm for topic modeling is Latent Dirichlet Allocation (LDA). Here is an example of topic modeling using LDA:

```
from sklearn.datasets import fetch_20newsgroups
from sklearn.feature_extraction.text import CountVectorizer
from sklearn.decomposition import LatentDirichletAllocation

# Load sample data
newsgroups = fetch_20newsgroups()

# Vectorize text data
vectorizer = CountVectorizer(max_features=1000)
X = vectorizer.fit_transform(newsgroups.data)

# Fit LDA model
lda = LatentDirichletAllocation(n_components=10, random_state=0)
lda.fit(X)

# Print top words in each topic
feature_names = vectorizer.get_feature_names()
for topic_idx, topic in enumerate(lda.components_):
    print("Topic #%d:" % topic_idx)
    print(" ".join([feature_names[i] for i in topic.argsort()[:-11:-1]]))
    print()
```

Output:

```
Topic #0:
edu cs article university writes science posting host computer reply
```

```
Topic #1:
god jesus christ bible believe faith christian christians sin church

Topic #2:
team game year games season players hockey nhl play league

Topic #3:
com bike dod cars article writes university ca just like

Topic #4:
windows dos ms software file version use files ftp os

Topic #5:
uk ac university posting host nntp nui subject manchester david

Topic #6:
drive scsi ide drives disk hard controller floppy bus hd

Topic #7:
key chip encryption clipper government keys public use secure law

Topic #8:
israel jews israeli arab arabs jewish lebanese lebanon peace state

Topic #9:
windows thanks know does help like using use software just
```

133. Web Application Deployment:

Web application deployment is the process of making a web application available for use on a server or hosting platform. This involves configuring the server environment, installing any necessary software dependencies, and uploading the application code to the server. Here is an example of deploying a Flask web application to a Heroku hosting platform:

```python
# app.py
from flask import Flask

app = Flask(__name__)

@app.route("/")
def hello():
    return "Hello World!"

if __name__ == "__main__":
    app.run()
```

```
# requirements.txt
Flask==2.0.2
gunicorn==20.1.0

# Procfile
web: gunicorn app:app

# Deploy to Heroku
# 1. Create a new Heroku app
# 2. Connect to the app using Heroku CLI
# 3. Add a Git remote to the app
# 4. Commit and push the code to the remote
# 5. Open the app in a browser
```

134. Web Development:

Web development refers to the process of creating websites and web applications. It involves the use of various technologies such as HTML, CSS, and JavaScript, along with server-side technologies such as PHP, Ruby on Rails, and Python's Django and Flask frameworks. Web development can be divided into two categories: front-end and back-end development. Front-end development deals with the client-side of a web application, which includes designing the user interface and handling user interactions. Back-end development, on the other hand, deals with the server-side of a web application, which includes handling data storage, processing user requests, and generating dynamic content.

Example:
Here is an example of a simple web application built with Flask, a Python web framework:

```
from flask import Flask, render_template

app = Flask(__name__)

@app.route('/')
def home():
    return render_template('home.html')

@app.route('/about')
def about():
    return render_template('about.html')
```

```
if __name__ == '__main__':
    app.run(debug=True)
```

This code creates a simple Flask application that has two routes, one for the home page and one for the about page. When a user navigates to the home page, Flask renders the `home.html` template, and when a user navigates to the about page, Flask renders the `about.html` template.

135. Web Scraping:

Web scraping is the process of extracting data from websites. It involves using automated tools to navigate through web pages and extract relevant information, such as product prices, stock market data, or news articles. Web scraping can be done using various programming languages, including Python, and it involves parsing HTML and/or XML documents to extract the desired information. The BeautifulSoup and Scrapy libraries are popular Python libraries used for web scraping.

Example:
Here is an example of a simple web scraping script that extracts the titles and links of the top news stories from the CNN homepage:

```python
import requests
from bs4 import BeautifulSoup

url = 'https://www.cnn.com/'

response = requests.get(url)

soup = BeautifulSoup(response.text, 'html.parser')

news_titles = []
news_links = []

for story in soup.find_all('h3', class_='cd__headline'):
    title = story.text.strip()
    link = story.find('a')['href']
    news_titles.append(title)
    news_links.append(link)

for i in range(len(news_titles)):
    print(news_titles[i])
    print(news_links[i])
    print()
```

This code uses the requests library to retrieve the HTML content of the CNN homepage, and then uses BeautifulSoup to parse the HTML and extract the titles and links of the top news stories. The resulting output is a list of news titles and links that can be used for further analysis.

50 ADVANCED LEVEL EXERCISES

The exercises in this book, and this section, are not arranged in any particular order according to the difficulty level. This may seem unorganized, but in fact, it grants readers the flexibility to skip ahead and find the information that they need at that particular moment. Furthermore, this is especially beneficial for students or readers who are more advanced in their studies as they may not need to cover the basics.

In this way, you can focus on the more challenging areas of the subject matter and progress at your own pace, which can be very rewarding. Ultimately, the lack of a prescribed order can be an advantage rather than a disadvantage, offering you the ability to customize your learning experience and make the most of your time and effort.

You can follow the order if you want, but you can also go directly to the exercise that you need to focus on.

The best way to learn is to enjoy yourself, so have fun coding your future.

LET'S START.

Advance Level Exercises

Exercise 1: File Parsing

Concepts:

- File I/O

- Regular expressions

Description: Write a Python script that reads a text file and extracts all URLs that are present in the file. The output should be a list of URLs.

Solution:

```python
import re

# Open the file for reading
with open('input_file.txt', 'r') as f:
    # Read the file contents
    file_contents = f.read()

    # Use regular expression to extract URLs
    urls = re.findall(r'http[s]?://(?:[a-zA-Z]|[0-9]|[$-_@.&+]|[!*\(\),]|(?:%[0-9a-fA-F][0
-9a-fA-F]))+', file_contents)

# Print the list of URLs
print(urls)
```

Exercise 2: Data Analysis

Concepts:

- File I/O

- Data manipulation

- Pandas library

Description: Write a Python script that reads a CSV file containing sales data and calculates the total sales revenue for each product category.

Solution:

```python
import pandas as pd

# Read the CSV file into a pandas dataframe
df = pd.read_csv('sales_data.csv')

# Group the data by product category and sum the sales revenue
total_revenue = df.groupby('Product Category')['Sales Revenue'].sum()

# Print the total revenue for each product category
print(total_revenue)
```

Exercise 3: Web Scraping

Concepts

- Web scraping

- Requests library

- Beautiful Soup library

- CSV file I/O

Description: Write a Python script that scrapes the title and price of all products listed on an e-commerce website and stores them in a CSV file.

Solution:

```python
import requests
from bs4 import BeautifulSoup
import csv

# Make a GET request to the website
response = requests.get('https://www.example.com/products')

# Parse the HTML content using Beautiful Soup
soup = BeautifulSoup(response.content, 'html.parser')

# Find all product titles and prices
titles = [title.text for title in soup.find_all('h3', class_='product-title')]
prices = [price.text for price in soup.find_all('div', class_='product-price')]

# Zip the titles and prices together
data = list(zip(titles, prices))

# Write the data to a CSV file
```

```
with open('product_data.csv', 'w', newline='') as f:
    writer = csv.writer(f)
    writer.writerows(data)
```

Exercise 4: Multithreading

Concepts:

- Multithreading

- Requests library

- Threading library

Description: Write a Python script that uses multithreading to download multiple images from a URL list simultaneously.

Solution:

```
import requests
import threading

# URL list of images to download
url_list = ['https://www.example.com/image1.jpg', 'https://www.example.com/image2.jpg', 'h
ttps://www.example.com/image3.jpg']

# Function to download an image from a URL
def download_image(url):
    response = requests.get(url)
    with open(url.split('/')[-1], 'wb') as f:
        f.write(response.content)

# Create a thread for each URL and start them all simultaneously
threads = []
for url in url_list:
    thread = threading.Thread(target=download_image, args=(url,))
    threads.append(thread)
    thread.start()

# Wait for all threads to finish
for thread in threads:
    thread.join()
```

Exercise 5: Machine Learning

Concepts:

- Machine learning

- Scikit-learn library

Description: Write a Python script that trains a machine learning model on a dataset and uses it to predict the output for new data.

Solution:

```python
import pandas as pd
from sklearn.model_selection import train_test_split
from sklearn.linear_model import LinearRegression

# Read the dataset into a pandas dataframe
df = pd.read_csv('dataset.csv')

# Split the data into training and testing sets
X_train, X_test, y_train, y_test = train_test_split(df[['feature1', 'feature2']], df['targ
et'], test_size=0.2, random_state=42)

# Train a linear regression model on the training data
model = LinearRegression()
model.fit(X_train, y_train)

# Use the model to predict the output for the testing data
y_pred = model.predict(X_test)

# Evaluate the model performance using the mean squared error metric
mse = ((y_test - y_pred) ** 2).mean()
print("Mean squared error:", mse)
```

In this exercise, we first read a dataset into a pandas dataframe. Then, we split the data into training and testing sets using the `train_test_split` function from the `sklearn.model_selection` module. We trained a linear regression model on the training data using the `LinearRegression` class from the `sklearn.linear_model` module. Finally, we used the trained model to predict the output for the testing data and evaluated the model performance using the mean squared error metric.

Exercise 6: Natural Language Processing

Concepts:

- Natural Language Processing

- Sentiment Analysis

- NLTK library

Description: Write a Python script that reads a text file and performs sentiment analysis on the text using a pre-trained NLP model.

Solution:

```python
import nltk
from nltk.sentiment.vader import SentimentIntensityAnalyzer

# Read the text file into a string
with open('input_file.txt', 'r') as f:    text = f.read()

# Create a SentimentIntensityAnalyzer object
sid = SentimentIntensityAnalyzer()

# Perform sentiment analysis on the text
scores = sid.polarity_scores(text)

# Print the sentiment scores
print(scores)
```

In this exercise, we first read a text file into a string. Then, we create a SentimentIntensityAnalyzer object from the nltk.sentiment.vader module. We use the polarity_scores method of the SentimentIntensityAnalyzer object to perform sentiment analysis on the text and get a dictionary of sentiment scores.

Exercise 7: Web Development

Concepts:

- Web Development

- Flask framework

- File Uploads

Description: Write a Python script that creates a web application using the Flask framework that allows users to upload a file and performs some processing on the file.

Solution:

```python
from flask import Flask, render_template, request
import os

app = Flask(__name__)

# Set the path for file uploads
UPLOAD_FOLDER = os.path.basename('uploads')
app.config['UPLOAD_FOLDER'] = UPLOAD_FOLDER

# Route for the home page
@app.route('/')
def index():
    return render_template('index.html')

# Route for file uploads
@app.route('/upload', methods=['POST'])
def upload():
    # Get the uploaded file
    file = request.files['file']

    # Save the file to the uploads folder
    file.save(os.path.join(app.config['UPLOAD_FOLDER'], file.filename))

    # Perform processing on the file
    # ...

    return 'File uploaded successfully'

if __name__ == '__main__':
    app.run(debug=True)
```

In this exercise, we first import the Flask module and create a Flask application. We set up a route for the home page that returns an HTML template. We set up a route for file uploads that receives an uploaded file and saves it to a designated uploads folder. We can perform processing on the uploaded file inside the `upload` function.

Exercise 8: Data Visualization

Concepts:

- Data Visualization

- Matplotlib library

- Candlestick Charts

Description: Write a Python script that reads a CSV file containing stock market data and plots a candlestick chart of the data.

Solution:

```
import pandas as pd
import matplotlib.pyplot as plt
from mpl_finance import candlestick_ohlc
import matplotlib.dates as mdates

# Read the CSV file into a pandas dataframe
df = pd.read_csv('stock_data.csv', parse_dates=['Date'])

# Convert the date column to Matplotlib dates format
df['Date'] = df['Date'].apply(mdates.date2num)

# Create a figure and axis objects
fig, ax = plt.subplots()

# Plot the candlestick chart
candlestick_ohlc(ax, df.values, width=0.6, colorup='green', colordown='red')

# Format the x-axis as dates
ax.xaxis_date()

# Set the axis labels and title
ax.set_xlabel('Date')
ax.set_ylabel('Price')
ax.set_title('Stock Market Data')

# Display the chart
plt.show()
```

In this exercise, we first read a CSV file containing stock market data into a pandas dataframe. We convert the date column to Matplotlib dates format and create a figure and axis objects. We plot the candlestick chart using the `candlestick_ohlc` function from the `mpl_finance` module. We format the x-axis as dates and set the axis labels and title. Finally, we display the chart using the `show` function from the `matplotlib.pyplot` module.

Exercise 9: Machine Learning

Concepts:

- Machine Learning

- Scikit-learn library

Description: Write a Python script that reads a dataset containing information about different types of flowers and trains a machine learning model to predict the type of a flower based on its features.

Solution:

```python
import pandas as pd
from sklearn.model_selection import train_test_split
from sklearn.linear_model import LogisticRegression
from sklearn.metrics import accuracy_score

# Read the dataset into a pandas dataframe
df = pd.read_csv('flower_data.csv')

# Split the data into training and testing sets
X_train, X_test, y_train, y_test = train_test_split(df[['sepal_length', 'sepal_width', 'pe
tal_length', 'petal_width']], df['species'], test_size=0.2, random_state=42)

# Train a logistic regression model on the training data
model = LogisticRegression()
model.fit(X_train, y_train)

# Use the model to predict the output for the testing data
y_pred = model.predict(X_test)

# Evaluate the model performance using the accuracy score metric
accuracy = accuracy_score(y_test, y_pred)
print("Accuracy:", accuracy)
```

In this exercise, we first read a dataset containing information about different types of flowers into a pandas dataframe. We split the data into training and testing sets using the `train_test_split` function from the `sklearn.model_selection` module. We trained a logistic regression model on the training data using the `LogisticRegression` class from the `sklearn.linear_model` module. Finally, we used the trained model to predict the output for the testing data and evaluated the model performance using the accuracy score metric.

Exercise 10: Data Analysis

Concepts:

- Data Analysis

- Recommendation Systems

- Collaborative Filtering

- Surprise library

Description: Write a Python script that reads a CSV file containing customer purchase data and generates a recommendation system that recommends products to customers based on their purchase history.

Solution:

```python
import pandas as pd
from surprise import Dataset
from surprise import Reader
from surprise import SVD
from surprise import accuracy
from surprise.model_selection import train_test_split

# Read the CSV file into a pandas dataframe
df = pd.read_csv('purchase_data.csv')

# Convert the pandas dataframe to a surprise dataset
reader = Reader(rating_scale=(1, 5))
data = Dataset.load_from_df(df[['customer_id', 'product_id', 'rating']], reader)

# Split the data into training and testing sets
trainset, testset = train_test_split(data, test_size=0.2)

# Train an SVD model on the training data
model = SVD(n_factors=50, n_epochs=20, lr_all=0.005, reg_all=0.02)
model.fit(trainset)

# Use the model to predict the output for the testing data
predictions = model.test(testset)

# Evaluate the model performance using the root mean squared error metric
rmse = accuracy.rmse(predictions)
print("RMSE:", rmse)

# Recommend products to customers based on their purchase history
for customer_id in df['customer_id'].unique():
    products = df[df['customer_id'] == customer_id]['product_id'].values
    for product_id in df['product_id'].unique():
        if product_id not in products:
            rating = model.predict(customer_id, product_id).est
            print(f"Customer {customer_id} might like product {product_id} with rating {rating}")
```

In this exercise, we first read a CSV file containing customer purchase data into a pandas dataframe. We convert the pandas dataframe to a surprise dataset using the Reader and Dataset classes from the surprise module. We split the data into training and testing sets using the train_test_split function from the surprise.model_selection module. We trained an SVD model on the training data using the SVD class from the surprise module. We used the trained model to predict the output for the testing data and evaluated the model performance using the root mean squared error metric. Finally, we recommended products to customers based on their purchase history using the trained model.

Exercise 11: Computer Vision

Concepts:

- Computer Vision

- Object Detection

- OpenCV library

- Pre-trained models

Description: Write a Python script that reads an image and performs object detection on the image using a pre-trained object detection model.

Solution:

```python
import cv2

# Read the image file
img = cv2.imread('image.jpg')

# Load the pre-trained object detection model
model = cv2.dnn.readNetFromTensorflow('frozen_inference_graph.pb', 'ssd_mobilenet_v2_coco_
2018_03_29.pbtxt')

# Set the input image and perform object detection
model.setInput(cv2.dnn.blobFromImage(img, size=(300, 300), swapRB=True, crop=False))
output = model.forward()

# Loop through the detected objects and draw bounding boxes around them
for detection in output[0, 0, :, :]:
    confidence = detection[2]
    if confidence > 0.5:
        x1 = int(detection[3] * img.shape[1])
```

```
        y1 = int(detection[4] * img.shape[0])
        x2 = int(detection[5] * img.shape[1])
        y2 = int(detection[6] * img.shape[0])
        cv2.rectangle(img, (x1, y1), (x2, y2), (0, 255, 0), 2)

# Display the image with the detected objects
cv2.imshow('image', img)
cv2.waitKey(0)
cv2.destroyAllWindows()
```

In this exercise, we first read an image file into a NumPy array using the `imread` function from the `cv2` module of OpenCV. We load a pre-trained object detection model using the `readNetFromTensorflow` function from the `cv2.dnn` module. We set the input image to the model and perform object detection using the `setInput` and `forward` methods of the model object. Finally, we loop through the detected objects and draw bounding boxes around them using the `rectangle` function from the `cv2` module.

Exercise 12: Natural Language Processing

Concepts:

- Natural Language Processing

- Topic Modeling

- Latent Dirichlet Allocation

- Gensim library

Description: Write a Python script that reads a text file and performs topic modeling on the text using Latent Dirichlet Allocation (LDA).

Solution:

```
import gensim
from gensim import corpora
from gensim.models import LdaModel

# Read the text file into a list of strings
with open('input_file.txt', 'r') as f:
    text = f.readlines()

# Remove newlines and convert to lowercase
text = [line.strip().lower() for line in text]
```

```
# Tokenize the text into words
tokens = [line.split() for line in text]

# Create a dictionary of words and their frequency
dictionary = corpora.Dictionary(tokens)

# Create a bag-of-words representation of the text
corpus = [dictionary.doc2bow(token) for token in tokens]

# Train an LDA model on the text
model = LdaModel(corpus, id2word=dictionary, num_topics=5, passes=10)

# Print the topics and their associated words
for topic in model.print_topics(num_words=5):
    print(topic)
```

In this exercise, we first read a text file into a list of strings. We preprocess the text by removing newlines, converting to lowercase, and tokenizing into words using the `split` method. We create a dictionary of words and their frequency and create a bag-of-words representation of the text using the `doc2bow` method of the dictionary object. We train an LDA model on the corpus using the `LdaModel` class from the `gensim.models` module. Finally, we print the topics and their associated words using the `print_topics` method of the model object.

Exercise 13: Web Scraping

Concepts:

- Web Scraping

- Beautiful Soup library

- Requests library

- CSV file handling

Description: Write a Python script that scrapes a website for product information and saves the information to a CSV file.

Solution:

```
import requests
from bs4 import BeautifulSoup
import csv
```

```
# Define the URL of the website to scrape
url = 'https://www.example.com/products'

# Send a request to the website and get the response
response = requests.get(url)

# Parse the HTML content of the response using Beautiful Soup
soup = BeautifulSoup(response.content, 'html.parser')

# Find all the product listings on the page
listings = soup.find_all('div', class_='product-listing')

# Write the product information to a CSV file
with open('products.csv', 'w', newline='') as f:
    writer = csv.writer(f)
    writer.writerow(['Product Name', 'Price', 'Description'])
    for listing in listings:
        name = listing.find('h3').text
        price = listing.find('span', class_='price').text
        description = listing.find('p').text
        writer.writerow([name, price, description])
```

In this exercise, we first define the URL of the website to scrape and send a request to the website using the `get` function from the `requests` module. We parse the HTML content of the response using Beautiful Soup and find all the product listings on the page using the `find_all` method. We write the product information to a CSV file using the `csv` module.

Exercise 14: Big Data Processing

Concepts:

- Big Data Processing

- PySpark

- Data Transformations

- Aggregation

- Parquet file format

Description: Write a PySpark script that reads a CSV file containing customer purchase data, performs some data transformations and aggregation, and saves the results to a Parquet file.

Solution:

```
from pyspark.sql import SparkSession

# Create a SparkSession object
spark = SparkSession.builder.appName('customer-purchases').getOrCreate()

# Read the CSV file into a Spark DataFrame
df = spark.read.csv('customer_purchases.csv', header=True, inferSchema=True)

# Perform some data transformations
df = df.filter(df['purchase_date'].between('2020-01-01', '2020-12-31'))
df = df.select('customer_id', 'product_id', 'price')
df = df.groupBy('customer_id').sum('price')

# Save the results to a Parquet file
df.write.parquet('customer_spending.parquet')
```

In this exercise, we first create a SparkSession object using the `SparkSession` class from the `pyspark.sql` module. We read a CSV file containing customer purchase data into a Spark DataFrame using the `read.csv` method. We perform some data transformations on the DataFrame using the `filter`, `select`, and `groupBy` methods. Finally, we save the results to a Parquet file using the `write.parquet` method.

Exercise 15: DevOps

Concepts:

- DevOps

- Fabric library

Description: Write a Python script that automates the deployment of a web application to a remote server using the Fabric library.

Solution:

```
from fabric import Connection

# Define the host and user credentials for the remote server
host = 'example.com'
user = 'user'
password = 'password'

# Define the path to the web application on the local machine and the remote server
```

```
local_path = '/path/to/local/app'
remote_path = '/path/to/remote/app'

# Create a connection to the remote server
c = Connection(host=host, user=user, connect_kwargs={'password': password})

# Upload the local files to the remote server
c.put(local_path, remote_path)

# Install any required dependencies on the remote server
c.run('sudo apt-get update && sudo apt-get install -y python3-pip')
c.run('pip3 install -r requirements.txt')

# Start the web application on the remote server
c.run('python3 app.py')
```

In this exercise, we first define the host and user credentials for the remote server. We define the path to the web application on the local machine and the remote server. We create a connection to the remote server using the `Connection` class from the `fabric` module. We upload the local files to the remote server using the `put` method of the connection object. We install any required dependencies on the remote server using the `run` method of the connection object. Finally, we start the web application on the remote server using the `run` method.

Exercise 16: Reinforcement Learning

Concepts:

- Reinforcement Learning
- Q-Learning
- OpenAI Gym library

Description: Write a Python script that implements a reinforcement learning algorithm to teach an agent to play a simple game.

Solution:

```
import gym
import numpy as np

# Create an OpenAI Gym environment for the game
env = gym.make('FrozenLake-v0')
```

```python
# Define the Q-table for the agent
Q = np.zeros([env.observation_space.n, env.action_space.n])

# Set the hyperparameters for the algorithm
alpha = 0.8
gamma = 0.95
epsilon = 0.1
num_episodes = 2000

# Train the agent using the Q-learning algorithm
for i in range(num_episodes):
    state = env.reset()
    done = False
    while not done:
        if np.random.uniform() < epsilon:
            action = env.action_space.sample()
        else:
            action = np.argmax(Q[state, :])
        next_state, reward, done, _ = env.step(action)
        Q[state, action] = (1 - alpha) * Q[state, action] + alpha * (reward + gamma * np.m
ax(Q[next_state, :]))
        state = next_state

# Test the agent by playing the game using the Q-table
state = env.reset()
done = False
while not done:
    action = np.argmax(Q[state, :])
    next_state, reward, done, _ = env.step(action)
    state = next_state
    env.render()
```

In this exercise, we first create an OpenAI Gym environment for the game using the `make` function from the `gym` module. We define the Q-table for the agent as a NumPy array and set the hyperparameters for the Q-learning algorithm. We train the agent using the Q-learning algorithm by looping through a specified number of episodes and updating the Q-table based on the rewards and next states. Finally, we test the agent by playing the game using the Q-table and visualizing the game using the `render` method.

Exercise 17: Time Series Analysis

Concepts:

- Time Series Analysis

- Data Preprocessing

- Data Visualization

- ARIMA model

- Statsmodels library

Description: Write a Python script that reads a CSV file containing time series data, performs some data preprocessing and visualization, and fits a time series model to the data.

Solution:

```python
import pandas as pd
import matplotlib.pyplot as plt
import statsmodels.api as sm

# Read the CSV file into a pandas dataframe
df = pd.read_csv('time_series.csv')

# Convert the date column to a datetime object and set it as the index
df['date'] = pd.to_datetime(df['date'])
df.set_index('date', inplace=True)

# Resample the data to a monthly frequency and fill any missing values
df = df.resample('M').mean()
df = df.fillna(method='ffill')

# Visualize the data
plt.plot(df)
plt.show()

# Fit an ARIMA model to the data
model = sm.tsa.ARIMA(df, order=(1, 1, 1))
results = model.fit()

# Print the model summary
print(results.summary())
```

In this exercise, we first read a CSV file containing time series data into a pandas dataframe. We convert the date column to a datetime object and set it as the index. We resample the data to a monthly frequency and fill any missing values using forward fill. We visualize the data using the `plot` function from the `matplotlib.pyplot` module. Finally, we fit an ARIMA model to the data using the `ARIMA` function from the `statsmodels.api` module and print the summary of the model using the `summary` method of the results object.

Exercise 18: Computer Networking

Concepts:

- Computer Networking

- TCP/IP Protocol

- Socket Programming

Description: Write a Python script that implements a simple TCP server that accepts client connections and sends and receives data.

Solution:

```python
import socket

# Define the host and port for the server
host = 'localhost'
port = 12345

# Create a socket object
s = socket.socket(socket.AF_INET, socket.SOCK_STREAM)

# Bind the socket to the host and port
s.bind((host, port))

# Listen for incoming connections
s.listen(1) print('Server listening on', host, port)

# Accept a client connection conn, addr = s.accept()
print('Connected by', addr)

# Send data to the client
conn.sendall(b'Hello, client!')

# Receive data from the client
data = conn.recv(1024)
print('Received:', data.decode())

# Close the connection
conn.close()
```

In this exercise, we first define the host and port for the server. We create a socket object using the `socket` function from the `socket` module and bind the socket to the host and port using the `bind` method. We listen for incoming connections using the `listen` method and accept a client connection using the `accept` method, which returns a connection object and the address of the client. We send data to the client using the `sendall` method of the connection object and receive data from the client using the `recv` method. Finally, we close the connection using the `close` method.

Exercise 19: Data Analysis and Visualization

Concepts:

- Data Analysis

- Data Visualization

- PDF Report Generation

- Pandas library

- Matplotlib library

- ReportLab library

Description: Write a Python script that reads a CSV file containing sales data for a retail store, performs some data analysis and visualization, and saves the results to a PDF report.

Solution:

```python
import pandas as pd
import matplotlib.pyplot as plt
from reportlab.lib.pagesizes import letter
from reportlab.pdfgen import canvas

# Read the CSV file into a pandas dataframe
df = pd.read_csv('sales_data.csv')

# Calculate the total sales by category and month
totals = df.groupby(['category', 'month']).sum()['sales']

# Plot the total sales by category and month
fig, axes = plt.subplots(nrows=len(df['category'].unique()), ncols=1, figsize=(8.5, 11))
for i, category in enumerate(df['category'].unique()):
    totals[category].plot(ax=axes[i], kind='bar', title=category)
plt.tight_layout()

# Save the plot to a PDF report
```

```
c = canvas.Canvas('sales_report.pdf', pagesize=letter)
c.drawString(50, 750, 'Sales Report')
c.drawString(50, 700, 'Total Sales by Category and Month')
plt.savefig('sales_plot.png')
c.drawImage('sales_plot.png', 50, 500, 500, 250)
c.showPage()
c.save()
```

In this exercise, we first read a CSV file containing sales data for a retail store into a pandas dataframe. We calculate the total sales by category and month using the `groupby` and `sum` methods. We plot the total sales by category and month using the `plot` function from the `matplotlib.pyplot` module and save the plot to a PNG file. Finally, we generate a PDF report using the `Canvas` and `Image` functions from the `reportlab` module.

Exercise 20: Machine Learning

Concepts:

- Machine Learning

- Convolutional Neural Networks

- Keras library

- MNIST dataset

Description: Write a Python script that trains a machine learning model to classify images of handwritten digits from the MNIST dataset.

Solution:

```
import tensorflow as tf
from tensorflow import keras
from tensorflow.keras import layers

# Load the MNIST dataset
(x_train, y_train), (x_test, y_test) = keras.datasets.mnist.load_data()

# Normalize the pixel values and reshape the data
x_train = x_train.astype('float32') / 255.0
x_test = x_test.astype('float32') / 255.0
x_train = x_train.reshape(-1, 28, 28, 1)
x_test = x_test.reshape(-1, 28, 28, 1)
```

```python
# Define the convolutional neural network model
model = keras.Sequential([
    layers.Conv2D(32, (3, 3), activation='relu', input_shape=(28, 28, 1)),
    layers.MaxPooling2D((2, 2)),
    layers.Conv2D(64, (3, 3), activation='relu'),
    layers.MaxPooling2D((2, 2)),
    layers.Flatten(),
    layers.Dense(10, activation='softmax')
])

# Compile the model
model.compile(optimizer='adam', loss='sparse_categorical_crossentropy', metrics=['accurac
y'])

# Train the model
model.fit(x_train, y_train, epochs=5, validation_data=(x_test, y_test))

# Evaluate the model on the test data
test_loss, test_acc = model.evaluate(x_test, y_test, verbose=2)
print('Test accuracy:', test_acc)
```

In this exercise, we first load the MNIST dataset using the `load_data` function from the `keras.datasets.mnist` module. We normalize the pixel values and reshape the data using NumPy. We define a convolutional neural network model using the `Sequential` class and various layers from the `layers` module of Keras. We compile the model using the `compile` method with the Adam optimizer and sparse categorical crossentropy loss function. We train the model using the `fit` method and evaluate the model on the test data using the `evaluate` method.

Exercise 21: Natural Language Processing

Concepts:

- Natural Language Processing

- Text Preprocessing

- Text Representation

- Topic Modeling

- Latent Dirichlet Allocation

- Gensim library

Description: Write a Python script that uses natural language processing techniques to analyze a corpus of text data and extract useful insights.

Solution:

```python
import gensim
from gensim import corpora
from gensim.models import LdaModel
from nltk.corpus import stopwords
from nltk.tokenize import word_tokenize
import pandas as pd

# Read the text data into a pandas dataframe
df = pd.read_csv('text_data.csv')

# Define the stop words and remove them from the text data
stop_words = stopwords.words('english')
df['text'] = df['text'].apply(lambda x: ' '.join([word for word in word_tokenize(x.lower
()) if word not in stop_words]))

# Create a document-term matrix from the text data
texts = df['text'].tolist()
tokenized = [word_tokenize(text) for text in texts]
dictionary = corpora.Dictionary(tokenized)
corpus = [dictionary.doc2bow(text) for text in tokenized]

# Perform topic modeling using LDA
num_topics = 5
lda_model = LdaModel(corpus, num_topics=num_topics, id2word=dictionary, passes=10)

# Print the topics and top words for each topic
for topic in lda_model.show_topics(num_topics=num_topics):
    print('Topic {}:'.format(topic[0]))
    print(', '.join(word for word, _ in lda_model.show_topic(topic[0])))

# Extract the topic distributions for each document
topic_dists = lda_model[corpus]
df['topic_dist'] = topic_dists

# Save the results to a CSV file
df.to_csv('text_data_topics.csv', index=False)
```

In this exercise, we first read a corpus of text data into a pandas dataframe. We define the stop words using the `stopwords` function from the `nltk.corpus` module and remove them from the text data using list comprehension and `apply` method of pandas. We create a document-term matrix from the text data using the `Dictionary` and `corpus` functions from the `gensim` module. We perform topic modeling using latent Dirichlet allocation (LDA) using the `LdaModel` function and extract the topic distributions for each document. Finally, we save the results to a CSV file using the `to_csv` method of pandas.

Exercise 22: Web Scraping

Concepts:

- Web Scraping

- HTML Parsing

- BeautifulSoup library

- CSV File I/O

Description: Write a Python script that scrapes data from a website using the BeautifulSoup library and saves it to a CSV file.

Solution:

```python
import requests
from bs4 import BeautifulSoup
import csv

# Define the URL to scrape url = 'https://www.example.com'

# Send a GET request to the URL and parse the HTML content
response = requests.get(url)
soup = BeautifulSoup(response.content, 'html.parser')

# Extract the data from the HTML content
data = []
for item in soup.find_all('div', {'class': 'item'}):
    name = item.find('h3').text
    price = item.find('span', {'class': 'price'}).text
    data.append([name, price])

# Save the data to a CSV file
with open('data.csv', 'w', newline='') as csvfile:
    writer = csv.writer(csvfile)
    writer.writerow(['Name', 'Price'])
    for row in data:
        writer.writerow(row)
```

In this exercise, we first define the URL to scrape using the `requests` library and parse the HTML content using the `BeautifulSoup` library. We extract the data from the HTML content using the `find_all` and `find` methods of the `soup` object. Finally, we save the data to a CSV file using the `csv` module.

Exercise 23: Database Interaction

Concepts:

- Database Interaction
- SQLite database
- SQL queries
- SQLite3 module

Description: Write a Python script that interacts with a database to retrieve and manipulate data.

Solution:

```python
import sqlite3

# Connect to the database
conn = sqlite3.connect('example.db')

# Create a cursor object
c = conn.cursor()

# Execute an SQL query to create a table
c.execute('''CREATE TABLE IF NOT EXISTS customers
             (id INTEGER PRIMARY KEY, name TEXT, email TEXT, phone TEXT)''')

# Execute an SQL query to insert data into the table
c.execute("INSERT INTO customers (name, email, phone) VALUES ('John Smith', 'john@example.
com', '555-1234')")

# Execute an SQL query to retrieve data from the table
c.execute("SELECT * FROM customers")
rows = c.fetchall()
for row in rows:
    print(row)

# Execute an SQL query to update data in the table
c.execute("UPDATE customers SET phone='555-5678' WHERE name='John Smith'")
```

```
# Execute an SQL query to delete data from the table
c.execute("DELETE FROM customers WHERE name='John Smith'")

# Commit the changes to the database
conn.commit()

# Close the database connection
conn.close()
```

In this exercise, we first connect to an SQLite database using the `connect` function from the `sqlite3` module. We create a cursor object using the `cursor` method of the connection object and execute SQL queries using the `execute` method of the cursor object. We retrieve data from the table using the `fetchall` method and print the results. We update data in the table using the `UPDATE` statement and delete data from the table using the `DELETE` statement. Finally, we commit the changes to the database and close the connection.

Exercise 24: Parallel Processing

Concepts:

- Parallel Processing

- Multiprocessing

- Process Pool

- CPU-bound tasks

Description. Write a Python script that performs a time-consuming computation using parallel processing to speed up the computation.

Solution:

```
import time
import multiprocessing

# Define a CPU-bound function that takes a long time to compute
def compute(num):
    result = 0
    for i in range(num):
        result += i
    return result

if __name__ == '__main__':
```

```
# Create a process pool with the number of CPUs available
num_cpus = multiprocessing.cpu_count()
pool = multiprocessing.Pool(num_cpus)

# Generate a list of numbers to compute
num_list = [10000000] * num_cpus

# Compute the results using parallel processing
start_time = time.time()
results = pool.map(compute, num_list)
end_time = time.time()

# Print the results and computation time
print('Results:', results)
print('Computation time:', end_time - start_time, 'seconds')
```

In this exercise, we first define a CPU-bound function that takes a long time to compute. We then create a process pool using the `Pool` function from the `multiprocessing` module with the number of CPUs available. We generate a list of numbers to compute and compute the results using the `map` method of the process pool. Finally, we print the results and computation time.

Exercise 25: Image Processing

Concepts:

- Image Processing
- Pillow library
- Image Manipulation
- Image Filtering

Description: Write a Python script that performs basic image processing operations on an image file.

Solution:

```
from PIL import Image, ImageFilter

# Open the image file
image = Image.open('example.jpg')
# Display the original image
image.show()
```

```
# Resize the image
image = image.resize((500, 500))

# Convert the image to grayscale
image = image.convert('L')

# Apply a Gaussian blur filter
image = image.filter(ImageFilter.GaussianBlur(radius=2))

# Save the processed image to a file
image.save('processed.jpg')

# Display the processed image
image.show()
```

In this exercise, we first open an image file using the `Image` class from the `Pillow` library. We resize the image using the `resize` method and convert it to grayscale using the `convert` method with the `'L'` mode. We apply a Gaussian blur filter using the `filter` method with the `GaussianBlur` class from the `ImageFilter` module. Finally, we save the processed image to a file using the `save` method and display it using the `show` method.

I hope you find these exercises useful! Let me know if you have any further questions.

Exercise 26: Machine Learning

Concepts:

- Machine Learning

- Scikit-Learn library

- Data Preprocessing

- Feature Engineering

- Model Training

- Model Evaluation

Description: Write a Python script that uses machine learning techniques to train a model and make predictions on new data.

Solution:

```python
import pandas as pd
from sklearn.model_selection import train_test_split
from sklearn.preprocessing import StandardScaler
from sklearn.linear_model import LogisticRegression
from sklearn.metrics import accuracy_score, precision_score, recall_score, f1_score

# Read the data into a pandas dataframe
df = pd.read_csv('data.csv')

# Split the data into training and testing sets
X_train, X_test, y_train, y_test = train_test_split(df.drop('target', axis=1), df['targe
t'], test_size=0.2, random_state=42)

# Scale the data using standardization
scaler = StandardScaler()
X_train_scaled = scaler.fit_transform(X_train) X_test_scaled = scaler.transform(X_test)

# Train a logistic regression model
model = LogisticRegression(random_state=42)
model.fit(X_train_scaled, y_train)

# Make predictions on the test set
y_pred = model.predict(X_test_scaled)

# Evaluate the model performance
accuracy = accuracy_score(y_test, y_pred)
precision = precision_score(y_test, y_pred)
recall = recall_score(y_test, y_pred)
f1 = f1_score(y_test, y_pred)

print('Accuracy:', accuracy)
print('Precision:', precision)
print('Recall:', recall)
print('F1 score:', f1)
```

In this exercise, we first read a dataset into a pandas dataframe. We split the data into training and testing sets using the `train_test_split` function from the `sklearn.model_selection` module. We scale the data using standardization using the `StandardScaler` class from the `sklearn.preprocessing` module. We train a logistic regression model using the `LogisticRegression` class from the `sklearn.linear_model` module and make predictions on the test set. Finally, we evaluate the performance of the model using metrics such as accuracy, precision, recall, and F1 score using the appropriate functions from the `sklearn.metrics` module.

Exercise 27: Web Development

Concepts:

- Web Development

- Flask framework

- HTML templates

- Routing

- HTTP methods

- Form handling

Description: Write a Python script that creates a web application using the Flask framework.

Solution:

```python
from flask import Flask, render_template, request

app = Flask(__name__)

# Define a route for the home page
@app.route('/')
def home():
    return render_template('home.html')

# Define a route for the contact page
@app.route('/contact', methods=['GET', 'POST'])
def contact():
    if request.method == 'POST':
        name = request.form['name']
        email = request.form['email']
        message = request.form['message']
        # TODO: Process the form data
        return 'Thanks for contacting us!'
    else:
        return render_template('contact.html')

if __name__ == '__main__':        app.run(debug=True)
```

In this exercise, we first import the `Flask` class from the `flask` module and create a new Flask application. We define routes for the home page and contact page using the route decorator. We use the render_template function to render HTML templates for the home page and contact page. We handle form submissions on the contact page using the request object and the POST method. Finally, we start the Flask application using the run method.

Exercise 28: Data Streaming

Concepts:

- Data Streaming

- Kafka

- PyKafka library

- Stream Processing

Description: Write a Python script that streams data from a source and processes it in real-time.

Solution:

```python
from pykafka import KafkaClient import json

# Connect to the Kafka broker
client = KafkaClient(hosts='localhost:9092')

# Get a reference to the topic
topic = client.topics['test']

# Create a consumer for the topic
consumer = topic.get_simple_consumer()

# Process messages in real-time
for message in consumer:
    if message is not None:
        data = json.loads(message.value)
        # TODO: Process the data in real-time
```

In this exercise, we first connect to a Kafka broker using the KafkaClient class from the pykafka library. We get a reference to a topic and create a consumer for the topic using the get_simple_consumer method. We process messages in real-time using a loop and the `value` attribute of the messages. We parse the message data using the `json.loads` function and process the data in real-time.

Exercise 29: Natural Language Processing

Concepts:

- Natural Language Processing

- NLTK library

- Tokenization

- Stemming

- Stop Words Removal

Description: Write a Python script that performs natural language processing tasks on a text corpus.

Solution:

```python
import nltk
from nltk.tokenize import word_tokenize
from nltk.stem import PorterStemmer
from nltk.corpus import stopwords

# Download NLTK data
nltk.download('punkt')
nltk.download('stopwords')

# Load the text corpus
with open('corpus.txt', 'r') as f:
    corpus = f.read()

# Tokenize the corpus
tokens = word_tokenize(corpus)

# Remove stop words
stop_words = set(stopwords.words('english'))
filtered_tokens = [token for token in tokens if token.lower() not in stop_words]

# Stem the tokens
stemmer = PorterStemmer()
stemmed_tokens = [stemmer.stem(token) for token in filtered_tokens]

# Print the results
print('Original tokens:', tokens[:10])
```

```
print('Filtered tokens:', filtered_tokens[:10])
print('Stemmed tokens:', stemmed_tokens[:10])
```

In this exercise, we first download the necessary data from the NLTK library using the `nltk.download` function. We load a text corpus from a file and tokenize the corpus using the `word_tokenize` function from the `nltk.tokenize` module. We remove stop words using the `stopwords` corpus from the NLTK library and stem the tokens using the `PorterStemmer` class from the `nltk.stem` module. Finally, we print the results for the original, filtered, and stemmed tokens.

Exercise 30: Distributed Systems

Concepts:

- Distributed Systems

- Pyro library

- Remote Method Invocation

- Client-Server Architecture

Description: Write a Python script that implements a distributed system using the Pyro library.

Solution:

```
import Pyro4

# Define a remote object class
@Pyro4.expose
class MyObject:
    def method1(self, arg1):
        # TODO: Implement the method
        return result1

    def method2(self, arg2):
        # TODO: Implement the method
        return result2

# Register the remote object
daemon = Pyro4.Daemon()
uri = daemon.register(MyObject)

# Start the name server
```

```
ns = Pyro4.locateNS()
ns.register('myobject', uri)

# Start the server
daemon.requestLoop()
```

In this exercise, we first define a remote object class using the `expose` decorator from the `Pyro4` library. We implement two methods that can be invoked remotely by a client. We register the remote object using the `register` method of a `Pyro4` daemon. We start the name server using the `locateNS` function from the `Pyro4` library and register the remote object with a name. Finally, we start the server using the `requestLoop` method of the daemon.

I hope you find these exercises helpful! Let me know if you have any further questions.

Exercise 31: Data Visualization

Concepts:

- Data Visualization
- Plotly library
- Line Chart
- Scatter Chart
- Bar Chart
- Heatmap
- Subplots

Description: Write a Python script that creates interactive visualizations of data using the Plotly library.

Solution:

```
import plotly.graph_objs as go
import plotly.subplots as sp
import pandas as pd

# Load the data into a pandas dataframe
df = pd.read_csv('data.csv')
```

```python
# Create a line chart
trace1 = go.Scatter(x=df['year'], y=df['sales'], mode='lines', name='Sales')

# Create a scatter chart
trace2 = go.Scatter(x=df['year'], y=df['profit'], mode='markers', name='Profit')

# Create a bar chart
trace3 = go.Bar(x=df['year'], y=df['expenses'], name='Expenses')

# Create a heatmap
trace4 = go.Heatmap(x=df['year'], y=df['quarter'], z=df['revenue'], colorscale='Viridis',
 name='Revenue')

# Create subplots
fig = sp.make_subplots(rows=2, cols=2, subplot_titles=('Sales', 'Profit', 'Expenses', 'Rev
enue'))
fig.append_trace(trace1, 1, 1)
fig.append_trace(trace2, 1, 2)
fig.append_trace(trace3, 2, 1)
fig.append_trace(trace4, 2, 2)

# Set the layout
fig.update_layout(title='Financial Performance', height=600, width=800)

# Display the chart
fig.show()
```

In this exercise, we first load a dataset into a pandas dataframe. We create several chart objects using the `Scatter`, `Bar`, and `Heatmap` classes from the `plotly.graph_objs` module. We create subplots using the `make_subplots` function from the `plotly.subplots` module and add the chart objects to the subplots using the `append_trace` method. We set the layout of the chart using the `update_layout` method and display the chart using the `show` method.

Exercise 32: Data Engineering

Concepts:

- Data Engineering

- SQLite

- Pandas library

- Data Transformation

- Data Integration

Description: Write a Python script that processes data from multiple sources and stores it in a database.

Solution:

```python
import sqlite3
import pandas as pd

# Load data from multiple sources into pandas dataframes
df1 = pd.read_csv('data1.csv')
df2 = pd.read_excel('data2.xlsx')
df3 = pd.read_json('data3.json')

# Transform the data
df1['date'] = pd.to_datetime(df1['date'])
df2['amount'] = df2['amount'] / 100
df3['description'] = df3['description'].str.upper()

# Combine the data df = pd.concat([df1, df2, df3], axis=0)

# Store the data in a SQLite database
conn = sqlite3.connect('mydb.db')
df.to_sql('mytable', conn, if_exists='replace', index=False)
```

In this exercise, we first load data from multiple sources into pandas dataframes using functions such as `read_csv`, `read_excel`, and `read_json`. We transform the data using pandas functions such as `to_datetime`, `str.upper`, and arithmetic operations. We combine the data into a single pandas dataframe using the `concat` function. Finally, we store the data in a SQLite database using the `to_sql` method of the pandas dataframe.

Exercise 33: Natural Language Generation

Concepts:

- Natural Language Generation
- Markov Chains
- NLTK library
- Text Corpus

Description: Write a Python script that generates text using natural language generation techniques.

Solution:

```
import nltk
import random

# Download NLTK data
nltk.download('punkt')

# Load the text corpus with open('corpus.txt', 'r') as f:
    corpus = f.read()

# Tokenize the corpus tokens = nltk.word_tokenize(corpus)

# Build a dictionary of word transitions
chain = {}
for i in range(len(tokens) - 1):
    word1 = tokens[i]
    word2 = tokens[i + 1]
    if word1 in chain:            chain[word1].append(word2)
    else:
        chain[word1] = [word2]

# Generate text using Markov chains
start_word = random.choice(list(chain.keys()))
sentence = start_word.capitalize()
while len(sentence) < 100:
    next_word = random.choice(chain[sentence.split()[-1]])
    sentence += ' ' + next_word

# Print the generated text
print(sentence)
```

In this exercise, we first download the necessary data from the NLTK library using the `nltk.download` function. We load a text corpus from a file and tokenize the corpus using the `word_tokenize` function from the `nltk` library. We build a dictionary of word transitions using a loop and generate text using Markov chains. We start by selecting a random word from the dictionary and then randomly select a next word from the list of possible transitions. We continue to add words to the sentence until it reaches a specified length. Finally, we print the generated text.

Exercise 34: Machine Learning

Concepts:

- Machine Learning

- Scikit-learn library

- Decision Tree Classifier

- Model Training

- Model Evaluation

Description: Write a Python script that trains a machine learning model using the scikit-learn library.

Solution:

```python
from sklearn import datasets
from sklearn.tree import DecisionTreeClassifier
from sklearn.model_selection import train_test_split
from sklearn.metrics import accuracy_score

# Load the iris dataset
iris = datasets.load_iris()

# Split the data into training and testing sets
X_train, X_test, y_train, y_test = train_test_split(iris.data, iris.target, test_size=0.3,
random_state=42)

# Train a decision tree classifier
clf = DecisionTreeClassifier()
clf.fit(X_train, y_train)

# Evaluate the model
y_pred = clf.predict(X_test)
accuracy = accuracy_score(y_test, y_pred)
print('Accuracy:', accuracy)
```

In this exercise, we first load the iris dataset from the scikit-learn library using the load_iris function. We split the data into training and testing sets using the train_test_split function. We train a decision tree classifier using the DecisionTreeClassifier class and the fit method. We evaluate the model using the predict method and the accuracy_score function from the sklearn.metrics module.

Exercise 35: Computer Vision

Concepts:

- Computer Vision

- OpenCV library

- Image Loading

- Image Filtering

- Image Segmentation

Description: Write a Python script that performs computer vision tasks on images using the OpenCV library.

Solution:

```python
import cv2

# Load an image
img = cv2.imread('image.jpg')

# Convert the image to grayscale
gray = cv2.cvtColor(img, cv2.COLOR_BGR2GRAY)

# Apply a median filter to the image
filtered = cv2.medianBlur(gray, 5)

# Apply adaptive thresholding to the image
thresh = cv2.adaptiveThreshold(filtered, 255, cv2.ADAPTIVE_THRESH_GAUSSIAN_C, cv2.THRESH_B
INARY, 11, 2)

# Apply morphological operations to the image
kernel = cv2.getStructuringElement(cv2.MORPH_RECT, (3, 3))
closed = cv2.morphologyEx(thresh, cv2.MORPH_CLOSE, kernel)

# Find contours in the image
contours, hierarchy = cv2.findContours(closed, cv2.RETR_TREE, cv2.CHAIN_APPROX_SIMPLE)

# Draw the contours on the original image
cv2.drawContours(img, contours, -1, (0, 0, 255), 2)

# Display the images
cv2.imshow('Original', img)
cv2.imshow('Thresholded', thresh)
cv2.imshow('Closed', closed)
cv2.waitKey(0)
```

In this exercise, we first load an image using the `imread` function from the OpenCV library. We convert the image to grayscale using the `cvtColor` function and apply a median filter to the image using the `medianBlur` function. We apply adaptive thresholding to the image using the `adaptiveThreshold` function and morphological operations to the image using the `getStructuringElement` and `morphologyEx` functions. We find contours in the image using the `findContours` function and draw the contours on the original image using the `drawContours` function. Finally, we display the images using the `imshow` function.

I hope you find these exercises helpful! Let me know if you have any further questions.

Exercise 36: Network Programming

Concepts:

- Network Programming
- Socket library
- Client-Server Architecture
- Protocol Implementation

Description: Write a Python script that communicates with a remote server using the socket library.

Solution:

```python
import socket

# Create a socket object
s = socket.socket()

# Define the server address and port number
host = 'localhost'
port = 12345

# Connect to the server
s.connect((host, port))

# Send data to the server
s.send(b'Hello, server!')

# Receive data from the server
data = s.recv(1024)
```

```
# Close the socket
s.close()

# Print the received data
print('Received:', data.decode())
```

In this exercise, we first create a socket object using the `socket` function from the socket library. We define the address and port number of the server we want to connect to. We connect to the server using the `connect` method of the socket object. We send data to the server using the `send` method and receive data from the server using the `recv` method. Finally, we close the socket using the `close` method and print the received data.

Exercise 37: Cloud Computing

Concepts:

- Cloud Computing

- Heroku

- Flask

- Web Application Deployment

Description: Write a Python script that deploys a Flask web application to the Heroku cloud platform.

Solution:

```
# Install the required libraries
!pip install Flask gunicorn

# Import the Flask library
from flask import Flask

# Create a Flask application
app = Flask(__name__)

# Define a route @app.route('/')
def hello():
    return 'Hello, world!'
```

```
# Run the application
if __name__ == '__main__':
    app.run()
```

In this exercise, we first install the required libraries for deploying a Flask web application to the Heroku cloud platform. We create a simple Flask application that defines a single route. We use the `run` method of the Flask object to run the application locally. To deploy the application to the Heroku cloud platform, we need to follow the instructions provided by Heroku and push our code to a remote repository.

Exercise 38: Natural Language Processing

Concepts:

- Natural Language Processing

- spaCy library

- Named Entity Recognition

- Text Processing

Description: Write a Python script that performs named entity recognition on text using the spaCy library.

Solution:

```
import spacy

# Load the English language model
nlp = spacy.load('en_core_web_sm')

# Define some text to process
text = 'Barack Obama was born in Hawaii.'

# Process the text
doc = nlp(text)

# Extract named entities from the text
for ent in doc.ents:
    print(ent.text, ent.label_)
```

In this exercise, we first load the English language model using the `load` function from the spaCy library. We define some text to process and process the text using the `nlp` function from the spaCy library. We extract named entities from the text using the `ents` attribute of the processed text and print the text and label of each named entity.

Exercise 39: Deep Learning

Concepts:

- Deep Learning

- TensorFlow library

- Convolutional Neural Network

- Model Training

- Model Evaluation

Description: Write a Python script that trains a deep learning model using the TensorFlow library.

Solution:

```python
import tensorflow as tf
from tensorflow.keras import datasets, layers, models

# Load the CIFAR-10 dataset
(train_images, train_labels), (test_images, test_labels) = datasets.cifar10.load_data()

# Normalize the pixel values
train_images, test_images = train_images / 255.0, test_images / 255.0

# Define the model architecture
model = models.Sequential([
    layers.Conv2D(32, (3, 3), activation='relu', input_shape=(32, 32, 3)),
    layers.MaxPooling2D((2, 2)),
    layers.Conv2D(64, (3, 3), activation='relu'),
    layers.MaxPooling2D((2, 2)),
    layers.Conv2D(64, (3, 3), activation='relu'),
    layers.Flatten(),
    layers.Dense(64, activation='relu'),
    layers.Dense(10)
])

# Compile the model
model.compile(optimizer='adam',
```

```
              loss=tf.keras.losses.SparseCategoricalCrossentropy(from_logits=True),
              metrics=['accuracy'])

# Train the model
model.fit(train_images, train_labels, epochs=10,
          validation_data=(test_images, test_labels))

# Evaluate the model
test_loss, test_acc = model.evaluate(test_images, test_labels, verbose=2)
print('Test accuracy:', test_acc)
```

In this exercise, we first load the CIFAR-10 dataset from the TensorFlow library using the `load_data` function. We normalize the pixel values of the images by dividing them by 255.0. We define a deep learning model architecture using the `Sequential` class from the TensorFlow library and various layers such as `Conv2D`, `MaxPooling2D`, `Flatten`, and `Dense`. We compile the model using the `compile` method and train the model using the `fit` method. We evaluate the model using the `evaluate` method and print the test accuracy.

Exercise 40: Data Analysis

Concepts:

- Data Analysis

- Pandas library

- Data Cleaning

- Data Manipulation

- Data Visualization

Description: Write a Python script that analyzes data using the pandas library.

Solution:

```
import pandas as pd
import matplotlib.pyplot as plt

# Load the data
df = pd.read_csv('data.csv')

# Clean the data
df.dropna(inplace=True)
```

```
# Manipulate the data
df['total_sales'] = df['price'] * df['quantity']
monthly_sales = df.groupby(pd.Grouper(key='date', freq='M')).sum()

# Visualize the data
plt.plot(monthly_sales['total_sales'])
plt.xlabel('Month')
plt.ylabel('Total Sales')
plt.show()
```

In this exercise, we first load data from a CSV file using the `read_csv` function from the pandas library. We clean the data by removing any rows with missing values using the `dropna` method. We manipulate the data by calculating the total sales for each transaction and grouping the data by month using the `groupby` method. We visualize the data by plotting the total sales for each month using the `plot` function from the matplotlib library.

Exercise 41: Data Science

Concepts:

- Data Science

- NumPy library

- pandas library

- Matplotlib library

- Data Cleaning

- Data Manipulation

- Data Visualization

Description: Write a Python script that performs data analysis on a dataset using the NumPy, pandas, and Matplotlib libraries.

Solution:

```
import numpy as np
import pandas as pd
import matplotlib.pyplot as plt
```

```
# Load the data
df = pd.read_csv('data.csv')

# Clean the data
df.dropna(inplace=True)

# Manipulate the data
df['total_sales'] = df['price'] * df['quantity']
monthly_sales = df.groupby(pd.Grouper(key='date', freq='M')).sum()

# Analyze the data
print('Total Sales:', df['total_sales'].sum())
print('Average Price:', df['price'].mean())
print('Median Quantity:', df['quantity'].median())

# Visualize the data
plt.plot(monthly_sales['total_sales'])
plt.xlabel('Month')
plt.ylabel('Total Sales')
plt.show()
```

In this exercise, we first load data from a CSV file using the `read_csv` function from the pandas library. We clean the data by removing any rows with missing values using the `dropna` method. We manipulate the data by calculating the total sales for each transaction and grouping the data by month using the `groupby` method. We perform some basic data analysis by calculating the total sales, average price, and median quantity. We visualize the data by plotting the total sales for each month using the `plot` function from the matplotlib library.

Exercise 42: Machine Learning

Concepts:

- Machine Learning

- scikit-learn library

- Support Vector Machines

- Model Training

- Model Evaluation

Description: Write a Python script that trains a machine learning model using the scikit-learn library.

Solution:

```
import numpy as np
from sklearn import datasets, svm
from sklearn.model_selection import train_test_split

# Load the iris dataset
iris = datasets.load_iris()

# Split the data into training and testing sets
X_train, X_test, y_train, y_test = train_test_split(iris.data, iris.target, test_size=0.2,
random_state=42)

# Train a support vector machine classifier
clf = svm.SVC(kernel='linear')
clf.fit(X_train, y_train)

# Evaluate the classifier
score = clf.score(X_test, y_test)
print('Accuracy:', score)
```

In this exercise, we first load the iris dataset from the scikit-learn library using the `load_iris` function. We split the data into training and testing sets using the `train_test_split` function from the scikit-learn library. We train a support vector machine classifier using the `SVC` class from the scikit-learn library with a linear kernel. We evaluate the classifier using the `score` method and print the accuracy.

Exercise 43: Web Scraping

Concepts:

- Web Scraping

- BeautifulSoup library

- HTML Parsing

- Data Extraction

Description: Write a Python script that scrapes data from a website using the BeautifulSoup library.

Solution:

```
import requests
```

```
from bs4 import BeautifulSoup

# Fetch the HTML content of the website
url = 'https://en.wikipedia.org/wiki/Python_(programming_language)'
r = requests.get(url)
html_content = r.text

# Parse the HTML content using BeautifulSoup
soup = BeautifulSoup(html_content, 'html.parser')

# Extract data from the HTML content
title = soup.title.string
links = soup.find_all('a')
for link in links:
    print(link.get('href'))
```

In this exercise, we first fetch the HTML content of a website using the `get` function from the requests library. We parse the HTML content using the `BeautifulSoup` class from the BeautifulSoup library. We extract data from the HTML content using various methods such as `title` and `find_all`.

Exercise 44: Database Programming

Concepts:

- Database Programming
- SQLite library
- SQL
- Data Retrieval
- Data Manipulation

Description: Write a Python script that interacts with a database using the SQLite library.

Solution:

```
import sqlite3

# Connect to the database
conn = sqlite3.connect('data.db')

# Create a table
conn.execute('''CREATE TABLE IF NOT EXISTS users
```

```
              (id INTEGER PRIMARY KEY AUTOINCREMENT,
               name TEXT NOT NULL,
               age INTEGER NOT NULL);''')

# Insert data into the table
conn.execute("INSERT INTO users (name, age) VALUES ('John Doe', 30)")
conn.execute("INSERT INTO users (name, age) VALUES ('Jane Doe', 25)")

# Retrieve data from the table
cur = conn.execute('SELECT * FROM users')
for row in cur:
    print(row)

# Update data in the table
conn.execute("UPDATE users SET age = 35 WHERE name = 'John Doe'")

# Delete data from the table
conn.execute("DELETE FROM users WHERE name = 'Jane Doe'")

# Commit the changes and close the connection
conn.commit()
conn.close()
```

In this exercise, we first connect to a SQLite database using the `connect` function from the SQLite library. We create a table using SQL commands and insert data into the table using SQL commands. We retrieve data from the table using SQL commands and print the data. We update data in the table and delete data from the table using SQL commands. Finally, we commit the changes to the database and close the connection.

Exercise 45: Cloud Computing

Concepts:

- Cloud Computing

- AWS

- Flask library

- Boto3 library

- Web Application Deployment

Description: Write a Python script that deploys a web application to the AWS cloud platform using the Flask and Boto3 libraries.

Solution:

```
# Install the required libraries
!pip install Flask boto3

# Import the required libraries
from flask import Flask
import boto3

# Create a Flask application
app = Flask(__name__)

# Define a route
@app.route('/')
def hello():
    return 'Hello, world!'

# Deploy the application to AWS
s3 = boto3.client('s3')
s3.upload_file('app.py', 'my-bucket', 'app.py')
```

In this exercise, we first install the required libraries for deploying a Flask web application to the AWS cloud platform. We create a simple Flask application that defines a single route. We use the `upload_file` method from the Boto3 library to upload the application to an AWS S3 bucket. Note that this is only a basic example and there are many additional steps involved in deploying a web application to the AWS cloud platform, such as creating an EC2 instance, setting up a load balancer, configuring security groups, and more.

Exercise 46: Natural Language Processing

Concepts:

- Natural Language Processing

- NLTK library

- Tokenization

- Part-of-Speech Tagging

- Named Entity Recognition

Description: Write a Python script that performs natural language processing on text data using the NLTK library.

Solution:

```python
import nltk

# Load the text data
text = '''Apple Inc. is an American multinational technology company headquartered in Cupe
rtino, California, that designs, develops, and sells consumer electronics, computer softwa
re, and online services. The company's hardware products include the iPhone smartphone, th
e iPad tablet computer, the Mac personal computer, the iPod portable media player, the App
le Watch smartwatch, the Apple TV digital media player, and the HomePod smart speaker. App
le's software includes the macOS and iOS operating systems, the iTunes media player, the S
afari web browser, and the iLife and iWork creativity and productivity suites. Its online
 services include the iTunes Store, the iOS App Store, and Mac App Store, Apple Music, and
iCloud.'''

# Tokenize the text
tokens = nltk.word_tokenize(text)

# Perform part-of-speech tagging
pos_tags = nltk.pos_tag(tokens)

# Perform named entity recognition
ne_tags = nltk.ne_chunk(pos_tags)

# Print the named entities
for chunk in ne_tags:
    if hasattr(chunk, 'label') and chunk.label() == 'ORGANIZATION':
        print('Organisation:', ' '.join(c[0] for c in chunk))
    elif hasattr(chunk, 'label') and chunk.label() == 'PERSON':
        print('Person:', ' '.join(c[0] for c in chunk))
```

In this exercise, we first load some text data. We tokenize the text using the `word_tokenize` function from the NLTK library. We perform part-of-speech tagging using the `pos_tag` function from the NLTK library. We perform named entity recognition using the `ne_chunk` function from the NLTK library. We print the named entities in the text data by checking if each chunk has a label of 'ORGANIZATION' or 'PERSON' using the `hasattr` function and `label` attribute.

Exercise 47: Big Data

Concepts:

- Big Data

- PySpark

- Apache Spark

- Data Processing

- MapReduce

Description: Write a PySpark script that processes data using the Spark framework.

Solution:

```python
from pyspark import SparkContext, SparkConf

# Configure the Spark context
conf = SparkConf().setAppName('wordcount').setMaster('local[*]')
sc = SparkContext(conf=conf)

# Load the text data
text = sc.textFile('data.txt')

# Split the text into words and count the occurrences of each word
word_counts = text.flatMap(lambda line: line.split(' ')).map(lambda word: (word, 1)).reduc
eByKey(lambda a, b: a + b)

# Print the word counts
for word, count in word_counts.collect():
    print(word, count)

# Stop the Spark context
sc.stop()
```

In this exercise, we first configure the Spark context using the `SparkConf` and `SparkContext` classes from the PySpark library. We load some text data using the `textFile` method. We split the text into words and count the occurrences of each word using the `flatMap`, `map`, and `reduceByKey` methods. We print the word counts using the `collect` method. Finally, we stop the Spark context using the `stop` method.

Exercise 48: Cybersecurity

Concepts:

- Cybersecurity

- Scapy library

- Network Analysis

- Packet Sniffing

Description: Write a Python script that performs security analysis on a network using the Scapy library.

Solution:

```python
from scapy.all import *

# Define a packet handler function
def packet_handler(packet):
    if packet.haslayer(TCP):
        if packet[TCP].flags & 2:
            print('SYN packet detected:', packet.summary())

# Start the packet sniffer
sniff(prn=packet_handler, filter='tcp', store=0)
```

In this exercise, we use the Scapy library to perform security analysis on a network. We define a packet handler function that is called for each packet that is sniffed. We check if the packet is a TCP packet and if it has the SYN flag set. If so, we print a message indicating that a SYN packet has been detected, along with a summary of the packet.

Exercise 49: Machine Learning

Concepts:

- Machine Learning

- Scikit-learn library

- Model Training

- Cross-Validation

- Grid Search

Description: Write a Python script that trains a machine learning model using the scikit-learn library.

Solution:

```python
from sklearn import datasets
```

```python
from sklearn.model_selection import cross_val_score, GridSearchCV
from sklearn.neighbors import KNeighborsClassifier

# Load the dataset
iris = datasets.load_iris()

# Split the dataset into features and target
X = iris.data
y = iris.target

# Define the hyperparameters to search
param_grid = {'n_neighbors': [3, 5, 7, 9], 'weights': ['uniform', 'distance']}

# Create a KNN classifier
knn = KNeighborsClassifier()

# Perform a grid search with cross-validation
grid_search = GridSearchCV(knn, param_grid, cv=5)
grid_search.fit(X, y)

# Print the best hyperparameters and the accuracy score
print('Best Hyperparameters:', grid_search.best_params_)
print('Accuracy Score:', grid_search.best_score_)
```

In this exercise, we use the scikit-learn library to train a machine learning model. We load a dataset using the `load_iris` function from the `datasets` module. We split the dataset into features and target. We define a dictionary of hyperparameters to search over using the `param_grid` variable. We create a KNN classifier using the `KNeighborsClassifier` class. We perform a grid search with cross-validation using the `GridSearchCV` class. We print the best hyperparameters and the accuracy score using the `best_params_` and `best_score_` attributes.

Exercise 50: Computer Vision

Concepts:

- Computer Vision

- OpenCV library

- Image Processing

- Object Detection

Description: Write a Python script that performs image processing using the OpenCV library.

Solution:

```python
import cv2

# Load the image
img = cv2.imread('image.jpg')

# Convert the image to grayscale
gray = cv2.cvtColor(img, cv2.COLOR_BGR2GRAY)

# Define a classifier for face detection
face_cascade = cv2.CascadeClassifier('haarcascade_frontalface_default.xml')
# Detect faces in the image
faces = face_cascade.detectMultiScale(gray, scaleFactor=1.1, minNeighbors=5)

# Draw rectangles around the detected faces
for (x, y, w, h) in faces:
    cv2.rectangle(img, (x, y), (x + w, y + h), (0, 255, 0), 2)

# Display the image with the detected faces
cv2.imshow('image', img)
cv2.waitKey(0)
cv2.destroyAllWindows()
```

In this exercise, we use the OpenCV library to perform image processing. We load an image using the `imread` function. We convert the image to grayscale using the `cvtColor` function. We define a classifier for face detection using the `CascadeClassifier` class and a pre-trained classifier file. We detect faces in the image using the `detectMultiScale` function. We draw rectangles around the detected faces using the `rectangle` function. We display the image with the detected faces using the `imshow`, `waitKey`, and `destroyAllWindows` functions.

SEE YOU SOON!

Congratulations on completing this book of Python exercises! We hope that you have found these exercises to be both challenging and rewarding, and that you have gained a deeper understanding of Python programming as a result.

Throughout this book, we have covered a wide range of topics, from basic syntax and data types to advanced topics such as machine learning and natural language processing. We have divided the exercises into three sections based on difficulty level, but we encourage you to explore all of the exercises to gain a comprehensive understanding of the language.

At our software company, we believe that programming is not just about writing code. It's about solving problems and creating solutions that make a difference in people's lives. We are constantly exploring new technologies and techniques to stay at the forefront of the industry, and we are excited to share our knowledge and experience with you through this book.

We also believe that practicing programming skills requires patience and persistence. You may not get the correct answer on the first try, and that's okay. The exercises in this book are designed to challenge you, and it's through struggling with difficult problems that you'll truly learn and grow as a programmer.

WHERE TO CONTINUE?

If you've completed this book of Python exercises and are hungry for more programming knowledge, we'd like to recommend some other books from our software company that you might find useful. These books cover a wide range of topics and are designed to help you continue to expand your programming skills.

1. "Master Web Development with Django" - This book is a comprehensive guide to building web applications using Django, one of the most popular Python web frameworks. It covers everything from setting up your development environment to deploying your application to a production server.

2. "Mastering React" - React is a popular JavaScript library for building user interfaces. This book will help you master the core concepts of React and show you how to build powerful, dynamic web applications.

3. "Data Analysis with Python" - Python is a powerful language for data analysis, and this book will help you unlock its full potential. It covers topics such as data cleaning, data manipulation, and data visualization, and provides you with practical exercises to help you apply what you've learned.

4. "Machine Learning with Python" - Machine learning is one of the most exciting fields in computer science, and this book will help you get started with building your own machine learning models using Python. It covers topics such as linear regression, logistic regression, and decision trees.

5. "Natural Language Processing with Python" - Natural language processing is a field that focuses on the interaction between computers and humans using natural language. This book will help you get started with building your own natural language processing applications using Python. It covers topics such as text preprocessing, sentiment analysis, and text classification.

All of these books are designed to help you continue to expand your programming skills and deepen your understanding of the Python language. We believe that programming is a skill that can be learned and developed over time, and we are committed to providing resources to help you achieve your goals.

We'd also like to take this opportunity to thank you for choosing our software company as your guide in your programming journey. We hope that you have found this book of Python exercises to be a valuable resource, and we look forward to continuing to provide you with high-quality programming resources in the future. If you have any feedback or suggestions for future books or resources, please don't hesitate to get in touch with us. We'd love to hear from you!

KNOW MORE ABOUT US

At Cuantum Technologies, we specialize in building web applications that deliver creative experiences and solve real-world problems. Our developers have expertise in a wide range of programming languages and frameworks, including Python, Django, React, Three,js, and Vue.js, among others. We are constantly exploring new technologies and techniques to stay at the forefront of the industry, and we pride ourselves on our ability to create solutions that meet our clients' needs.

If you are interested in learning more about our Cuantum Technologies and the services that we offer, please visit our website at www.cuantum.tech. We would be happy to answer any questions that you may have and to discuss how we can help you with your software development needs.

CONCLUSION

In conclusion, we hope that you have found this book of Python exercises to be a valuable resource in your journey to become a proficient Python programmer. By working through these exercises, you have gained practical, hands-on experience with the language and have developed problem-solving skills that will be invaluable as you continue to work on more complex projects.

Whether you are a beginner with no programming experience or an experienced programmer looking to expand your skills, this book has provided you with a comprehensive set of exercises to challenge and develop your Python programming abilities. From basic syntax and data types to advanced topics such as machine learning and natural language processing, the exercises in this book cover a wide range of topics, providing you with a well-rounded understanding of the language.

We believe that programming is not just about writing code; it's about solving problems and creating solutions that make a difference in people's lives. At our software company, we are committed to creating software that delivers creative experiences and solves real-world problems. We are constantly exploring new technologies and techniques to stay at the forefront of the industry, and we are excited to share our knowledge and experience with you through this book.

As you continue on your journey to become a proficient Python programmer, we encourage you to continue to explore new technologies and techniques, and to practice and develop your skills. The field of programming is constantly evolving, and there is always something new to learn. We hope that this book has provided you with a solid foundation in Python programming, and we wish you all the best in your future programming endeavors.

www.cuantum.tech

Printed in Great Britain
by Amazon

55293351R00183